Engaging the culture

Christians at work in education

Edited by Richard Edlin & Jill Ireland

National Institute for Christian Education
PO Box 7000
Blacktown NSW 2148
Australia

National Library of Australia
Cataolguing-in-Publication Data

    Engaging the culture : Christians at work in education.

    Bibliography.
    Includes index.
    ISBN 0 9752422 1 0.

    1. Christian education. 2. Christian teachers. 3.
    Teaching - Religious aspects - Christianity. I. Edlin,
    Richard J., 1951- . II. Ireland, Jillian.

    371.071

Cover design by Taninka Visuals
Tanya van der Schoor Ph: 61 2 4284 0344 Email: tanya@taninka.com.au

Printed by Openbook Print
205 Halifax Street, Adelaide, South Australia 5000

Unless otherwise noted, the Scripture quotations in this publication are from the New International Version (NIV) of the Bible

Contents

Preface

Jill Ireland

Jill Ireland followed up an honours degree in English and French with Masters research at Oxford University on John Donne and TS Eliot, made possible through the Caltex Woman Graduate of the Year Awards. She recently completed a Masters degree in education with NICE.

Jill and her engineer husband Stephen have five children aged 10—20. They helped establish Bega Valley Christian College. Jill's recent research has been in educational policy formation and children's literature. Her doctoral research is on Year 12 English texts in all states and the International Baccalaureate Diploma. Jill was one of the editors of *Pointing the Way* (NICE, 2004). In her spare time Jill teaches medieval to modern literature and Practical Reasoning at the University of Wollongong's Bega campus.

A National Board member of CPCS, Jill has served on the NICE Council for eleven years. She recognises structured professional development from a Christian perspective as vital for teachers in Christian school communities, so they maintain their distinctiveness over future decades.

Engaging the culture as Christians at work in education requires alertness to presuppositions, tenacity and willingness to change. It is not something we do alone, but a challenge we take on communally. The contributors to this book are a diverse group of people—infants teachers and university lecturers, parents and principals, early in their careers and very experienced. They approach the challenge of cultural engagement from different angles, as they seek to "take every thought captive" (2 Cor 10:5) and apply a Christian worldview in practice. Richard Edlin and Rod Thompson tackle the challenge of separating reformed worldview and reformed (or Reformed) theology, clarifying a source of confusion for many, and illustrating how broadly a reformed worldview can be applied.

Jack Fennema challenges us to explain the purposes of Christian education in ways that resonate with young people, so they move from being subjects to being participants. He outlines the distinctive responsibilities of the three groups of stakeholders in Christian schooling—students, parents and teachers—and looks strategically at what can be achieved if these roles are understood wisely as complementary rather than competing. Likewise **Ken Dickens** tackles areas of contention about the differing roles of churches and Christian schools. He faces the hard issue of conflicting ideas about Christian schooling within and between congregations: "… in some churches it is a mark of orthodoxy to have your children in a Christian school. In others it is an indication of a lack of commitment to evangelism." There are circles in which this subject is taboo, but the presuppositions behind these approaches are uncovered here in a way that is very constructive.

Richard Edlin's perceptive chapter on why we think the way we do makes a substantial contribution to an important discussion: how do we identify those unexamined assumptions adopted from our culture which warp our Christian worldview? Dr Edlin's experience overseeing education for missionary children in numerous countries has given him a unique insight into breaking the habits of cultural idolatry. His chapter is also an accessible introduction to Socrates, Plato and Aristotle, whose influence is still palpable even in today's classrooms. Both Edlin and Tim Charles examine how philosophies and theoretical perspectives from diverse times and places can collide, influencing each other in ways which profoundly affect the task of Christian education, often without us noticing.

Trevor Cooling observes that many Christians suppress their curiosity about faith issues which are implicit, difficult or paradoxical, deferring to theological "experts" who decide for them. He compares two models of being theologically faithful—faithful transmission and theological contextualisation. His chapter offers a persuasive rationale for seeing theological curiosity as a virtue, which need not lead to liberalism or a downgrading of the authority of the Bible as God's directing Word. **Richard Edlin's** second chapter takes these insights deeply into our educational context. He outlines the potential for "reformed critical realism" to energise the Christian school's faithful engagement with the world, by transforming both attitudes and actions. This is a challenge which is taken up by **Coralie Harris** in her recognition that every action reflects a core belief. The reader can enter Coralie's infants classroom as she reflects on her actions, realising how she has unconsciously privileged some ideas over others, hampering the working out of her worldview as a Christian teacher. She reminds us that it is not only lesson content which should be biblical, but also our teaching and assessment methods. Her chapter models how intensely practical theory can be.

David Smith's article puts the searchlight on the way different teaching areas have their own cultures to which belief can relate in various ways. He demonstrates how the culture of second language education can resist or be influenced by Christian approaches to teaching and learning. His use of metaphor as leitmotiv is compelling and illuminating: he characterises language education as hospitality to the stranger, and language teaching as the provision of a home. Smith's approach through metaphor could be seen as embodying scriptural principles imaginatively, and with the sort of fruitful curiosity which Cooling and Edlin are proposing.

Jeanette Woods' research tackles the significance of religious factors in developing students' resilience—the ability to recover from adversity. She succinctly summarises her findings, which have many applications in the context of Christian schooling in an increasingly pluralist culture. Her chapter also models the value of couching research on religious issues in terms that postmodernist academia can accept, without avoiding the key implications for our community of schools. This is part of being in the marketplace of ideas, and not sidelining issues of faith to a private sphere, away from the "real" world.

From his own experience of the idolatry of sport, **Mike Goheen** explores a nuanced view of sport as part of God's creation which can be faithfully celebrated by his people. He offers a defensible rationale of competition which dovetails with a Christian worldview while not overlooking the challenges that arise in the competitive context. In a culture where sport can be treated as a god, it is important that Christian teachers and parents think through the implications of Goheen's approach.

Mitch O'Toole, like Ken Dickens, points out the dampening of authentic inquiry which can occur when approaches to a controversial issue are adversarial, polarised and lacking in respect. In a very insightful chapter on the changeable nature of scientific models, O'Toole uses the evolution debate as a microcosm of how society responds to competing theories over time. He also shows how changes in scientific models can leave the curriculum behind and identifies the value in science of the concept of reformed critical realism that has become one of the unifying themes of this book.

Charles Justins shows that biblical theology and Christian worldview need to be embodied in ways which are plausible. His outline of how these factors might interact to increase the impact of Christian education upon communities with diverse cultures and faith backgrounds connects with the contention of David Smith and Coralie Harris, that sometimes we need to begin at the point of our approach in the classroom, and work back to the ideas which underlie it, rather than assuming greater insight comes when working from theory to practice. The illustrations used by Smith and Harris seem to have great explanatory power, and it is hoped that they will fuel further investigations by teachers in classrooms of many kinds.

The intertextual connections between various contributions in this volume can be taken as metaphors for the ongoing conversation which enriches our experience of Christian education in diverse local and national context—as parents, teachers and students who are often surprised by where God takes us on our communal faith journey.

Acknowledgments

The editors would like to thank all those who have contributed to this book, particularly Annette Edlin, who could be described as the "stage-manager" of the drama of blending manuscripts from around the country and across the world into a coherent piece of work with the potential to influence the heart, mind and will of many who are serving God's kingdom through Christian education.

Introduction:
What's with this "reformed" idea in Christian education?

Richard Edlin
Principal, National Institute for Christian Education

Richard Edlin is the principal of the National Institute for Christian Education (NICE), a government-accredited, degree-granting postgraduate teacher training organisation based in Sydney, Australia. Although Richard his wife, Annette, and their three adult children currently all live in Australia, the Edlins have travelled the world in their commitment to the cause of Christian education. Richard has written many books and articles on Christian education, as well as producing videos and other ICT media on the subject. His experience includes over 30 years of teaching and administration in both secular and Christian educational contexts in both the developed and the developing world. His earned doctorate in teacher education is from the University of Alabama. In 2005, he was awarded a rare honorary doctorate from Kosin University in Busan, Korea, for his international contribution to Christian education.

Rod Thompson
Lecturer, National Institute for Christian Education
Lecturer, Masters Institute

Rod Thompson is a lecturer with the National Institute for Christian Education and is currently seconded to the Masters Institute in Auckland, New Zealand, where he is the Director of the Centre of Worldview Studies. He and his wife Rosanne ventured to New Zealand at the beginning of 2004, having previously spent all of their married lives in Mt Druitt in the western suburbs of Sydney. They have four children. Rod previously taught in both government and Christian schools and has also served as a Presbyterian minister for some 15 years. Rod completed doctoral studies concerning the foundational relationship of the Bible to education, at Macquarie University in 2003.

Christians involved in education are a wondrously heterogeneous bunch. Look inside many Christian schools, and you'll find committed Christian parents and teachers from a host of different backgrounds—Anglicans, Presbyterians, Baptists, Pentecostals, Adventists, and so on.

When this diverse group of people hear the Christian education message as presented by groups such as the National Institute for Christian Education (NICE), it often resonates with them. "Where has this been all my life?" is a not uncommon response. "My main regret," say others, "isn't that I didn't know this stuff before now, but that I didn't know that I didn't know it." Their spirits resonate with the biblically authentic ideas of celebrating the lordship of Christ over all of life in the education provided in Christian schools. There is something intuitively attractive about NICE's commitment to strive to position the gospel, and not western cultural forces, as the primary shaper of how we think and live. Christian parents see it as a God-honouring and dynamic expression of the type of education that they want for their children. For Christian teachers, NICE study unfolds a dynamic and transformational way of understanding and applying an approach to the teaching and learning process that gives full expression to their desire to bring every thought into subjection to Jesus Christ.

But there is a problem. This exciting approach to Christian education often seems to carry with it the tag "reformed." Ken Dickens, NICE senior lecturer, suggests that a reformed understanding will help us be biblically faithful in our education. Rod Thompson, another NICE lecturer, advocates the foundational necessity of a reformed way of thinking about the Scriptures. Richard Edlin, NICE principal, talks about reformed critical realism as if it were the best paradigm for Christians to adopt in order to avoid the idolatries of both modernity and postmodernity. Edlin constantly uses the terms "reformed/reformational" and "biblically authentic" as if the latter fits seamlessly within the former. Mike Goheen, a scholar respected by NICE, is an ordained Reformed Church minister.

The problem is, of course, that some fine Christians involved in education who like the NICE perspective, are uncomfortable with this apparently inescapable link between faithful Christian education and the word "reformed." Surely one doesn't have to be reformed to be a good Christian parent, board member, or teacher involved in Christian education? Furthermore, the term is often linked with John Calvin of the Reformation, and although many Christians in education find Calvin's views to be attractive, others find them to be extreme and even repugnant.

So why this emphasis on reformed? Surely it cannot mean the abandonment of cherished denominational links or theological perspectives just because John Calvin didn't like them! What does it mean when NICE talks about being reformed in education, but still being able to celebrate one's own Presbyterian, Anglican, Pentecostal, Baptist, or Adventist heritage?

There is a way forward that does not require that Christians adopt a reformed theological perspective. What is needed is a recognition of the distinct differences between a *reformed worldview*, which nests comfortably within many evangelical denominational traditions, and a *reformed theology* which is appropriate for a more limited range of denominational heritages. In other words, Christians in education can (and should) be reformed in worldview terms without having to be a Calvinist or be reformed theologically or denominationally. Though there is an obvious coherence between a reformed theology and a reformed worldview, it is not necessary to be reformed theologically in order to be reformed in terms of worldview.

In the remaining section of this paper we seek to expand on this key difference between a reformed theology and a reformed worldview. We wish to acknowledge the input of Dr Mike Goheen for alerting us to this helpful distinction.

A reformed theology compared to a reformed worldview

The term theology has come to be widely used to mean "the systematic study of the fundamental ideas of the Christian faith" (McGrath, 2001, p. 139). Like all areas of systematic study—such as biology or anthropology or physics—theology is shaped by foundational worldview assumptions—ways of looking at the world that issue from one's culture and being rather than from thought-out cognitive systems. The sum of these foundational assumptions makes up our worldview. Worldview beliefs are often pretheoretical, and they give meaning to the details of our everyday lives. They also provide the necessary grounding for disciplines of study such as theology.

Christians may be influenced by theological systems of thought such as Calvinism, Anglicanism, Adventism or Presbyterianism, but their primary faith experience is grounded in the Bible itself as God's revelation from which worldview beliefs arise in the context of everyday life. For example, Calvinism's acronym of TULIP is a theological construct, whereas acknowledging the lordship of Christ over all things is an inevitable worldview response to a faithful reading of the whole Bible as God's written word. On the one hand, reformed theology is a systematic theological tradition that is reflected in documents like the Canons of Dordt or the Westminster Confession. On the other hand, a reformed worldview is an almost gut-level living response that Christians exploring education as a faithful response to the authority of the whole Bible might seek to live by. A reformed worldview assumes that all of the Bible is foundational for all of life.

Characteristics of a reformed worldview

Wherever Christians are seeking to live in the light of the transformational authority of the Bible for all of life, they are living out a reformed worldview. The following three features are key touchstones of this theologically transcending reformed worldview:

Appreciation of the inherent goodness of creation

When God made the world, he said over and over again, "It is good." And it is still good. Human fashioning of creation, or the fruits of human stewardly endeavours (for example, governments, buildings, cultures, Apple computers and so on) is also a godly calling. As Paul reminded his hearers in Athens in Acts 17, every human thought and action is a faithful or unfaithful response to the inescapable reality that life's central driving force is the search to know God. Thus the daily experience of Christians faithfully exercising this calling in every aspect of life is one of gratitude, wonder, and responsive discipleship.

The devastating impact of sin across the whole of creation

The unbroken line of human sin from Adam to us today, has distorted humankind's ability to live obediently before God. It has impacted all of creation which groans under God's judgement and longs for restoration. We live in the light of this unbearable tension daily in every aspect of creation—marriages break up, bodies decay, governments war, parents abort, power corrupts—and economic rationalism, with its insatiable appetite for human sacrifice, dominates education. However, though sin distorts, it does not eradicate the stamp of God's character and goodness in creation.

Christ's comprehensive restoration of all creation.

The gospel truly is good news. God has said "Yes" to his world and "No" to sin in the death and resurrection of Jesus. For further discussion of this point, see The cross and our calling (Redeemer University College, 2003 pp. 1-3). He is reclaiming all things – trees, rocks, elephants, kangaroos, kiwis, governmental structures, music, art, space and aviation, technology, the imagination, and education, and he empowers his people to be transformational witnesses to this gospel in the twenty-first century. Because of this gospel, reformed Christians live this worldview in hope in their everyday lives and callings, as God's ambassadors calling to all people everywhere to repent and live lives of obedient service to and worship of their Creator. All other options lead to despair, chaos, unfulfilment and death. The glory of Christian education is to explore the meaning of this restoration. As children in

Christian schools learn about the world and their places and tasks in it, they will discover the glorious hope of the Christian for lives of fulfilled service now and for eternity as they are challenged with the celebration of the lordship of Christ over everything.

Historical and contemporary precedents for the term reformed

We have chosen to use the term reformed in this article (and more widely throughout this book) for both historical and contemporary reasons.

Historically, the term reformed recalls the fundamental rediscovery during the reformation of the centrality for all people of the entire scriptures for everyday life. It is exactly this reformed characteristic that is critical for a biblically faithful worldview today—including the biblically faithful nurture of children and their preparation to be culture formers under Christ's lordship.

The term reformed or reformational also embodies a dynamic, contemporary perspective in modern life. Just as the reassessment of religion was a key feature of the reformation of old, so too in contemporary twenty-first century Christianity it presupposes a commitment to be involved in a humble, continual, ongoing assessment of one's worldview in contemporary life. This is what Edlin has referred to elsewhere as a holy and dynamic disequilibrium that always acknowledges the human frailty of our stewardly response to God's revelation, and allows our paradigms to be open to reformulation in the light of subsequent, biblically-derived insights into God, his character in Jesus Christ, and his calling on our lives. The use of the term reformed as a prefix to the philosophical position known as critical realism is another appropriate and contemporary use of the term.

Reformed is a term widely used in this book and in Christian education courses offered by groups such as NICE. It is not used in a theological attempt to proselytise on behalf of a reformed theology or a reformed denominational position—though there is an obvious coherence between a reformed worldview and a reformed theology. Rather, the term is used in a worldview context, wherein Christians of a wide variety of evangelical denominations and traditions can adopt it as a most appropriate description of a way of looking at and living in the world that is biblically authentic and which gives transformational direction to dynamic and biblically faithful Christian education. As such, it is commended to Christians of goodwill everywhere (whatever their theological persuasion) as a profound and helpful way of describing that which we do in the cause of Christian education.

References

McGrath, A. 2001. *Christian theology: An introduction* (3rd ed.). Oxford, UK: Blackwell

Redeemer University College. 2003. *The cross and our calling.* Retrieved 23 August 2005 from www.biblicaltheology.ca/blue_files/Cross&Calling.pdf

Chapter 1

Transforming education: Parents

Jack Fennema
Professor of Education, Emeritus, Covenant College

Dr Jack Fennema earned his BA from Calvin College and an EdD from the University of Georgia. Later he acquired an MA in marriage and family therapy from the Reformed Theological Seminary.

Dr Fennema has taught and been an administrator in K–12 Christian schools for 25 years. He has taught and served as director of graduate programs at Dordt College and Covenant College, where he is presently Professor of Education, Emeritus. He also served as Vice President at Trinity Christian College and as Executive Director of the Ontario Alliance of Christian Schools in Canada.

Dr Fennema is author of *Nurturing children in the Lord* and, in 2005, of *The religious nature and biblical nurture of God's children*. He and his wife Barbara live near Columbus, Ohio.

Abstract

This chapter explores the roles and responsibilities of parents in the formal education of their children. Questions addressed are: Should parents send their children to a Christian school? Why or why not? To what kind of Christian school should parents send their children? Many types exist. What should be the purpose of Christian education? Here, the unique nature of kingdom education is described. Questions continue: How does kingdom education impact the curriculum? Knowing in the four basic relationships of life is explored. The final question asked is: What are the responsibilities of parents to their Christian school? Indeed, if parents are responsible for the education of their children, they must then be involved in a responsible manner.

Parents are the people primarily responsible for the education of children. That doesn't mean that they are the ones who have to do the actual teaching, but they are the ones who are commissioned by God to make certain that children receive an education that is God-centered and God honouring. This was true during the Old Testament era (see Deut 6:1–9 and Ps 78:1–8). This was also true in the early church. The apostle Paul tells fathers in particular to bring up their children in "the nurture and admonition of the Lord" (Eph 6:4 KJV). This nurture includes instruction and correction, and both must be "of the Lord". The state is never mentioned in the Bible as being responsible for education. Even the church's role in education is secondary to that of the parents. Consequently, one of the most important choices that parents must make is that of a school for their children.

> *Parents are the people primarily responsible for the education of children… they are the ones who are commissioned by God to make certain that children receive an education that is God-centered and God honouring.*

This chapter explores the role and responsibilities of parents in the formal education of their children. Key questions are posed; biblical answers are sought. Education that is biblically transformed begins with parents who themselves view their nurturing responsibilities through eyes and minds that have already been transformed through a relationship with Christ and his way of being in the world.

Should parents send their children to a Christian school?

Where in the Bible does it say: "Parents, send your children to a Christian school"? The answer is, "It doesn't." During biblical times children were educated at home by their parents or by tutors, and, for Jewish children, the synagogue provided religious training, as well. Schools, as they are today, did not exist back then. The questions to be addressed, then, are: "What guidance does the Bible provide in answering schooling questions?" and "Is a Christian school the place that can best provide my children with the education the Lord desires for them?" Answers to these questions need to be framed within two cautions. Parents are to make certain that their educational purposes are correct, and they are to be *pro*active rather than *re*active in their decision-making.

Educational purposes need to be correct

Some Christian parents send their children to secular schools to be evangelists; the great commission has provided them with the answer to the "Which school?" question. While there may be a nugget of merit in this purpose, it ignores the primary reason for education, that of preparation for life. The purpose of formal education is designed to equip students for living life—learning the content, skills, and values necessary to function fully and successfully as adults. Even though education should be as authentically life-like as possible, it is meant to be *preparation for* life. Doing evangelism as elementary or secondary students lies outside the scope of the primary purpose for education.

Decisions should be *pro*active rather than *re*active

Making educational choices reactively rather than proactively can be tempting. Unhappiness with a particular school system, for whatever the reason, however, should not be the primary basis for choosing another. The point of reference is wrong. Christian parents must seek first to be biblically faithful in their decision-making. Their questions should be: "What would God have us do?" "What guidance can the Bible provide?" and "Which choice would be the most obedient?"

What, then, does the Bible say about the education of children? On which godly principles can parents base their educational decisions? A cardinal truth of Scripture provides the core of the answer: *Jesus is Lord of all.* The Father has given the Son "all authority in heaven and on earth" (Matt 28:18; see also Dan 7:13–14;). If parents can confess this with heartfelt conviction, the answers to their educational questions will follow, for the lordship of Jesus Christ is the pivotal truth for education. This is true because Christ is Lord of the two main components of education: the students and the curriculum.

Christ is the Lord of children

Children don't really belong to parents; they belong to God through Christ. Parents have been designated by God to be his stewards—caretakers—of children. Yes, as stated above, parents are responsible for the nurture of their children, but that is *delegated* authority. Children are a trust given to parents by God. Paul calls the children of believing parents holy (1 Cor 7:14). To be holy is to be set apart for godly purposes and service. God has consecrated these children to himself. They belong to him.

Parents, in turn, are to consecrate their children back to God. Jesus said, "Let the little children come to me, and do not hinder them, for the kingdom of God belongs to such as these" (Mark 10:14). Hannah consecrated her child Samuel to God. She brought him to the house of the Lord and dedicated him with the words: "I prayed for this child, and the Lord has granted me what I asked of him. So now I give him to the Lord. For his whole life he will be given over to the Lord" (1 Sam 1:27–28).

Secular education has removed all references to God, declaring him irrelevant.

What does it mean to "be given over to the Lord" educationally? Moses' explanation to the people of Israel about how to nurture their children remains applicable today. Parents were instructed to teach their children the commands, decrees and laws of God, in particular the command "to love the Lord your God with all your heart and with all your soul and with all your strength" (Deut 6:1,5). Moses continued: "Now choose life, so that you and your children may live and that you may love the Lord your God, listen to his voice, and hold fast to him. For the Lord is your life ..." (Deut 30:19–20). Moses was telling God's people that life is all about God. Thus, the nurture of children is all about God, for they belong to him, and they are to live life in obedience and praise before his face.

This nurture in the things of God is not a part-time job. It is to take place 24/7, both in the privacy of one's home and in the marketplace.

Talk about (these commandments) when you sit at home and when you walk along the road, when you lie down and when you get up. Tie them as symbols on your hands and bind them on your foreheads. Write them on the doorframes of your houses and on your gates (Deut 6:7–9).

Life before the Lord is not dualistic—part sacred and part secular. All of life has been declared holy by God, for he is sovereign and Christ is Lord of all. Nurture in the home is to be holy to the Lord; nurture outside of the home is to be holy to the Lord, as well.

Christ is the Lord of this world

The curriculum of a school is, by its very nature, religious. For example, the curriculum in most schools is both secular and humanistic; thus, the religion that provides its direction is secular humanism. Secular education has removed all references to God, declaring him irrelevant to all that has happened, is happening, and will happen. The mighty acts of God have been replaced by the accomplishments of humankind; thus, the education is also humanistic. Education that omits any reference to God and his Word fails to teach students to think from a biblical worldview. Sadly, this tends to neutralise even the finest of Christian students from becoming discerning Christian thinkers. Their minds have not been developed to operate from a Christian perspective, and, consequently, much of their effectiveness in the marketplace will have been neutralised from the beginning.

In contrast, the curriculum within a school that acknowledges the lordship of Christ over all things views the world and life within it as sacred, holy unto the Lord. The psalmist writes: "The earth is the Lord's, and everything in it, the world and all who live in it" (Ps 24:1). Zechariah writes that on the day of Christ's return when every knee will bow acknowledging his lordship, the words "holy to the Lord will be inscribed on the bells of the horses and the cooking pots" (14:20). What appears common to people today will be shown at that time as having been sacred all along. The bowing of the knee at the name of Jesus will have broad implications.

A curriculum that is based on secular humanism is at best only partially true and at worst a lie. God mandates that his children be taught the truth and the whole truth—truth that is centred in Christ, the living truth. If Christ is Lord of all, every part of the curriculum heralds his kingship, for either Christ is Lord of all or Christ is not Lord at all.

An education that acknowledges the lordship of Christ over children and the curriculum is not an option—it is a command.

To what kind of Christian school should parents send their children?

Just as there are many different kinds of churches, there are many different kinds of Christian schools. Two criteria exist that can help select a Christian school: 1) Transformation by the Spirit and the Word, and 2) Faithfulness to the Word.

Schools that are transformed by the Spirit and the Word

Just as salvation by Jesus Christ calls for a complete transformation, schools that seek to be Christ-honouring need to be transformed as well. To begin, cosmetic changes aren't enough. Such modifications as placing Scripture verses on the bulletin boards or having students wear uniforms, as noble as these changes may be, do not make a school Christian. Next, adding godly components isn't enough, either. Providing morning devotions, chapels, biblical studies programs, and a strict set of rules, as noble as these may be, also do not make a school Christian. Instead, to create a Christ-honouring school the light of the world and the light of the Word must illumine every facet of the educational enterprise in a transforming way. The Spirit of Christ and biblical norms must permeate all thought and practice within the school. Every policy and every activity, from the classroom to the athletic fields to the boardroom, must bring pleasure and glory to God.

Schools that are faithful to the Word

As alluded to above, Christian schools sometimes fall into the trap of responding to the wrong reference point as the norm. Rather than seeking, first and foremost, to be faithful to Scripture, the plumbline for decision-making is other schools. This may result in one of two opposite quests: either being "distinctive from" or being "the same as".

Some Christian schools base their reason for existence on being distinctive from secular schools. This goal isn't all bad, but it can become a trap. Such schools tend to react rather than act. The wiser approach is to begin with Scripture to elicit the guidelines for doing education in a Christ-honouring manner. Usually a school that seeks first to be biblically faithful will also become rather distinctive from other schools as well. Distinctiveness may indeed be the outcome, but it should not be the primary goal. Since even secular schools, because of God's common grace, inadvertently do a number of things God's way, distinctiveness, per se, is not always valid. Every school, whether secular or Christian, is only more-or-less faithful to God's norms for education. Hence, Christian schools need to be humbly cautious about seeking to be distinctive in all ways from secular schools and, in so doing, establishing their corner on the truth.

Other Christian schools want it all. They desire to have every bell and whistle that their secular counterparts have, plus a Christian testimony. Once again, brick and mortar, the quest after high achievers and winning athletic teams are not necessarily bad things, but they may reflect misplaced priorities. The story from the first chapter of the book of Daniel is a wonderful illustration of the foolishness of God trumping the wisdom of this world. Faithfulness to God's word resulted in

Daniel and his friends being found "ten times better in every matter of wisdom and understanding" (1:20). Too often, however, faithfulness to Scripture can take on a secondary role to highly visible activities that receive greater public acclaim. Paul's admonition to Timothy, although not literally applicable, in concept does apply: "For physical training is of some value, but godliness has value for all things, holding promise for both the present life and the life to come" (1 Tim 4:8). The major aspects of Christian education must always remain the major emphasis in time, energy, and money spent.

Every Christian school is different from the next. It is important, then, to investigate a school carefully to determine the degree to which the Spirit and the Word have transformed it and the degree to which it is faithful in actual practices to biblical norms for education.

What should be the purpose of Christian education?

Parents send their children to Christian schools for many different reasons. These may include: safety from bad things happening in other schools; quality academics; schooling with other Christians; high moral and behavioural standards; inclusion of prayer, bible study, and chapel; and the teaching of God's truth. Some parents might even say that the whole is greater than the sum of these parts. It may be the whole package.

Yet, if parents were asked to describe the outcomes they desire for their children after a number of years of Christian schooling, many would be hard-pressed to paint a coherent picture. They know that they are seeking to be obedient to the biblical injunction to educate their children in the Lord, but they are less certain of the differences that 12 years of Christian education will make formatively in the lives of their children.

An examination of Christ's earthly ministry can be helpful in developing biblically based outcomes for Christian education, for children are called to be disciples of Jesus in today's world. The practices of Christ are to be as emulated by his followers today as they were in his time.

Christian education equips students for kingdom service

The central focus of Christ's earthly ministry was the renewal of God's kingdom on earth. The first petition of the Lord's Prayer points to this: "Your kingdom come, your will be done on earth as it is in heaven" (Matt 6:10). Christ's followers were told that the first thing they should be seeking is the kingdom of God and his righteousness (Matt 6:33).

God's kingdom had been established on earth at the dawn of creation. God's sovereign rule and ways of doing things were present in unchallenged form. Life was good, the way God had created it to be. But humankind's fall into sin changed all of that. God's good creation became infected by sin. Human beings were alienated from God and became eternally lost, and creation itself was subject to the bondage of decay (Rom 8:21). In God's love and grace, however, Christ was anointed King by the Father and given all authority on earth to reverse the effects of the fall. John writes: "The reason the Son of God appeared was to destroy the devil's work" (1 John 3:8b). He did this through his ministry, his death, and his resurrection. Matthew records: "Jesus went throughout Galilee, teaching in their synagogues, preaching the good news of the kingdom, and healing every disease and sickness among the people" (4:23). After his earthly mission had been accomplished and shortly before his return to the Father, Christ as head of his church commissioned his body to continue doing that which he had begun. Because he had been given all authority on earth, they were to "go and make disciples of all nations, baptising … and teaching them to obey everything" that he had commanded them (Matt 28:19–20). They were to actively seek the renewal of Christ's kingdom on earth by reversing the effects of the fall, just as Christ had done. They were to declare that Jesus is Lord of all and to herald the coming of his kingdom. Christian education is to equip Christ's young disciples to be active citizens of his kingdom. To do that, kingdom education includes several specific tasks.

> *Christian education is to equip Christ's young disciples to be active citizens of his kingdom.*

1. Kingdom education equips students to think with the mind of Christ.

Disciples of Christ need to be taught how to think and act in a manner that often runs counter to the culture in which they live. Their minds are to be transformed through the Spirit and Word of God. The Bible is to be used as glasses through which to view the world correctly and as light to discern God's truth from Satan's lies. Students are to be taught to evaluate life and the world through a worldview based on the doctrine of all things: God created all things good; the fall into sin affected all things in creation; Christ's redemption provided reconciliation for all things; and when Christ returns to establish his kingdom in fullness, all things will be made new.

2. Kingdom education equips students to fulfil the cultural mandate.

The kingdom task given to humankind by God in the beginning was to rule and have dominion over creation as citizens of his kingdom on earth (Gen 1:28; 2:15). God's image-bearing representatives were to take care of creation as stewards and to develop creation's potential as culture formers. Every area of life was under God's sovereign rule. Every activity of humankind, whether work or play, was to bring glory to God. Talents were to be developed and products created that would form a culture that served God in holiness. Although sin has profaned God's good creation, the original mandate has never been abrogated. It continues to be pivotal as a basis and outcome of Christian education.

3. Kingdom education equips students to herald Christ's coming kingdom.

Christ began the renewal of the kingdom of God during his earthly ministry, but that kingdom will not be fully established until he returns when all things will be made new. Therefore, Christ's kingdom is already with us in part but not yet with us in fullness. The kingdom renewal work of Christ is to continue, however, until the day of his return. Just as Christ reversed the effects of sin through healing and restoring, his disciples today are commissioned to apply justice, righteousness, and love to a world that groans for deliverance. The ethics of the consummated kingdom, the perfect shalom of Christ, are to be applied to society, culture, and the natural world right now. In doing so, two messages must be proclaimed: "This world belongs to Christ, for Jesus is Lord of all!" and "The King is coming again!"

4. Kingdom education equips students to be prophets for the 21st century.

Jesus, our chief prophet and living truth, desires to impact every issue of this day and age through modern-day prophets. The creation of prophetic voices will require the training of discerning minds, students who can apply the truths of Scripture to the headlines of the day. They must be prepared to be Christ's voice in the world, proclaiming his lordship and his ways of doing things. They must be guided to live lives of truthful integrity in the classroom, on the playing field, in their social lives, and in the workplace.

5. Kingdom education equips students to be priests for the 21st century.

Jesus, our only high priest, continues to provide his healing balm to a hurting world through his disciples. Students are to be trained as evangelists, sharing the good news of the kingdom of Christ. They are also to be equipped for healing ministries that help the marginalised and disenfranchised. They are to be prepared for ministries of reconciliation as peacemakers in families, churches, and society. They are to be shown how to give a cup of water in Christ's name.

6. Kingdom education equips students to be kings for the 21st century.

Jesus, our eternal king, has been given all authority on earth right now, and his followers need to be trained to proclaim his kingly rule as his ambassadors in the here-and-now, as well. Servant leadership is to be taught. Students must learn how to rule in justice and righteousness in areas over which they have been given responsibility and authority. They are to be prepared to be faithful stewards and responsible developers of creation and culture.

Christian education is kingdom education. Indeed, there is a purpose to it all.

How does kingdom education impact the curriculum?

If the purpose of Christian education is to equip young citizens of Christ's kingdom to serve as his ambassadors in his world, the curriculum of the school must reflect this approach to education. It, too, must be transformed by the Spirit and Word of God. Simply adapting a curriculum from secular education is not sufficient.

One way to approach curriculum in a manner that is consistent with Scripture is seeking "to know" through the four basic relationships of life—knowing God, knowing others, knowing creation, and knowing one's self. Knowing in the biblical sense is more than simply cognitive mastery; it is holistic. Just as people are commanded to love God with their entire beings—heart, soul, mind, and strength, so students are "to know" with their heart, head, and hands. Learning within Christian schools includes a cognitive understanding of the truth, a heartfelt commitment to the truth, and an obedient response to the truth. It is hearing the Word and doing the Word; it is both revelation and response.

1. Knowing God

The first of all commandments is to love God totally. That is a proper place for a Christian school curriculum to begin, for to love God, one must know God. God has revealed himself through his Son, his Spirit, his Word, and his world. Every subject in the curriculum needs to point to God through Christ, for all things were created by him and for him, all things hold together in him, all things have been reconciled through him, and all things are under his lordship (Col 1:15–20). But the primary curriculum area dealing with knowing God is biblical studies. Students need to be biblically literate if they are to view and understand life and the world through the lens of Scripture. With Christ at the centre, students are to gain an understanding of the great themes of the Bible, such as creation, the fall, redemption, and the consummation. They need to become scholars of the Bible, learning to handle correctly the word of truth (2 Tim 2:15). They need to be able to find answers in the Bible to life's questions.

Although the primary task of the Christian school is education rather than evangelism, the desire should be present that every student will know God through Christ in a personal way. Only by knowing God in personal relationship can a student know others, creation, and one's self in a truly meaningful manner.

2. Knowing others

The second of all commandments is to love one's neighbour. This, too, is a curricular area of prime importance. The social science subjects of history, geography, political science, and economics fall into this category. The behavioural science subjects of sociology and anthropology serve as supplements. Church history, world religions, literature, and art and music history and appreciation can be included, as well. Christian schools should consider teaching these subjects from a cultural studies or humanities approach because of their unified view of the world, in which all things are held together in Christ.

Equipping students to fulfil the great commission is a legitimate part of this curriculum area, for the greatest of all love acts is to lead others to Jesus. Evangelism skills can be honed through both local and cross-cultural ministry efforts.

The school itself serves as a living curriculum forum in this area, for students are to be taught how to live in community and function together as the body of Christ. Zero tolerance for putdowns is stressed, biblically based conflict resolution skills are taught, and reconciliation and restoration practices are encouraged.

3. Knowing creation

The original cultural mandate referred primarily to taking care of and developing the natural and physical world. Such stewardship continues to be important today. The curricular areas of life, physical, and earth science, maths, and computer science serve to equip students for this. Psalm 19 is particularly relevant in the knowing creation process:

The heavens declare the glory of God;
  the skies proclaim the work of his hands.
Day after day they pour forth speech;
  night after night they display knowledge (verses 1–2).

Students need to ask certain questions as they explore God's revelation of himself through his creation. How does God reveal himself and his truth through the natural world? And, what, indeed, is being communicated?

4. Knowing one's self

Part of being a caretaker of creation is learning how to take care of one's self. This is not an exercise in narcissistic love; rather, it is a healthy appreciation for being the special creation of the divine potter (Isa 64:8; Ps 8:4–5). It is biblically legitimate for students to learn to understand themselves, to respect themselves, and to care for themselves.

Self-understanding begins with the biblical account of being "fearfully and wonderfully made" (Ps 139:14) as image–bearers of God (Gen 1:27). It continues with the unwrapping of natural talents and spiritual gifts.

This curricular area includes health and physical education, the fine and performing arts, and psychology. The language skills of listening, speaking, writing, and reading are also important in self-development.

In summary, the Christian school may teach subjects that go by the same names as subjects in secular schools, and the content and skills may be similar at times, but the entire framework of the curriculum has been transformed. Christian education is knowing in relationship. The knowing is holistic and responsive; the relationships begin with God. The direction is toward the face of God; the purpose is to bring glory to God through responses of obedience and praise.

What are the responsibilities of parents to their Christian school?

Parents need to have a vested interest in the Christian school in which they have enrolled their children. The relationship to the school must be more than just the purchase of services, for God continues to hold parents responsible for the nurture of their children. Yes, parents can delegate some of that responsibility to teachers, and, true, teachers need to be able to function in loco parentis, but certain responsibilities do continue. These include responsibilities to themselves as parents, to other parents, and to the teachers.

Parents' responsibilities to themselves

Parents need to understand the education that is being provided for their children some 30 to 40 hours each week. Reading this chapter is a good beginning, but it is only a beginning. Parent education within a Christian school may be as important as student education, for the home and school must work in tandem with each other to maximise their effectiveness in providing godly nurture. All parents, but board members in particular, should gain a certain level of expertise in the philosophy, psychology, and curriculum development of Christian education. The school should make books and workshops available for that purpose.

Parent-directed schools mean parent-involved schools. Volunteering, serving on committees and the board, attending school events are all important ways to partner with one's own children in their education. The venture of Christian education works much better when parents are involved, and this investment reaps eternal benefits.

Parents' responsibilities to other parents

Christian schools differ from each other in their approaches to education. Parents are members of churches that differ in theology. These differences can be a problem or they can be a blessing.

Diversity in the body of Christ should be embraced and enjoyed.

Before parents enrol their children in a particular Christian school, they should thoroughly investigate the school to determine their degree of compatibility. If there is agreement on the essentials, parents should feel encouraged to enrol their children, for the basic unity necessary to function in community will be present. But diversity within that unity will also be present. Parents need to allow room for differences on minor theological matters, for the school is a school, not a church. In fact, diversity in the body of Christ should be embraced and enjoyed. By attending a school that includes families from many different churches, students can better learn the essentials of their faith and why they and others believe as they do (Acts 17:11).

Parents' responsibilities to administrators and teachers

One of the best contributions parents can make toward the unity of the body is to follow the Matthew 18 principle religiously when they deal with administrators and teachers. If a problem exists, they must go directly to the person involved. They must not discuss the matter with anyone else. Rather, they are to keep it between the two of them. Then, they are to seek a win–win solution, one that both parties can feel good about. If no solution is forthcoming, they should invite a mutually agreed-upon third party to listen to both sides and offer suggestions for an amicable resolution. Parents who go first to other parents, the administrator, or, worse yet, to a board member before going to the teacher do incalculable damage to relationships and to the school. This is a sin and cannot be allowed to take place in a school consecrated to Christ.

Parents should expect teachers to know how to teach Christianly in a biblically faithful manner. After all, that is a primary reason for enrolling one's children in a Christian school. It is a reasonable expectation. But, realistically, teachers have their own professional growth journey to walk. They themselves need to be taught how better to teach in a transformed manner. Happily, resources exist to help teachers grow as Christian educators. Books, conventions, workshops, courses, and academic degree programs are available. Parents owe teachers two things in this regard. They need to keep the teachers' feet to the fire to grow professionally as Christian educators. High expectations should be developed and they need to be codified as policy. Secondly, however, the resources must also be provided. The time and the money for professional development must be built into the school structure and budget. The dividends of this investment will soon become evident in the classroom.

In conclusion, God has given parents the responsibility to nurture their children in his ways. One of the avenues through which to do this is the Christian school. In choosing a school, however, parents need to be discerning, for not all Christian schools are the same. Christian schools need to be faithful to the educational norms provided by Scripture. Once committed to a school, parents have the responsibility to assist the school in remaining faithful and in understanding how better to do education Christianly. Transformed education needs parents whose hearts, minds and actions are also being transformed by the Spirit and the Word.

Questions for discussion

1. Is enrolling one's children in a Christian school an act of obedience to God? Defend your answer from Scripture.

2. Describe the different kinds of Christian schools of which you are aware. How might each of them defend from Scripture their particular approach to education?

3. In what ways do the different purposes of Christian schools translate into policies and practices that differ as well?

4. Identify parts of the curriculum of your Christian school that have been transformed and are rightly in line with biblical norms.

5. Describe life in a world in which Christ's kingdom had been fully actualised. What would that world look like?

6. Why is following the Matthew 18 principle so important for Christian institutions? Provide examples from your own experience.

7. How important is it for parents to understand the Christian nature of the education being provided their children? Why?

8. How can board members determine the degree to which teachers who apply for positions in a Christian school are able to teach in a biblically faithful manner?

9. List several reasons why Christian education is a valid alternative to secular education.

Transforming education: Teachers

Jack Fennema

Professor of Education, Emeritus, Covenant College

Dr Jack Fennema earned his BA from Calvin College and an EdD from the University of Georgia. Later he acquired an MA in marriage and family therapy from the Reformed Theological Seminary.

Dr Fennema has taught and been an administrator in K–12 Christian schools for 25 years. He has taught and served as director of graduate programs at Dordt College and Covenant College, where he is presently Professor of Education, Emeritus. He also served as Vice President at Trinity Christian College and as Executive Director of the Ontario Alliance of Christian Schools in Canada.

Dr Fennema is author of *Nurturing children in the Lord* and, in 2005, of *The religious nature and biblical nurture of God's children*. He and his wife Barbara live near Columbus, Ohio.

Abstract

This chapter examines the roles of teachers in the transforming of education. The area of biblical epistemology is explored first—one knows through divine revelation, both special, the Bible, and general, the creation. Next, biblical ontology is dealt with—truth for Christians is centred in the person of Jesus Christ. Thus it is dynamic and interactive, and calls for an obedient response. Pedagogy is examined next—how to instruct according to biblical principles, followed by exploring the biblical purpose of Christian education. A creation-fall-redemption-consummation worldview is then cited as a key component of Christian education. The chapter concludes with the admonition for teachers to remain faithful. Faithfulness to the Word of God is the foundation of teaching that transforms.

Teaching is one of the highest of all callings. Jesus was a teacher (Matt 23:10), and teaching is cited as one of the gifts of the Spirit (Rom 12:7). Teachers are vitally important to our world because they serve as primary guides for the next generation. The nature of the world some 20 or 30 years from now depends greatly on the type of nurture received by today's youth, and teachers play a very formative role in that process.

The influence of teachers on students cannot be overestimated. Luke writes: "… everyone who is fully trained will be like his teacher" (6:40). That is both a wonderful opportunity and an awesome responsibility! In fact, James cautions: "Not many of you should presume to be teachers, … because you know that we who teach will be judged more strictly" (3:1). Because teachers have great influence, they will be held to greater accountability.

> *Teaching is one of the highest of all callings. Jesus was a teacher, and teaching is cited as one of the gifts of the Spirit.*

This chapter examines the role of teachers in the transforming of education. Before proceeding, however, a need must be recognised and a caution issued.

First, the need: In order for teachers to be transformers of education, the Holy Spirit must have transformed them; they must be born again. The requirement that all teachers in Christian schools must have hearts regenerated by the Spirit of God is not simply an attempt to be exclusive; it is a necessary component for transforming education. The apostle Paul explains the reason for this: "The person without the Spirit does not accept the things that come from the Spirit of God but considers them foolishness, and cannot understand them because they are spiritually discerned" (1 Cor 2:14). If teachers are to have access to the "full riches of complete understanding", they must "know the mystery of God, namely, Christ, in whom are hidden all the treasures of wisdom and knowledge" (Col 2:2–3). Understanding (and thus teaching) the wisdom and knowledge hidden in Christ requires a heart indwelt by the Spirit of Christ. Only then can a teacher understand reality as God created it.

Second, the caution: Don't confuse "transformed" education with "distinctive" education; rather, "transformed" education is "faithful" education—faithful to the Word of God. There is a difference between the two terms. At times, teachers who received their training in secular schools or who have taught in them sense that *all* teaching in Christian schools must be distinctive from that which they experienced in secular schools. This can result in abnormal attempts to Christianise such subjects as maths or grammar or spelling. Because God's general revelation is, indeed, general to all humankind, and because in God's providence all humankind can have common grace insights into his truth, a sizeable portion of secular education may, in fact, be quite similar to Christian education.

All schools are more-or-less faithful to the Word of God. One would expect secular schools to be less faithful to the Word and Christian schools to be more faithful, but, sadly, that is not always the case. Seeking to be faithful is an intentional and comprehensive activity that must be worked at. It is far more than simply placing a Bible verse over a lesson. Teachers who seek to transform need to be faithful to the Word in their epistemology, ontology, pedagogy, purposes and worldview. This is no small task.

Transformed teaching is faithful to the Word in *epistemology*

Pretend that you are a graduate student in a secular university and are attending a class on learning theory. The professor has posed the question, "How do we know?" He explained that this is the fundamental question of epistemology, one of the key areas of philosophy. Since all teachers are committed to teaching the truth, how can they know that their sources for truth are reliable? What, indeed, is a reliable source? Those are fundamental questions for all teachers to wrestle with, for teaching is all about knowing the truth. How would you answer the question, "How do we know?"

In today's postmodern world, the answer given by most students might be that truth is found within each individual. Since the process for determining truth is subjective, truth is unique to each person. And since truth is not absolute, it could also change with time and circumstances. There is no universal truth for all people, simply many particular truths.

Older students who grew up during the modern era might provide a different answer. Truth for them can be determined through research and the scientific method. The process is objective. Since reality is lawful and predictable, truth is constant and can be known by rational minds. If something is observable and measurable, it can be known. Empirical data are the vehicles by which one can know the truth. Universals exist. Truth is absolute.

But what answer should a Christian give? Would the answer agree or disagree with the first two? Actually, a biblical view of knowing does have both subjective and objective dimensions, but there is much more to the process. The Christian's answer to the epistemological question of how we know is: we know through divine revelation. God chose to reveal himself, his truth, his way of salvation, and his blueprint for life through three modes: Jesus, the Bible, and the creation. We have all heard about education's three r's (reading, 'riting and 'rithmatic). For the Christian, however, the foundational fourth r of education is revelation.

God's revelation through Jesus

The apostle John wrote: "In the beginning was the Word, and the Word was with God, and the Word was God" (John 1:1). The apostle Paul wrote: "[Christ] is the image of the invisible God" and "God was pleased to have all his fullness dwell in him" (Col 1:15 & 19). And the author of Hebrews wrote:

In the past God spoke to our ancestors through the prophets at many times and in various ways, but in these last days he has spoken to us by his Son, whom he appointed heir of all things, and through whom he made the universe. The Son is the radiance of God's glory and the exact representation of his being, sustaining all things by his powerful word (1:1–3).

God the Father has been most fully made known through Jesus the Son, "who, being in very nature God," took on the very nature of a human being, so that God and people could be reconciled (Phil 2:6–8; 2 Cor 5:18–19). *God has revealed himself through Jesus.*

A proper goal for Christian teachers is that every one of their students will come to know God personally by exercising saving faith in Jesus. Transformed students are an important part of transformed education.

God's revelation through the Bible

We have all heard of 3-D or 3-dimensional glasses that provide virtual reality in movie theatres. The Bible functions in a similar manner as a person dons the eyeglasses of the Word and peers out into creation. This time, one more dimension is added—the transcendent. The Bible, in this sense, serves as 4-D glasses through which to view created reality as God intended. A biblical worldview frames the subject under study to provide insight and understanding from above.

The Bible also acts as a light to ferret out Satan's lie from God's truth. The darkness of this world is destroyed by the Light of the world and of the Word. Discernment can be taught through shining the normative word of Scripture on that which is being studied.

Glasses are not helpful if they are not worn, and light is not helpful if it remains unlit. The Bible, too, must be studied and applied diligently if it is to effectively provide godly understanding to the rest of the curriculum. This calls for a strong biblical literacy program for Christian schools, one that focuses on the major biblical themes of creation, fall, redemption, and the consummation of the kingdom, viewed through the person of Jesus. The Bible is God's specific or special revelation of himself.

God's revelation through creation

Jesus is also central to God's revelation of himself through creation, for he is the Word through whom all things were made and in whom all things hold together and are sustained (John 1:3; Col 1:17; Heb 1:3). Ps 19 states:

The heavens declare the glory of God;
*   the skies proclaim the work of his hands.*
Day after day they pour forth speech;
*   night after night they display knowledge.*
There is no speech or language
*   where their voice is not heard.*
Their voice goes out into all the earth,
*   their words to the end of the world* (1–4a).

God communicates with us through his Word or *Logos* for creation. The apostle Paul tells us: "… since the creation of the world God's invisible qualities—his eternal power and divine nature—have been clearly seen, being understood from what has been made … (Rom 1:20). Creation serves as God's natural or general revelation of himself to humankind.

Creation—now expanded to include all of society and culture—is the source of curriculum for the Christian school. The voice of God can be heard through created reality as it is unfolded in the various disciplines. Teachers and students are to be attuned to what God is saying.

God's revelation of himself has been communicated through three distinct modes; but the message is unified and consistent in each mode, whether it is Jesus, the Bible, or creation. One must know Jesus before one can understand the Bible. And one must correctly understand the Bible before one can interpret creation. In all cases, the Holy Spirit is necessary for illumination.

Knowing as a dynamic process

One part of the answer to the epistemological question of how we know is through divine revelation. But there is a second part to the answer, one that deals more with process than with product. In the Old Testament the Hebrew word *yadah* was used to communicate the concept of knowing. The word *yadah* connotes a comprehensive and dynamic approach to knowing truth or another person. One understands with one's mind, one commits to that understanding with one's heart, and one responds to that commitment through active obedience. Knowing is a holistic and total process. This is illustrated in the command to love God with one's heart, soul, mind, and strength. God is to be known or loved with one's entire being. Knowing is a covenantal or relational activity. Thus, knowing in a Hebrew or biblical sense stands in stark contrast to knowing in a Greek sense—only rationally and in an objective, non-relational manner.

Helping students to know in a biblical way has profound implications for the classroom. Teaching and learning must move beyond the simple transmission of information, which reflects more the Greek model. It must include understanding, heart commitment, and opportunity to respond. The heart commitment part is a bit more problematic, for that is really the work of the Holy Spirit rather than that of the teacher. But teachers can pray for and with students in this regard. Teachers, however, can certainly provide opportunities to act upon the truth that is learnt, for "doing the truth" is part of biblical knowing (John 3:21 NKJV). God's revelation always calls for an obedient response, motivated by submission (i.e., honour), thankfulness, and praise. The lessons experienced in Christian schools are to be holistic and relational, reflecting the Bible's definition of knowing.

Transformed teaching is faithful to the Word in ontology

What is truth? That is a central question of ontology, another one of the key areas of philosophy. This question was posed in quite a unique setting some two thousand years ago. Pilate, the Roman governor of Judea, asked this question of Jesus, perhaps somewhat rhetorically (John 18:38). He framed his question in Greek thought, however—that truth could be known cognitively and then mastered. Pilate didn't realise that the person standing before him had already stated: "*I* am the truth"

(John 14:6). The Bible's view of truth is that it is a person—alive, dynamic, and life-changing. Truth is the Master. It is not some thing to be mastered. Just as biblical knowing calls for an obedient response, the biblical view of truth is that truth always requires obedience. If one knows the truth, one is to obey the truth, for truth is the word of God. Truth is God's Word—Jesus (John 17:17; 1:1).

When Jesus identified himself as the truth, he couched it in the phrase: "I am the way and the truth and the life" (John 14:6). That way-truth-life sequence carries special meaning for Christian education. First, life in and through Jesus is a legitimate goal for Christians and, subsequently, for Christian education. Eternal life versus eternal death has always been a central issue in God's economy. Moses presented this challenge to the people of Israel many years before:

This day I call heaven and earth as witnesses against you that I have set before you life and death, blessings and curses. Now choose life, so that you and your children may live and that you may love the Lord your God, listen to his voice, and hold fast to him. For the Lord is your life … (Deut 30:19–20).

Jesus said: "I have come that they may have life, and have it to the full" (John 10:10). The abundant life found in Jesus lasts for all eternity, but it begins in the here-and-now. That life is what all Christian teachers desire for their students.

Second, Jesus stated that he (and only he) is the way to that life. But he also said that the way to that life is through the truth (or the Truth). In a very real sense, the Christian school, as the purveyor of truth, leads children through truthful teaching to life as it was meant to be lived—abundantly, to the fullest! For it is the truth that (or, the Truth who) sets them free to be able to appropriate that life (John 8:32). Christian teachers who know the Truth person-

> *Life in and through Jesus is a legitimate goal for Christians and, subsequently, for Christian education.*

ally and have submitted to the truth themselves have a wonderful opportunity to introduce their students to the living Truth who is the Way to the fullness of life. So, Christian teacher: Teach the truth—boldly! Lead your students to life in the one who is Life.

A biblically faithful view of ontology should transform classrooms. To begin, teachers must be aware that they are to teach God's truth. This could be propositional truth or it could be experiential truth, but lesson plans should identify the truth to be taught. Next, this truth, which is alive, dynamic, and life-changing, needs to be taught in that same manner. Christian education should never be boring education! Finally, truth demands obedience, for it is God speaking. Lesson plans, again, need to incorporate activities of response. The truth is something (or some One) to be lived out in real life.

Transformed teaching is faithful to the Word in *pedagogy*

Instructing through show and tell

Question: Does the Bible provide examples or illustrations of the best way to nurture or teach children? From our finite, human viewpoint, that would seem to be an excellent thing for God to have provided. Parents and teachers could simply follow the prototype provided and get it right every time! But, interestingly, God chose not to provide us with such a model. No parents (or teachers) in the biblical account got it right. In the very first family, the older son killed his younger brother. The spousal conniving and the sibling rivalries within the families of the patriarchs—Abraham, Isaac, and Jacob—left much to be desired. Samuel turned out well, but, then, his parents didn't raise him. The priest Eli did. David, the man after God's own heart, was not very effective as a parent. In the New Testament era, the two most notable figures, Jesus and Paul, were not married, thus they had no children. Timothy could be cited as an exemplary young man, but he had an unbelieving father. And on it goes.

The closest thing to a biblical model for the nurture of children is actually found with Old Testament Israel. It was not exemplified by any one particular family, but by all families in the community. There, indeed, was a Hebrew way of instructing children in the things of the Lord. It was the apprenticeship model: illustrate by example, explain while doing. Today we might call it show and tell. It is living life before children as it is meant to be lived and it is simultaneously explaining to children what is being done and why. This approach is, perhaps, best described in the portion of Scripture often cited as the primary rationale for Christian education: Deuteronomy 6:4–9. It begins with the Hebrew *Shema* and then continues into a description of unified and holistic instruction.

Hear, O Israel: The Lord our God, the Lord is one. Love the Lord your God with all your heart and with all your soul and with all your strength. These commandments that I give you today are to be upon your hearts. Impress them on your children. Talk about them when you walk along the road, when you lie down and when you get up. Tie them as symbols on your hands and bind them on your foreheads. Write them on the doorframes of your houses and on your gates.

Loving God is a 24/7 proposition. It is to be lived out before one's children both privately and publicly. And it is to be talked about continually. The Passover feast was probably the classic example of this mode of instruction. Every time the ceremony was celebrated the historic symbolism of each part was explained and the faithfulness and mighty acts of God were described (Exod 12:24–27).

Teachers can and should use many different methods and strategies to teach their lessons. But the large and central themes of Christian education must be modelled through show and tell. The abundant life in Christ to which teachers are guiding their students is to be lived before them daily.

Instructing through connections

Most educators believe that good pedagogy involves the seeing and making of connections. But not all educators understand that a covenantally relational God is the reason behind a world designed with such connectedness. The four basic relationships of life—God-others-creation-self—reflect a unified and connected cosmic system. Secular educators would omit the foundational God-relationship, but they do see the world as being organic and systemic—i.e., connected. Biblically faithful pedagogy intentionally incorporates relationship or connectedness into the teaching–learning process, for the concept of relationship helps to define both the creation and the Creator.

Many teachers seek to teach in an integrated or integral manner, because they believe that that is good pedagogy. And they are right. But when Christian teachers are asked for a Christian or biblical rationale for integrated units, they often are stuck for an answer. That answer, simply stated, is that all of created reality is an interrelated and interdependent unity held together and sustained by Jesus—the Word or Logos for creation (John 1:1–3; Col 1:16–17; Heb 1:1–3). If teachers want to accurately represent the cosmos and reality to their students, they must demonstrate creation's unity and connectedness, for that is the way things are. This means that integral units and a humanities approach to the curricula of a Christian school should definitely have a place.

But there is more. Most educators today define the term "meaningful learning" as learning that is connected with previous learning or knowledge. Most agree that unless students can connect the lesson of the day with something familiar, something they already know, learning will not take place. Learning is a Velcro process. For retention, the new must be attached to the old. The reason for this is that students have been created with mental schemata that resemble schematic drawings—a cognitive maze of interconnections that provide insights for understanding. In fact, the integral unity of students' cognitive structures mirrors the integral unity of the creation being studied. One was designed to provide understanding of the other.

Christian education is education that "seeks first the kingdom" so that God's will may be done and his kingdom come, on earth.

The relational unity and connectedness of the educational process lacks ultimate meaning, however, unless it is connected to God's kingdom purpose for it all. Christian education is teleological education. God is guiding the world and life within it toward his own predetermined conclusion. The creation and all within it are teleological in nature— moving with purpose toward a known end. In order to reflect accurately these realities of life, education must be teleological in its nature, as well. The first three chapters of Genesis provide the kingdom context; the last three chapters of Revelation provide the goal and outcome. The four gospels provide the central message. Events of life have purpose and movement. The King is coming! At a time already known to the Father, Christ's eternal kingdom will be established in fullness. Christian education is education that "seeks first the kingdom" so that God's will may be done and his kingdom come, on earth. Students must be made aware of this so that they can see the connection between their studies and God's kingdom purposes for this world and life within it.

Transformed teaching is faithful to the Word in *purpose*

The purposes people give for education are directly linked to the purposes they give for life. The behaviourist might seek happiness through a reduction of the negative and an increase of the positive. The humanist might seek self-actualisation, "Be all that you were meant to be." The materialist might seek possessions. The humanitarian might seek to leave this world a better place. And, on it goes. Secular private education educates students toward some of the goals listed above or simply toward entrance into a quality university. Secular public education educates toward productive citizenship. This would involve the ability to become gainfully employed and to function responsibly within a community. But what about Christian schools?

In secular education, it is all about us. Christian educators must not fall into that trap. For them it must be all about God. The purpose of Christian education is to equip students to live life before God as God designed it to be. For us to understand what that life looks like, we must go to the Word of God, his blueprint for life. The Bible has much to say about living life, but there are three summary statements that seem to encapsulate the rest: the love commandments; the great commission; and the cultural mandate.

The love commandments

The bottom line for the Christian is to love God—totally. Next, it is to love others as much as we love ourselves. The first of the love commandments is a summary of the first four of the Ten Commandments given to Moses. The second of the love commandments summarises the remaining six commandments of the Decalogue (Matt 22:37–40).

If loving God is the number one rule for life, loving God must also be the top priority for the Christian school. All curricula and activities must guide students toward God so that they can know and love him more fully. Since this primary focus on God is totally missing from secular education, Christian educators cannot and must not go to their secular counterparts for guidance on the purpose of education. They must begin with God and his Word and guide their students toward the "chief end of man", as the Westminster Catechism puts it, which is to "glorify God and enjoy him forever". Lessons must point students toward God and equip them to serve their neighbours through loving actions.

Loving God with our mind and heart and strength comport well with biblical approaches to knowing and to truth. The idea of loving God with our minds in particular is an interesting concept for both teachers and students to explore. The Bible speaks of being transformed by the renewing of our minds (Rom 12:2), of having the mind of Christ (1 Cor 2:16) and of taking every thought captive to make it obedient to Christ (2 Cor 10:5). Teaching students to think Christianly or in a biblically faithful manner is an important equipping task of the Christian school.

The great commission

The commission that Jesus gave his disciples shortly before his ascension to heaven (Matt 28:18–20) includes several statements that are sometimes overlooked. The great commission is typically seen as the command to share the good news about Jesus to a lost world; it is evangelistic. Whether evangelism should be taught in the school or the church or the home is open to debate, but the need for evangelism is beyond dispute. This, however, is where the precise wording of the commission takes on added meaning.

The words "make disciples of all nations" move beyond saving souls. Discipling involves nurture—both instruction and correction. Thus, as mentioned previously, it calls for showing and telling. Nurturing students toward becoming fully equipped disciples of Jesus is the goal of the Christian school; it includes, but is more comprehensive than, being born again.

The words "teaching them to obey everything I have commanded you" are comprehensive, as well, for "everything" means every thing. A clue to what is included may be found in the preceding statement: "All authority in heaven and on earth has been given to me. Therefore …" The word "therefore" is there for a reason. Christ's authority or rule or kingship provide the basis both for "discipling the nations" and "teaching everything". The gospel of which this commission is speaking is the full-orbed or cosmic gospel of the kingdom. It involves being born again, for the kingdom (i.e., God's rule) begins in one's heart, but it quickly expands into all of nature, society, and culture. Again, Christian schools are, in essence, kingdom schools. In this sense, the great commission actually leads back to the original cultural mandate.

The cultural mandate

Loving God involves obeying God. Jesus said: "If you love me, you will obey what I command" (John 14:15). Part of that loving obedience is to teach everything that was previously commanded. This includes the mandate given to Adam and Eve in the beginning: have dominion over creation as my representatives, as my image bearers. The original cultural mandate (Gen 1:28; 2:15) included populating the earth, taking care of it and developing its potential. This was to be done for the glory of God and for the welfare of both humankind and the creation itself. It was the original pathway to loving God and loving one's neighbour. And it was a kingdom mandate in that it instructed humankind to rule in God's name. As life moved beyond the original garden, the cultural mandate that focused primarily on the natural world expanded into a more encompassing cultural mandate that included society and culture as well. The world and all life within it were to acknowledge God's rule. God's kingdom was established on earth. Mankind was to seek the fuller establishment and development of that kingdom. Seeking the kingdom was the primary task given in the beginning.

The cultural mandate has never been abrogated; it is still in effect. In fact, it provides foundational impetus for Christian education today. Christian schools are to prepare stewards and developers of God's world for his glory. They are to be culture formers in the name of Christ, who has been given all authority to be King over all things.

The purposes for Christian education are quite different from the purposes that drive secular education. In fact, they are radically different, for they emerge from God's revelatory Word. The education that seeks to accomplish these purposes is to be equally as radical. It is not simply secular education with a Christian veneer. It is transformed education, from its core through all activities, both in and out of the classroom. For Jesus is Lord of all things.

Transformed teaching is faithful to the Word in *worldview*

The essence of Christian education is teaching and learning that is couched in a biblically faithful perspective. Teachers must frame each of their lessons in a biblical worldview. A worldview grid, if you will, is to be placed on the aspect of created reality under study, and the material is to be interpreted and evaluated against both the narrative and propositional truth of Scripture. The Bible serves as eyeglasses through which general revelation can be viewed with transcendent clarity; it is light by which truth can be discerned in the midst of darkness. Teaching from a biblical worldview is the primary way to foster the mind of Christ in students. It helps them to break free from the conforming thought patterns of this world to the transforming insights of the Word and the Spirit. It helps them to think Christianly, a primary objective of the Christian school.

> *The Bible serves as eyeglasses through which general revelation can be viewed with transcendent clarity; it is light by which truth can be discerned in the midst of darkness.*

One biblical worldview that has been quite useful within the educational scene is that of creation-fall-redemption-consummation. It is important, though, not to apply this worldview in rote, rationalistic, or objective fashion, for the truth found in Jesus is alive, dynamic, and life-changing. Each of these four areas should be viewed in the light of the Light, for Scripture states: "In (his) light we see light" (Ps 36:9b). Jesus Christ, as the Logos for and in creation, is to be centrally present in every lesson.

The creation-fall-redemption-consummation worldview can be incorporated into lessons by asking a series of questions:

1. **What was God's original intent for the portion of created reality under study?** What are the creation norms—the way things should be for this particular aspect of reality? If the subject were the family, questions might include: What defines a family according to God's original intent? What is the God-given purpose of the family? What, according to Scripture, are its roles, responsibilities, and rules?

2. **Because of the fall, things no longer work the way they were intended. In what ways has this portion of created reality been affected by the fall, the presence of sin, and/or the spirit(s) of the times?** In a study of the family, questions might be: How has sin negatively affected the institution and sanctity of marriage and the family? How have the definition and the purpose of marriage been distorted by sin? How have family relationships been weakened through a misinterpretation of roles, responsibilities, and rules?

3. **Just as sin pervasively and comprehensively affects all things, the redemption of Christ covers all things, as well. What actions could or should be taken to bring reconciliation or restoration or redemption to this portion of created reality?** For the family: What steps could be taken to strengthen marriages and families? How can sin and its effects be removed from families? How can biblical norms be promoted within families?

4. **When Christ returns, all things will be made new. All of created reality will become fully sanctified. It will not only be whole—its original creation state, it will be complete. What might this portion of created reality look like in the new heaven and the new earth?** What impact should this "already" of the kingdom have on us today as we live in the "not yet"? Answers to these questions for the family might have a rather interesting twist to them, for there will be no marriage in heaven. Parental and sibling relationships may be altered, as well. In response to his own question, "Who are my mother and my brothers?" Jesus answered: "Whoever does God's will is my brother and sister and mother" (Mark 3:35). With the consummation of Christ's kingdom, the old order will have passed away; the new order will have been established. All things will be made new, including families.

5. **Worldview is a necessary tool for biblically faithful teaching and learning, for it is the vehicle by which students can be taught to think in a godly manner.**

But worldview can teach discernment in another way, as well. Since all persons have (religious) worldviews that direct all of their thoughts and practices, it is important to analyse the impact of worldview on their lives and works. Their worldviews can be ascertained by asking certain questions: Where are these people coming from? How do they answer the big questions of life and the world? Can we see the influence of their worldviews on their work? To what degree are their worldviews in alignment with Scripture? What portion of their thought and practice is redeemable? What portion should Christians not embrace? Literary works, films, and music should be analysed, evaluated and understood for their portrayal of worldviews. The sometimes-subtle worldview messages are far more important to be discerned and concerned over than the sometimes more obvious foul language or moral indiscretions.

Within the Christian school a biblical worldview is to be taught and learnt; but it is also an important tool to be applied in the studies and lives of students.

Transformed teaching is faithful to the Word in remaining faithful

This chapter began by explaining that if teachers are to be transformers of education for Christ, they must have hearts that have been transformed by the Spirit of Christ. They must be born again. But there is more. Yes, teachers must be transformed; but teachers must also remain transformed, both personally and professionally.

First, remaining transformed personally. Most students remember the lessons taught by their teachers' lives more than the lessons taught by their teachers' words. That is called incarnational teaching—truth embodied in a person. Jesus was the master incarnational teacher; teachers today are to emulate him. Like the apostle Paul, teachers should be able to say to their students: "Follow my example, as I follow the example of Christ" (1 Cor 11:1). John Piper is reported to have said that you can't commend what you don't cherish. Howard Hendricks purportedly said something similar indicating that if you want your students to bleed for a cause, you must be willing to let them haemorrhage. The only way for teachers to cherish and to haemorrhage for the cause of Christ is to remain in Jesus, the vine. Jesus said, "I am the vine; you are the branches. If you remain in me and I in you, you will bear much fruit; apart from me you can do nothing" (John 15:5). Remaining in the vine includes daily devotions and weekly church involvement. Sanctifying music, films and reading material should be part of the mix. What is ingested experientially becomes a natural part of what is lived and taught. To be healthy and alive and vibrant in Christ, one must faithfully feed on the bread of life and drink of the new wine—Jesus. Apart from him, there is no transforming power.

Second, remaining transformed professionally. Being a Christian teacher must be more than a job and a paycheque. It must be viewed as a high calling that requires continual growth. Learning to teach Christianly is a life-long effort. One never really arrives. Every year of teaching should include professional development oriented from a Christian perspective. It is a core responsibility for every Christian teacher to identify institutions and courses that examine teaching and learning from a biblically authentic worldview perspective, and then enrol in these courses. All the better if this responsibility is shared by the principal and board so that whole communities of teachers can be given the time and resources to study together.

The proper goal of transformed Christian teaching is faithfulness to the Word of God. This faithfulness includes knowing through revelation and relationship, active obedience to the truth by doing the truth, teaching by word and example, equipping for fulfilment of God's mandates, commands and commissions, and the nurturing of discerning Christian minds. The way to faithfulness in these areas is through personal and professional faithfulness.

Questions for discussion

1. What things can believing teachers see or understand that unbelieving teachers cannot see or understand? Why is it important for Christian teachers to be able to discern the things of the Spirit?

2. What are some pitfalls of making distinctiveness the primary goal of Christian education? Can you provide illustrations?

3. Is it okay that some teaching in a Christian school might be the same as or similar to some teaching that takes place in a secular school? Why or why not? Can Christian and secular teachers collaborate over certain educational matters, or do they have nothing in common? Explain your answer.

4. Select one of the lessons you teach. How might it be taught from a postmodern perspective? A modern perspective? A revelatory perspective?

5. Again, select a lesson you teach. How might the lesson be taught from a Greek view of truth? From a biblical view of truth?

6. Can you identify times when Jesus taught using the show and tell approach? If yes, when?

7. List the different connections a lesson may have. Why are connections necessary for learning? In which ways is God a God of connections or relationships?

8. In which ways are the love commands, the great commission, and the cultural mandate related to education? Is equipping students for obedient fulfilment of these a proper goal for Christian education? Why or why not?

9. Why is worldview the heart and soul of Christian education? Explain your answer.

10. Do you believe that a Christian teacher will be ineffective without personal and professional growth? Explain your answer.

Chapter 3

Transforming education: Students

Jack Fennema
Professor of Education, Emeritus, Covenant College

Dr Jack Fennema earned his BA from Calvin College and an EdD from the University of Georgia. Later he acquired an MA in marriage and family therapy from the Reformed Theological Seminary.

Dr Fennema has taught and been an administrator in K–12 Christian schools for 25 years. He has taught and served as director of graduate programs at Dordt College and Covenant College, where he is presently Professor of Education, Emeritus. He also served as Vice President at Trinity Christian College and as Executive Director of the Ontario Alliance of Christian Schools in Canada.

Dr Fennema is author of *Nurturing children in the Lord* and, in 2005, of *The religious nature and biblical nurture of God's children*. He and his wife Barbara live near Columbus, Ohio.

Abstract

Students need to understand the reasons they are enrolled in a Christian school. This chapter cites learning-to-live-the-abundant-life as the primary reason, and that Jesus is the way and truth leading to that life. Life begins by accepting Jesus as Saviour and declaring him to be Lord. Jesus is the way. But Jesus is also the truth—a topic that the Christian school can deal with as no other school can. The necessity of the armour of God is emphasised—it's a dangerous world out there! Each piece is examined for its stated place and purpose. Finally, various facets of the abundant life in Christ are reviewed—what it means to live life in him, both privately and publicly. It is ultimately a life of reconciliation and obedience.

> *If your 13-year-old child or student asked you why he or she should attend a Christian school, what would you say?*

Here is a question for parents and teachers: If your 13-year-old child or student asked you why he or she should attend a Christian school, what would you say? And, would your answer to this question be able to convince this young adolescent of the merit of Christian education? Most of us would be able to give our children some rationale for attending a Christian school, but explaining that rationale to a 13-year-old in a convincing manner is no easy task. Yet that is the goal of this chapter: first, to identify the biblical rationale for Christian education and then to explain that rationale in a manner that might make sense to the children we are seeking to educate. This chapter, then, is written initially for parents and teachers, but the message is ultimately for sons, daughters, and students.

The reason you should attend a Christian school is ...

Children are enrolled in Christian schools for many different reasons, some *re*active and some *pro*active. The students themselves may enjoy attending their particular Christian school because of friends who also attend there, friendly and caring teachers, feelings of safety and security, interesting and challenging subjects, and the availability of a wide variety of extra-curricular activities. Some may cite the Christian atmosphere, values, and teaching, as well. Typically, though, students do not understand the philosophical, theological, or even the biblical rationale that underlies the enterprise called Christian education. Consequently, most would not be able to articulate a well-thought-out reason for choosing a Christian school over a high-quality public school in their neighborhood.

The answer to the why question that truly cuts to the chase comes in the form of another question: How then shall we live? Education is all about living life. Why, then, should children attend a Christian school? Answer: To learn how to live life *as intended* in the *real* world. The italicised words are the key to the answer. "As intended" is defined by the Bible, and "real" is reality as God created it. Even the word "life" may need to be further defined. Jesus spoke of the nature of the life he provides: "I have come that [you] may have life, and have it to the full" (John 10:10). Other versions speak of having that life abundantly. Either way, life in Christ is full or complete beyond measure. It extends far beyond finite comprehension. It is life as it was designed by God to be.

An aspect of this life that is vitally important for children and young people to understand is that life in Christ is one part of a two-part choice. It is an either-or proposition. There are no additional options. Moses made this very clear as he confronted the people of Israel with this choice:

I set before you today life and prosperity, death and destruction. For I command you today to love the Lord your God, to walk in his ways, and to keep his commands, decrees, and laws; then you will live ...

This day I call heaven and earth as witnesses against you that I have set before you life and death, blessings and curses. Now choose life, so that you and your children may live and that you may love the Lord your God, listen to his voice, and hold fast to him. For the Lord is your life ... (Deut 30:15–16, 19–20)

The choice is between the full or abundant life in Christ and death. Both feet must be planted firmly on one side of the line or the other. Placing one foot on each side is not an option.

One other aspect that deserves attention is that life as it is meant to be lived is available right now. Generally, we speak of eternal life. Yes, life in Christ will last into all eternity, but for children the immediacy of life is more compelling and real. Eternity is a long way off for them. The abundant life will begin for them the moment they choose Christ as Lord and Saviour.

The Christian school, in cooperation with the Christian home and church, is in the business of equipping students to live life to the fullest. This equipping process is outlined very succinctly by one of Jesus' great "I am" statements: "I am the way and the truth and the life" (John 14:6a). The way to life begins with Jesus, who is the Way. It then proceeds through the truth, the currency of any school, the Christian school in particular. Jesus is the Truth, and, of course, he is also the Life. Each of these three stepping-stones—the way, the truth, and the life—will be examined for the manner in which it transforms education for students.

Jesus is the Way

The way to life as it was meant to be lived begins with Jesus, for he is the door or the gate through whom one must pass (John 10:7,9) to be reconciled with the Father, the source and giver of all life. And, no one can come to the Father except through Jesus (John 14:6b). For students to have access to and appropriate the abundant life, they must accept Jesus as their Saviour and declare him to be their Lord.

Accepting Jesus as Saviour

Within every Christian school classroom, some students have been born again or regenerated by the Holy Spirit and some have not. This is simply true. Even though only God really knows which students have experienced the new birth, the fact that followers of Jesus exhibit the fruit of his Spirit does provide some clue. These include: love, joy, peace, patience, kindness, goodness, faithfulness, gentleness, and self-control (Gal 5:22–23a).

A debate exists within Christian school circles whether evangelism should be a part of the school's purpose. Some Christian school advocates believe that the spiritual condition of children should be the concern of the home and the church but not of the school, which should focus solely on education. Some schools, however, especially those that are ministries of a church, see evangelism as a key if not primary component of the school's mission. Without seeking to resolve this issue here, an argument can be made that the spiritual condition of students is, indeed, germane to fulfilling the educational mission of any Christian school.

Simply stated, unless the Holy Spirit dwells within the hearts of students, they cannot comprehend or discern the big picture of the kingdom of Christ that the school is seeking to inculcate. Stated another way, students who have not experienced the new birth do not have access to the riches of the new life in Christ; thus, the fulfilment of the central task of the Christian school, that of equipping students to live life as intended in the real world, will have limited success. Not-yet-believers and unbelievers do not have ears that hear or eyes that see the things of the Spirit. Scripture is clear on this. "The man without the Spirit does not accept the things that come from the Spirit of God, for they are foolishness to him, and he cannot understand them, because they are spiritually discerned (1 Cor 2:14). Consequently, the regeneration of all students should be the desire and prayer of both parents and teachers.

Life as intended is to centre on loving God with one's entire being, including one's mind. Students who do not (yet) love Jesus cannot love the Father. The full or abundant life is found in God, and Jesus is the only Way.

Confessing Jesus as Lord

It is vitally important that students understand that the purpose of the new birth is more than simply an escape from hell. Its central purpose is proactive rather than reactive. It is to live life in Christ as God intended. Yes, students are "saved from", but their focus is to be on being "saved for." Being a follower of Jesus is more than a product of cheap grace or easy believism. It is a costly venture that calls for submission to Jesus as Lord. It involves dying to self. For it is all about Jesus, not about them.

Students must answer the question that Jesus asks of all who want to follow him: "Who do you say that I am?" The apostle Paul provides the proper answer: "… if you confess with your mouth, 'Jesus is Lord', and believe in your heart that God raised him from the dead, you will be saved. For it is with your heart that you believe and are justified, and it is with your mouth that you confess and are saved" (Rom 10:9–10). Belief with one's heart calls for total submission to the will of God in one's life; confessing that Jesus is Lord calls for a life that is sold-out to doing God's will. Both feet must be placed uncompromisingly within the kingdom of God.

Living for Jesus involves personal lordship over one's lifestyle. This includes purity, holiness, integrity and other biblical virtues. The fruit of the Spirit is exhibited. But living for Jesus also includes cosmic lordship, for Christ has been given authority over all things. He is King over a kingdom that touches every walk of life. Followers of Jesus are to seek first that kingdom, so that his kingdom may come and his will be done on earth.

> *Living for Jesus involves personal lordship over one's lifestyle.*

Students who are have experienced renewal from above will be progressively conformed into the very likeness of Christ, who himself is the "image of the invisible God" (Rom 8:29; Col 1:19), for they are becoming new creations. They are to decrease so that Christ may increase, for it is no longer they who live, but Christ who lives in and through them. The true knowledge, righteousness, and holiness of God that were lost with the Fall will be restored, at least in part (Col 3:9–10; Eph 4:22–24).

Jesus is the Truth

The abundant life in Christ begins for students the moment that they accept Jesus as their Saviour and Lord. They don't need a Christian school for that to happen. But unless students can understand how to fully appropriate and live that new life, their ministry as ambassadors for Christ in the world will be limited. They will not be able to maximise their full potential as citizens of Christ's kingdom on earth. The Christian school plays a vital role in the equipping of students to live in the world as followers of Christ.

Perhaps a deficit example can best illustrate this. The problem that Christians have with public education is more one of omission than commission. Public schools can be faulted more for what they don't do than for what they do. They have systematically eliminated any authoritative, normative, or redemptive reference to God from virtually every aspect of the school, the curriculum in particular. The reason this is so problematic for Christians is that, first, it is in direct conflict with the greatest of commandments to love God totally. Second, it denies that the world and life within it is all about God. It is an education that through omission declares that God is irrelevant to anything that has happened, is happening, or will be happening in the world. In this, it is both humanistic and secular. The devastating effect of dismissing God from 13 years of education (15,000+ hours) is that the mind of Christ cannot be developed in students. Even committed Christians tend to have their ability to understand how to minister in the marketplace muted. Their witness tends to become myopic, limited to sacred parts of life. They are unable to recognise how Christ is Lord of all things in society and culture, because they have been systematically desensitised to this fact day-in and day-out. Consequently, their impact as heralds and ambassadors of Christ's kingdom is, in effect, neutralised.

Unhappily, Christian schools can fall into a similar trap if they fail to teach that Christ is Lord of all things and that all of life is sacred. The Christian school can play a vital role in equipping students to live life as intended in the real world only if it places every aspect of the school—the curriculum in particular—under Christ's lordship. Only then can students learn to love God with all their minds. Only then can the discerning mind of Christ be developed in them.

As mentioned previously, the currency of schools is teaching the truth. Christian schools proclaim Jesus as the truth through whom students can be set free to live life fully. In the crucifixion of Christ, the shackles of sin that restrain the mind were broken. Eyes can now see, ears can hear, minds can comprehend "the mystery of God, namely, Christ, in whom are hidden all the treasures of wisdom and knowledge" (Col 2:2b–3). Students are shown how to walk in the truth so that they may obediently do the truth. The truth is the way to the life and it is a way of life.

Students are equipped in the truth through several means. They study God's general and special revelation, and they put on the whole armor of God, which involves praying in the Spirit.

Studying God's general revelation

God has revealed himself through his Son Jesus and through the Bible. But his earliest revelation came through the world he created. The apostle Paul tells us: "… since the creation of the world God's invisible qualities—his eternal power and divine nature—have been clearly seen, being understood from what has been made …" (Rom 1:20). The psalmist David concurs:

The heavens declare the glory of God;
the skies proclaim the works of his hands.
Day after day they pour forth speech;
night after night they display knowledge.
There is no speech or language
where their voice is not heard.
Their voice goes out into all the earth,
their words to the ends of the world.
(Ps 19:1–4a)

God's revelation of himself through creation is called general revelation, for it is available to all people, no matter what their relationship with God might be. It is from this general revelation that the curriculum of all schools is drawn, but it is only the Christian school that acknowledges the Author.

Using the eyeglasses of the Bible

Students can study the Bible during their devotions at home and as part of the educational program of their churches. But the Christian school teaches the Bible for a very special purpose: to understand general revelation more accurately and fully. In one sense, the Bible serves as 4-D glasses for students. They can study the three-dimensional world on their own, but to understand the transcendent dimension of the world in which they live, they need to use the eyeglasses of Scripture. It is from the Bible that a worldview is developed and applied to each of the disciplines taught. Biblical discernment is provided by viewing the world through the lens and in the light of Scripture. Vision that has been blurred by sin becomes clear; things that cannot be seen in darkness become observable in the light of the Word. The mysteries of God can be revealed.

Putting on the whole armour of God

Two kingdoms exist in this world: the kingdom of light and the kingdom of darkness, and the two kingdoms are in conflict. To be effective soldiers of the King, students must be equipped for the spiritual warfare in which they will be engaged. Different pieces of military equipment are listed by the apostle Paul in his letter to the Ephesians (6:10–18). The helmet of salvation and the sword of the Spirit—the Word of God—have already been mentioned as part of the equipping of young saints. Truth is described as a belt to be worn, for knowing and employing the truth revealed through the Word and the world is necessary for the successful living of life and the fighting of its battles in the name of Christ. The breastplate of righteousness is knowing what is right as God has determined it to be. Feet shod with readiness follow, as the righteous peace or shalom of Christ is actively applied to a broken and hurting world. Once again, students are called to image the true knowledge, righteousness and holiness found in Jesus. And, finally, faith replaces fear. When under attack, fear can create panic, but faith enables one to stand firm. Paul states elsewhere:

For though we live in the world, we do not wage war as the world does. The weapons we fight with are not the weapons of the world. On the contrary, they have divine power to demolish strongholds. We demolish arguments and every pretension that sets itself up against the knowledge of God, and we take captive every thought to make it obedient to Christ (2 Cor 10:3–5).

Kingdom citizens must be equipped with special armour and weapons if they are to carry out the work of their king in his world.

Within the Christian school, the light of the Word is used to destroy the lies of the evil one in the world, and the preserving salt of truth is used to redeem that which is true, noble, right, pure, lovely, admirable, excellent or praiseworthy (Phil 4:8). Truth is applied, discernment is exercised, and every thought is taken captive for Christ, who is Lord and King of all. Kingdom citizens must be equipped with special armour and weapons if they are to carry out the work of their king in his world.

Praying in the Spirit

In fitting conclusion to the "armour of God" passage, Paul instructs: "And pray in the Spirit on all occasions with all kinds of prayers and requests" (Eph 6:18). For it is "'not by might nor by power, but by my Spirit', says the Lord Almighty" (Zech 4:6). Every part of the equipping process in the Christian school must be bathed in prayer. The transformation of young hearts and minds is more than a pedagogical formula. It is a supernatural activity of the Spirit of Christ. Truth is designed to transform, and the Holy Spirit is the divine agent through whom transformation takes place, for he is the One who illumines and empowers. His presence in the classroom is to be invoked often and sincerely. For, in the words of Jesus, "Apart from me you can do nothing" (John 15:5c).

The Christian school is a place specially designed to equip children and young people to represent Christ in the world over which he is Lord of all things. Christian schools are to teach, in the words of the hymn writer, "living for Jesus a life that is true"—true to Jesus, true to the Bible and true to the world created and held together by Christ's powerful presence. Christian schools equip for a life of honouring God, serving others and enjoying God's good creation—life as God designed it to be.

The pathway to that life is through the truth. This truth both frees students to become everything God created them to be and at the same time demands an obedient response from them. It is truth that transforms students so that they can serve as instruments of transformation in God's world.

Understood within this context, Christian education is not an option for believers; it is a command. God expects children whom he has consecrated—declared holy, set apart for him (1 Cor 7:14)—to be nurtured toward loving him, serving others and caring for and developing his world. They are to be separated for holiness unto the Lord. This is the life he desires for them; it is living life before the face of God.

Jesus is the Life

Several questions might be posed by students at this point. "What does this full life look like in reality?" "In what ways will it personally affect my life?" "How is Jesus involved?" "How is the Christian school involved?" It is one thing to say, "Jesus is the life", which indeed is a true statement from Scripture, but what does that mean, practically speaking? All good questions.

A life of shalom

The new life, the full life, is a life of shalom. The word *shalom* is Hebrew for "peace" and is used today as a Jewish greeting or farewell. It is a word that implies a total sense of well-being, of harmony and fulfilment through relationship with God, others, the world and even with one's self. Things are the way they are supposed to be: whole, balanced, in sync. It is life that is fulfilled—filled with fullness.

Adam and Eve experienced shalom before sin entered the world. Perfect shalom or peace was then lost with the Fall and can only be regained through the Prince of Peace, Jesus. His words are: "Peace I leave with you; my peace I give you. I do not give to you as the world gives. Do not let your hearts be troubled and do not be afraid (John 14:27). The apostle Paul writes: "Do not be anxious about anything, but in everything, by prayer and petition, with thanksgiving, present your requests to God. And the peace of God, which transcends all understanding, will guard your hearts and minds in Christ Jesus" (Phil 4:6–7). The perfect peace of God—a deep-seated need within every person—is found only in Christ Jesus.

The need for shalom can be subdivided, if you will, into a series of needs that have been part of being human since the beginning.

1. **The need to be loved.** The kind of love craved is sacrificial—seeking the recipient's welfare. It is unconditional—based on who the person is, not on what the person does. It is unending—it can be counted on. This love provides safety and security, provision and protection. Only God provides this love perfectly, but parents provide it next best.

2. **The need to belong.** All persons need to be in meaningful relationship with others, part of a broader community. They need to experience the dignity of a task that contributes to the welfare of the whole. They need to love and to serve others. They need to be loved, needed, valued and respected by others.

3. **The need for achievement.** This is the need to be a creator, to form a product, to complete a task. It is achieving a goal, accomplishing a purpose. Closure is involved.

4. **The need for competency.** This focuses more on the process than the product. Persons desire competency in a field or activity. They need to be good at something, able to do something really well—develop and fine-tune a talent.

5. **The need to know.** All human beings possess an inherent desire to know and to understand. They have a built-in quest for knowledge. They want to know how things work, their cause-and-effect. They enjoy finding answers to questions and solving problems and mysteries. They want to have new experiences and adventures. They like exploring new places and accepting new challenges.

6. **The need to self-actualise.** This need involves becoming everything a person was created to be—the "I need to be me". It is coming to know one's self intimately, fully acting on that knowledge and existentially enjoying the process. It is fulfilment of one's person, passions and potential. It is a lifetime of giving birth to oneself.

7. **The need for transcendence.** This is the human need to find ultimate meaning and answers to life's foundational questions. This is the need to belong to Someone far greater than oneself. It is relating to and being embraced by God. It is experiencing his perfect shalom. It is the desire to worship him.

In a quest to fill this need, persons either turn to the true God or they turn to idols and exchange *"the truth of God for a lie, and [worship] and [serve] created things rather than the Creator ..."* (Rom 1:25).

Granted, secular education can meet a number of these needs, at least to some degree. But it is only Christian education that seeks and is able to meet all of these needs in the person and power of Jesus. And, it is only a school committed to seeking first the kingdom of God that can create a whole that is greater than the sum of the parts: the full life of shalom in Jesus.

A life of personal fullness

Jesus provides life to students personally. Again, students do not necessarily need the Christian school for that to happen. By personally acknowledging Jesus as the way to the Father they can experience the peace of his forgiveness and restoration no matter where they attend school. They can also appropriate the security of having Jesus as Lord over their personal lives. And, they can exhibit and enjoy the fruit of the Spirit.

The Christian school does, however, assist students to grow personally in the Lord. That may not be the primary goal of the school, but it certainly is an important part of what the school is seeking to accomplish. The essence of the Christian school mandate, though, is equipping students to live life as intended in the real world. In so doing, the Christian school seeks to move students beyond their personal world into the world as cosmos.

A life of fullness in God's cosmos

Only education that is illumined and empowered by the Word and the Spirit can equip students to live life as intended by God in his created reality. Reality for many children and young people today is what they see and experience in their subjective worlds. Tragically, much of that reality is an illusion. The truth of God cannot be found in it. The normativity of God's Word too often feels abnormal to them, and the abnormalities created by the Fall often appear to be normal. In addition, the lie that this world belongs to the evil one rather than to Jesus, to whom all authority has been given, permeates the thinking of many Christian youth. This erroneous view of the world causes them to hunker down as if in a city of refuge, waiting to be rescued when Jesus returns. In contrast, the Christian school stands as a boot camp to educate, train and equip young citizens of Christ's kingdom to wage war, demolish strongholds, and take every thought captive to make it obedient to Christ. The Christian school is not simply a luxury for parents who can afford it; it is a place necessary for preparing kingdom youth for their kingdom task. This task encompasses and engages the entire world as cosmos, the world for which Jesus died (John 3:16).

The apostle Paul writes about this cosmos, God's created reality, in his letter to the church in Rome:

The creation waits in eager expectation for the sons of God to be revealed. For the creation was subjected to frustration, not by its own choice, but by the will of the one who subjected it, in hope that the creation itself will be liberated from its bondage to decay and brought into the glorious freedom of the children of God.

We know that the whole creation has been groaning as in the pains of childbirth right up to the present time (Rom 8:19–22).

The world for which Jesus died includes all people on earth and all of creation. With the advent of sin the creation was cursed; with the advent of Christ the bonds of the curse were broken. Jesus' words on the cross, "It is finished" (John 19:30), signalled the shattering of the curse. The creation now waits "in eager expectation" (Rom 8:19) for citizens of the kingdom to further the liberation and give birth to its potential for the glory of God as originally intended. The primary purpose of the Christian school is to prepare students for just such a task. The road passes through the cross and the Great Commission, for reconciliation must take place, but it continues through the crown and the cultural mandate of Genesis 1, as well. Both the cross and crown of Jesus are to be acknowledged in the purpose and activities of the Christian school.

A life of reconciliation and obedience

Students (and all persons) who have been transformed into new creations by Christ are given the ministry of reconciliation. They are Christ's ambassadors—his presence—within the world over which he is King (2 Cor 5:17–21). The ministry of reconciliation is holistic. It involves all things—society, culture and nature. It includes the liberation of both people and creation. It is, in fact, appropriating the Christian life to the fullest as intended. All aspects of God's perfect peace cited above are present.

New creations in Christ are progressively conformed to the likeness of Jesus and thus become restored image-bearers of God. Once again they possess and can exercise true knowledge, righteousness and holiness. They do this through the divine offices within which Jesus himself functioned. He was our chief Prophet, our only High Priest, and our eternal King. Students, as his image-bearers are, in turn, to function as prophets, priests, and kings within his world.

The Christian school equips its students to be 21ˢᵗ century prophets. As recipients of true knowledge they are equipped to become God's spokespersons. They are taught to represent his thinking in all things, because the entire world belongs to God and is presently governed by his Son. It is truly all about him. Students are prepared to function as his prophetic voice in the marketplaces of today, providing his answers to contemporary issues and problems.

Fulfilling the office of prophet requires a discerning mind that understands how the norms of Scripture apply to families, politics, work, recreation and other facets of society, culture and the natural world. One of the most important responsibilities that a Christian school has is to develop Christian minds within its students. These are minds that no longer conform to the pattern of this world but are transformed by the Word and the Spirit. They are minds that can analyse and evaluate what the world has to offer through a biblical worldview or grid. They are minds that understand the creation order that is present in each discipline studied in school— how Jesus as the Logos holds created reality together in a lawful and intentional manner. Christian education is designed to teach students how to love God with their minds. In so doing, students are equipped to be the prophetic voice of Christ in today's world.

> *One of the most important responsibilities that a Christian school has is to develop Christian minds within its students.*

The Christian school also equips its students to be 21ˢᵗ century priests. As recipients of true holiness, they are equipped to become God's healing agents. As mediating bridge-builders, students can in the name of Christ bring reconciliation and peacemaking to alienated people. This begins with the restoration provided by Jesus between the Father and a lost world. It continues with the renewal of human relationships and the relationship between people and creation. As healers, students are called to restore broken people and a hurting world. The divine balm of Gilead is to be applied to the human pain and suffering caused by sin.

Fulfilling the office of priest requires a caring heart, a mind that understands and feet "shod in readiness". The spectrum of healing opportunities ranges from evangelism to healthcare to the environment. The natural, social and behavioural sciences are prime avenues through which to equip kingdom youth to bring strategic shalom to people and places ravaged by the effects of sin. One does not have to look far to see the need for a cup of water in the name of Christ. Jesus said: "Whatever you

[do] for the least of these ... you [do] for me" (Matt 25:40). Priestly service is both an activity and an outcome of Christian education.

Finally, the Christian school equips its students to be 21st century kings. As recipients of true righteousness, they can be kingly kingdom-seekers who act in the name of Christ with justice, righteousness and mercy. They are to be taught to do what is right. The prophet Micah summarises this with the words:

He has shown you, O man, what is good.
   And what does the Lord require of you?
To act justly and to love mercy
   and to walk humbly with your God. (6:8).

At the dawn of history, God appointed his image-bearers to be his representative rulers over creation, and he issued the following mandate:

"Be fruitful and increase in number; fill the earth and subdue it. Rule over the fish of the sea and the birds of the air and over every living creature that moves on the ground."

The Lord God took the man and put him in the Garden of Eden to work it and take care of it (Gen 1:28; 2:15).

This cultural mandate is still in effect today, and students are to be equipped to carry it out. To do so, they must become thoroughly familiar with every aspect of God's general revelation, the world over which they are to be caretakers and stewards. This involves studying the content of the various school disciplines. It also requires viewing the skill areas—the maths, computer, language—as tools with which to rule over and develop creation. Students are to rightly divide God's special revelation to determine how to rule in a righteous manner. And they are to be taught how to be servant-leaders as they exercise the authority given to them in the various arenas of life. This is especially important if their responsibilities include the powerless, those who have been marginalised or disenfranchised. The seeking of Christ's kingdom and his righteousness requires a servant's heart.

Summary

Students in Christian schools need to know the reason they are enrolled in their alternative school. This means, first of all, that parents and teachers must personally think through a biblically faithful rationale for this decision and, then, be able to state that rationale in a way that resonates with students. No small task.

All schools seek to prepare their students for life. They all seek to provide answers to the question: How then shall we live? Since schools define the purpose of life differently, they also educate students in a variety of ways. The Christian school believes that life is to be lived before the face of God—*coram Deo*. Thus, its purpose and program reflect that ideal.

The Christian life is positive, not negative. It begins now, not in the sweet by and by. It transforms all things, not just a sacred part of life. It begins with Jesus as the Way to the Father. It then proceeds through Jesus as the Truth who sets one free. The Christian school specialises in truth that is found in Jesus and in God's special and general revelation. Students are taught to embrace the truth so that they can become engaged in living life to its fullest.

Life in Jesus is a life of shalom—life as it was created to be, life as every person yearns for it to be. This life is full-orbed; it is both personal and cosmic in scope. The curriculum of the Christian school is full-orbed as well, as it teaches the lordship and kingship of Jesus over his world as cosmos. Each discipline seeks to equip students in a particular facet of kingdom citizenship.

The Christian life begins with Jesus; it then passes through being born again back to the Genesis 1 mandate to rule and subdue as God's agents in his world. The journey moves forward toward the culmination of Christ's kingdom, when every knee will bow and all things will be placed under his feet.

The youth of Christ's kingdom are called to learn how to live life *as intended* in the *real* world so that they can assume their roles and responsibilities as kingdom citizens. The Christian school exists to equip them to do that as 21st century prophets, priests and kings living life before the face of God—*coram Deo*.

Questions for discussion

1. Write a brief statement in language 13-year-olds would understand, explaining the purpose and goals of your Christian school. Try it out on them, and then discuss the results with another parent or teacher.

2. Ask your children or students to explain why a person should become a Christian. Did their answers include life as it is described in this chapter?

3. Can a child or young person accept Jesus as Saviour without also accepting him as Lord? If yes, what would that look like? If no, why not?

4. Explain the difference between personal lordship and cosmic lordship. How does each impact the Christian school?

5. What is so unique about the Christian life that prohibits secular schools from equipping students to live that life?

6. Do you agree with the statement: "The problem Christians have with public education is more one of omission than commission"? Explain your answer.

7. Should the equipping of youth with "the whole armour of God" be more the business of the home and church than the school? Why or why not?

8. Review the seven aspects of shalom listed in this chapter. Would you add any? Delete any? Explain your answer.

9. What has the ministry of reconciliation to do with being a prophet, priest and king? What is the role of Christian education in this process?

10. Explain what is meant by the statement: "The Christian life begins with Jesus; it then passes through being born again back to the Genesis 1 mandate to rule and subdue as God's agents in his world. The journey moves forward toward the culmination of Christ's kingdom …" Explain the relationship of each part of that statement to the task of the Christian school.

Chapter 4

Inhabiting the mindfield

Why we think the way we do, and what to do about it

Richard Edlin

Principal, National Institute for Christian Education

Richard Edlin is the principal of the National Institute for Christian Education (NICE), a government-accredited, degree-granting postgraduate teacher training organisation based in Sydney, Australia. Although Richard, his wife, Annette, and their three adult children currently all live in Australia, the Edlins have travelled the world in their commitment to the cause of Christian education. Richard, has written many books and articles on Christian Education, as well as producing videos and other ICT media on the subject. His experience includes over 30 years of teaching and administration in both secular and Christian educational contexts in both the developed and the developing world. His earned doctorate in teacher education is from the University of Alabama. In 2005, he was awarded a rare honorary doctorate from Kosin University in Busan, Korea, for his international contribution to Christian education.

Abstract

This chapter examines the powerful but largely unrecognised forces that control our thinking patterns and processes in Western society. It acknowledges that as Christians we desire that everything, including how we think, reflects our willing submission to the lordship of Christ. In reality, however, our thinking tends to reflect unwittingly the lordship of philosophies that have shaped the modern (and postmodern) Western world. Greek philosophers are examined as one example of the pagan, theistically committed nature of our thinking. Examples are given of how this constrains our reading of Scripture and warps the shape of our educational goals and practices. The chapter concludes with a few suggestions, focused on a repositioning in our lives of the full story of the Bible, that can lead us to celebrate the lordship of Christ over how we think and live as Christians in the 21st century.

Introduction

Why do we Christians think the way that we do, particularly in education, when so often these thought patterns are at variance with biblical perspectives? Consider the four examples below that illustrate the point.

1. Knowing truth

When asked to explain what truth is, many of us attempt to encapsulate it in a definition that focuses on accuracy of ideas. The Bible seems to understand truth in a different way that goes beyond the world of concepts and ideas. Consider that Jesus did not say "I've come to tell you about the truth"; rather he said, "I am the truth" (John 14:6). For Jesus, and the Bible, although truth obviously has a strong cognitive aspect, truth first of all is relational. If we ignore this, then we will have all sorts of trouble with Rahab for example, who lied when telling Jericho's soldiers that the Jewish spies had run off when in fact she was hiding them in her house. In the books of Hebrews and James, because she was trothful (faithful in relationship) to her new-found God and his servants (Josh 2; Heb 11:31; Jas 2:25), Rahab is commended

> *The Bible seems to understand truth in a different way that goes beyond the world of concepts and ideas.*

for this "untruth". But many of us have trouble endorsing the Bible's commendation of Rahab because we reduce truth to cognitive concepts. Perhaps we think about truth in this limited way because of ingrained, Western cultural tendencies which are at variance with a fully flowered biblical mindset concerning truth.

2. Examinations tell us when a student knows something

As a second example, why do we as Christian educators teach as if genuine knowing consists in being able to accurately repeat a series of ideas in a written test? Ask most teachers (and most examination/qualifications agencies and politicians as well) how we are able to determine that our students know something, and we'll tell you that students demonstrate knowledge through the sitting of examinations. We often reward this abstract academic achievement in end-of-year prize-giving ceremonies. Why do we think like this? A biblical concept of knowing insists that people don't really know something until they live it out in their lives in service and worship of God. Consider the biblical concept of knowing in the example of Adam and Eve. Adam *knew* his wife Eve, and they bore a son. Forgive the pun, but this knowing was much more than just a piece of knowledge conceived in Adam's head! As Jack Fennema says elsewhere in this book, "Knowing in the biblical sense is more than simply cognitive mastery; it is holistic … Students are 'to know' with their heart, head and hands. Learning within Christian schools includes a cognitive understanding of the truth, a heartfelt commitment to the truth and an obedient response to the truth. It is hearing the Word and doing the Word; it is both revelation and response." Sadly, and usually without even realising it, when I look back on how I understood knowing in my classroom, I assumed this non-biblical understanding of the concept. Maybe again, the impact of the Greeks on my Western educational training and living has had something to do with it!

3. Academic success and titles

Consider the issue of how we as teachers prepare children for life beyond school. Even if not stated, an assumption of our educational culture is that if a child is capable of extended abstract thought, then he or she should naturally consider going to university and obtaining a degree. After all, this career path in our Western world leads to a higher status and higher income, in the years ahead, and usually to an all-round better person. But why do we think this way, given that our cultural commitment to the superiority of abstract academic achievement and its attendant status-level over manual labour has no biblical foundation? Despite their intellectual skills, Jesus did not demean carpentry and Paul continued to employ his manual skill of tentmaking right throughout his life. The title, Doctor, may be a useful tool in procuring a complementary upgrade in airline travel, but in Christian terms it is absolutely no indicator of the value or fulfilment of a person. The answer lies in the elitist view of abstract ideas and knowledge that we have inherited from that great Greek philosopher, Plato.

4. Controversy about asking questions

Finally, consider the issue of encouraging students to ask questions in class. This is one area of dramatic difference between Western pedagogy and Eastern pedagogy. In the West, students are encouraged to question, and teacher training programs are replete with instructional techniques that encourage an inquisitive environment. In Asian schools following a Confucian model, however, it is often assumed that to ask teachers questions is insulting and contrary to good relationships. Why do we in the West so highly value this instructional technique which is decried by quality educators in other cultures? What would Jesus do if he was a fellow teacher in my school? Which model more accurately reflects a biblically authentic pattern in my cultural setting?

A biblical calling to be made new in our minds

Why do we think the way that we do? In one sense, this may seem to be a silly question. "We just do!" one might be tempted to respond. But that is not the case—we don't just do. How we think (which is an important governor in what we think) is not a neutral, naïve activity. It reflects particular powerful beliefs about the world and our place and task in it. It is a rich and complicated process, developed and honed over centuries of reflection, conditioning and reinforcement. As Kanitz (2005) has commented, in our thinking "We are starting with [an unacknowledged] densely populated intellectual ground with various worldviews firmly entrenched and others competing for space" (p. 105). The fact that we today are largely unaware of this only adds to its power and authority over us.

As educators, and in particular as Christian educators, as we seek to bring every thought into captivity to Jesus Christ (2 Cor. 10:5), it behoves us to develop an awareness of the culturally bound forces that shape how we think. In fact, God's Word urges us as an act of worship to God, to be much more deliberate and vigilant in proactively reforming patterns of the mind including why we think the way that we do. In his letter to his friends in Colossae, Paul urged them not to be led astray by ideas and thought-patterns based on human ideas, but to base their ideas and thought-patterns on the revelation of Jesus Christ, through whom all things hold together (Col 1:8). Paul also urged his readers to work hard at not being conformed to the prevailing secular culture, but to be "transformed by the renewing of their minds" (Rom 12: 1–2). Finally, consider what Paul said when writing to Christians in Ephesus, that city already famous in Paul's day for great philosophers like Heraclitus. Paul challenged them to be different from the licentious and hedonistic individualism of their culture and to be like Jesus, highlighting his underlying thesis that being born again into Christ has as one of its foundation stones "being made new in the attitude of your minds" (Eph 4:17 – 5:2).

It's crucial that we recognise the almost subliminal activity inherent in why we think the way that we do. We don't consciously think about breathing, but we take several breaths each minute to sustain our bodies. Similarly, we don't usually think about how we think, yet how we think (i.e. why we think the way we do) gives form and structure to our mental processes that enable us to comprehend, discern and interact with the world in a coherent manner. As Christians, our failure to realise the impact of putting ideas together may have led us to exclude biblically informed perspectives from our core decision-making. It may also be leading us Christian educators to function antithetically to the gospel we proclaim in many of our educational activities. Sadly, Harry Blamires' (1963) comment of several decades ago still haunts Christians in education today: "We are observing the sly process by which the Christian mind de-Christianises itself without intending to do so" (p. 69). Sire (2000) goes so far as to lament that when Christian educators and scholars typically succumb to a pagan intellectual perspective, they are living a lie:

I suspect that there are many more Christian academics than those whose academic papers reflect a Christian worldview … [In many areas of study] revealed truths of the Christian worldview are so relevant that not to bring them into the picture constitutes living a lie (p. 219).

The Western mind

This chapter limits the discussion of how we think to the context of people predominantly impacted by the Western mind. Patterns identified are those that have developed within a Western tradition rather than, for example, the Eastern traditions of Confucianism or Daruma's Zen Buddhism. The same issue needs to be addressed, of course, by those whose thinking has been shaped by Eastern episte-mological and philosophical traditions but this exploration needs to be done by scholars who are well versed in understanding those traditions.

What then is this contemporary Western mind that is at the core of shaping our thinking? Tarnas (1991) equates "Western mind" with "worldview" but although this is helpful, "worldview" extends the notion beyond the more limited concept of cognition that is the focus here. However, this paper does endorse the centrality of the notion of worldview or big story that we inhabit, and the associated contention that this worldview or story both informs, and is informed by, the way that we think.

Kok's (1998) otherwise helpful publication on this matter defines the Western mind as "the theoretical investigation and account of the diversity, dimensions, and interrelatedness of the cosmos" (p. 3). However, this definition could apply to a pattern of thinking derived from many cultural traditions, not just the West.

The term "Western mind" could usefully be considered to be the dynamic, cumulative amalgam of specific thoughts, ideas and cognitive processes that have gained credence through the epochs of human history progressing from classical (mainly Greek or Hellenistic), through Christianity, the medieval period, the renaissance and modernity, and onto the postmodernity of today.

> *For the Christian engaging cautiously in the world of ideas, our understanding must be embedded within a Christian frame of reference.*

Although this definition offered above has merit, for the Christian it remains incomplete. Philip Jackson's (1992, p. 12) comment that even our definitions are a part of our argument serves to remind us that definitions are not neutral or objective, but are philosophically laden expressions of a particular point of view. For the Christian engaging cautiously in the world of ideas, our understanding must be embedded within a Christian frame of reference. To live and move and have our being in Christ, means that we declare that our understanding of thinking and why we think the way that we do needs to commence with, and flow out of, a Christian set of presuppositions. As an aside, we implore non-Christian writers in this area to recognise and declare their own presuppositional starting points as well!

To be consistent then, in a very real sense Christian educators seeking to understand the concept and implications of why we think the way we do in the Western world need to start with a biblically authentic understanding of that world. We start, therefore, with an acknowledgment of the creative and sustaining authority of the eternal God of the Bible over all that is. We recognise that human beings, though created perfect, marred God's creation by sin and have thus contaminated every aspect of reality (including thinking and culture). Wonderfully, and in a preordained manner, God, by the incarnation and substitutionary crucifixion and resurrection of Jesus Christ, provided a way for the world (including humanity) to be reconciled to himself. This in turn provides those who accept it with the dynamic to live now and for eternity in a personal relationship with this Creator-sustainer God as we celebrate his lordship over everything—including mental processes.

Great philosophers such as Socrates, Plato and Aristotle discovered valuable insights from which we can learn. However, in that they did their thinking outside of a creaturely submission to the God of the Bible, their discoveries were distorted and tended to elevate one aspect of the creation (rationality for example) to the position of ultimate authority which belongs to God alone. This means that in our analysis of their thinking, Christian educators must recognise the pre-existing and idolatrous cultural commitments of the reflections of these pagan philosophers, and critique them accordingly. In passing, we should also recognise that even the assumption that the process of cognitive analysis will enable us to discern truth is itself a philosophically laden position that needs exploration. As Kok (1998, p. 23) has commented, analysis follows assumptions and confessions, and not the other way around.

Focus on Greek or Hellenistic traditions

Many strands are woven together in the fabric that determines why we think the way we do in the contemporary west. The discussion in this chapter is limited to the heritage of the Greeks, and especially Socrates, Plato and Aristotle, and the re-emergence of some of their ideas in the neoplatonic period. Although there are other vital subsequent intellectual streams such as the renaissance, modernity and postmodernity, they will not be discussed here (a succinct and useful overview of their place in shaping our contemporary thinking can be found in an article by Goheen (2004) in *Pointing the way: Directions for Christian education in the new millennium*).

Early Hellenistic thinking

The centuries of Homer, with his anthropomorphic view of the gods (ascribing to them human form, characteristics and behaviour), are often described as the pre-dawn of Western thought. In this period up until around the fifth century BC, myth and legend merged into reality. This is well captured in the *Iliad* and the *Odyssey*, which Tarnas (1991) describes as "a collective primordial vision" (p. 24). Yet, at this time, powerful intellectual forces began to appear on the stage of human history which have enduring influence today. Democritus (460–370 BC) gave us atomic theory and perhaps provided Plato, 150 years later, with a platform from which to develop his two-worldy perception of reality (dualism). Pythagoras (582–507 BC), within an overtly religious context, helped us to understand mathematical forms. Parmenides (510 BC–c 450 BC) asserted the primacy of logic as the determiner of reality. Heraclitus (535–475 BC) recognised the uncertainty caused by change in the world, but claimed that it could be best come to terms with through a rational, fiery, ordering power of the universe called the *logos*. Therefore John was not saying something radically new in his gospel when he said that in the beginning was the *logos*, and the *logos* was with God and the *logos* was God. What John did announce that was stunningly radical and counter-culturally interpersonal, was the incarnation—that the *logos* became flesh and dwelt among us in Jesus Christ!

We should also remember the sophists and orphists who were important during this classical Greek period. The individualistic sophists reduced the purpose of debate from determining truth to the mere winning of an argument (hence the derogatory use of the term sophistry today). The incipient dualism of the orphics had a great influence on Plato and subsequent Western thought.

The School of Athens (Raphael, c 1511)

Although the aforementioned people and movements are important, there are three giants of Greek thought who have had the most enduring impact on why we think the way that we do in the modern Western world. These men are Socrates, Plato and Aristotle, all depicted in Raphael's 500-year-old mural in the Vatican. At the request of Pope Julius II, the young Raphael Sanzio painted a fresco originally entitled *Knowledge of Causes* but which has been known to posterity as *The School of Athens*. The panorama (depicted below) was an attempt to bring into one place

many of the famous Greek sages—even though they did not all live at the same time. Raphael also used his imagination to embellish historical records in depicting the physical appearances of his subjects (it is suggested, for example, that Heraclitus in the picture was given the face of Raphael's contemporary, Michelangelo).

The painting provides a convenient platform from which to launch a brief discussion of the central figures from the Greek culture who have equipped us (for better and for worse) in the 21st century to think the way that we do. Raphael left no chart by which to name his assembled figures. However, by their various actions and activities in the painting, many can be identified. Socrates, Plato and Aristotle can be recognised conclusively. After reading this chapter, readers might like to identify our three philosophers in Raphael's picture, using the comments made about each of them in this chapter. A coloured version of *The School of Athens* can be viewed on many sites on the World Wide Web.

The influence of Socrates (c 469–399 BC)

Much of what we know about Socrates we know through Plato, a disciple of Socrates, and the one who recorded Socrates' wisdom in his own *Dialogues*. For Socrates, the best way to identify the truth or otherwise of assumptions or opinions was to challenge them with a constant stream of questions which frequently exposed the assumptions to be ignorance masquerading as wisdom. Socrates' view was that "to know virtue … one has to take apart, analyse, test the worth of every statement … in order to find its true character" (Tarnas, 1991, p. 34). For Socrates, once one had pursued an idea vigorously enough through this technique, then good insight would be attained and correct thinking and living would be the inevitable consequence. His questioning style, imbued as it was with a genuine desire to seek after truth, was not universally endorsed, particularly by some in positions of power. Ultimately, it led Socrates to be put on trial and condemned to die by drinking a mixture laced with deadly hemlock.

Socrates' style of critical scepticism, called the socratic method or socratic dialectic, lives on today. In pedagogical circles, we contrast direct instruction (not in vogue in the West) with the laudable socratic method which is deemed to inspire the enquiring mind, give students ownership in the learning process, and help lead to an improved and more enlightened position in everything from scientific enquiry to the causes of events in history. Though frequent questioning is seen as a blight on education in some other cultures, so important is the socratic method in Western education, that whole courses in Bachelor of Education degrees are devoted to equipping teacher trainees with effective questioning skills and strategies and to keeping teachers from falling into the trap of continuous direct instruction. A classroom is not considered to be a good classroom unless individual children are encouraged and empowered to question as an integral part of their learning activities. This is not only true of the student. Teachers are encouraged to consider themselves to be reflective practitioners, which involves the responsibility of questioning one's own understanding and delivery styles. The concept of formative evaluation as opposed to summative evaluation is predicated upon teachers being reflective interrogators of their own teaching styles and content.

At this point, we are not evaluating the merits of the socratic method. The intention here is to show that our thinking about what makes good teaching and about why we think that questioning is a good practice is not neutral or intuitive. It is not just the way things are. It is a particular individualistic pedagogical tradition and approach that is deplored in some cultures but is lauded in our own, and is a heritage from the teaching and learning style made popular by Socrates. This is why Raphael in his great fresco shows Socrates remonstrating or arguing (look at the use of his hands).

The influence of Plato (c 427–347 BC)

Plato is at the centre of Greek thought. He focused his thinking on the search for truth. However, he believed that it was impossible to discover this elusive reality in the imperfect and constantly changing environment of the world in which we live. The inconstant material world and our experience of it cannot be trusted. We must seek the pure form of truth in the unadulterated world of ideas or forms. We must look elsewhere, into the world of ideas, wherein exists the true reality of the forms of things that we experience in everyday life. This is why Raphael shows Plato in the fresco pointing upward, out of our own tainted, experiential situation. Further-more, since the unseen but perfect or ideal world of ideas is the really true world, then true knowledge is theoretical knowledge, and true wisdom is the process of disengaging ourselves from the world of experience and rigorously searching for the reality that is beyond.

Two illustrations help us to comprehend Plato's position. As I write this chapter, I am looking over beautiful Lake Tarawera in New Zealand, with its majestic and currently inactive volcano looming in the background. Consider the boats that I can see in the small boat harbour in the foreground. I can see many kinds of boats: big, little, fat, sleek, fast, slow, white, red and so on. But which one is the real boat? Plato's answer is that none of them are. They all embody some of the realities of what it is to be a boat, but none of them is the real, perfect boat. The real, perfect form of a boat doesn't exist in the world of experience, but only in the world of ideas. Therefore to find what it is to understand a real boat, we need to elevate our thinking from the inadequacy of experienced reality and contemplate the world of ideas—a serious and challenging task. Only then will we truly be able to understand the essence or unchanging idea or form of the boat, from which all experienced boats are derived but of which they are an inadequate image.

The second illustration is the famous allegory of the cave which Plato himself relates in *The Republic* (translated and cited in Ozmon & Carver, 2003, pp. 41–43). In this witty story which is somewhat reminiscent of Orwell's *Animal Farm*, Plato tells of unenlightened people who have spent their entire lives imprisoned in a cave and who are only able to face the cave's back wall. The light of a fire projects shadows of the outside world onto the back wall. Because of their position and ignorance, the pathetic prisoners mistake the hazy shadow on the wall for the glorious reality that exists outside the cave. They spend their energies seeking to understand the shadows, rewarding those who are best at describing their form and predicting their appearance, while all the time ridiculing any suggestion of a fuller reality that exists beyond the shadows. In Plato's analysis, our world of experience is the paltry world of shadows and real wisdom involves seeing beyond this shadowy den to the fullness of the world of ideas where one can find the real ordering principles of life.

> *The concept today that education which informs the mind of possibilities beyond current knowledge and experience will lead to the betterment of the individual and of society is a legacy of Plato.*

Because real knowledge is found in this other world of ideas, and therefore knowledge and activities limited to interaction with this present world are inferior and of less value, Plato further argued that those few who engaged in the cognitive journey beyond the temporal world towards real truth could be regarded as philosopher-kings. They were worthy of elevated status and respect, and must share their wisdom with others. They also were the best choices for positions of power since they had the required insights to rule for the greater good of the rest of humanity which did not possess their superior insight.

The concept today that education which informs the mind of possibilities beyond current knowledge and experience will lead to the betterment of the individual and of society is a legacy of Plato. It is so pervasive that we can scarcely imagine education any other way. We believe that, as the world of ideas in the classroom raises their horizons and understandings to better and more extended possibilities for living, all children will be able to live and act in a more appropriate and fulfilling way. The perspective that intellectual pursuits and the study of ideas (white collar work) is fundamentally a better thing to do than manual labour (blue collar work) is also a product of platonic thinking. Therefore in schooling we lament the taking up of an apprenticeship by an intellectually gifted teenager and counsel him or her to stay on at school and go to university and so have a more fulfilling life. When statistics are released and endorsed which demonstrate that those with a university degree are able to earn higher incomes than those without, at least in part we are reflecting and reinforcing Plato's superiority of the cerebral professions over more manual vocations.

Teaching students to think is at the core of platonic or idealist pedagogy. According to Ozmon & Carver (2003), good platonic teachers would be defined as those who encourage their students to think morally and independently, and who consider ideas and truth beyond what they see, not just limiting investigation to the minutiae of any particular situation or data set. Postmodern or radical constructivist perspectives concerning the relative nature of truth do not fit comfortably within a platonic way of thinking.

Neoplatonism

Although misplaced in terms of chronological order, it is appropriate at this point to consider neoplatonism, which was the re-emergence of platonic thinking from the third to the fifth century AD. With Plotinus as its principal protagonist, neoplatonism focused on Plato's two-world dualism and on the concept of a mystical other as the controlling force in the superior world of the upper realm. This Absolute Good was the transcendent removed reality from which emanated the lower, baser world inhabited by human beings. Neoplatonism continued the platonic priorities for education. It also gave the Christian church a dualistic or dichotomous view of nature and grace which viewed the present world as inherently evil—something from which to be delivered at the return of Jesus when all Christians will be translated from the present dark world to the new perfect world somewhere else in the hereafter. This set of assumptions is a lingering infection that continues to poison much of contemporary Western Christianity.

Aristotle (484–322 AD)

"In his lifetime he was famous; since his death he has overshadowed our history" (Henderson, 2003, p. 56).

For over 20 years Aristotle studied at Plato's feet in the Academy. After Plato's death, Aristotle left the Academy, only to return to Athens several years later and establish his own competing learning centre, the Lyceum. Aristotle came to reject Plato's central thesis of another-world centredness and contended that true reality was here among us in the physical and tangible world in which we live.

Aristotle is the father of empiricism, where real knowledge (not just Plato's imperfect shadow) is gained through a reasoned and logical analysis of our five-sense experience of the world we inhabit. This is why Raphael places Aristotle alongside Plato his mentor, but with Aristotle's hands firmly stretched earthward. At the Academy, one studied transcendent ideas. At the Lyceum, one experimented with the immanent world of experience.

In Aristotle, we have the origins of positivism and modernism: sensory experiences, and the interpretive, logical analysis of an active intellect (he called this *nous*) are sufficient to comprehend universal truth. Though various stages of Aristotle's thinking revealed an enduring platonic component, his focus on the physical world and strong logical methodology provided the core components from which later scientific investigation could develop.

Despite the development of a contemporary postmodern perspective, most of our Western classrooms continue to reflect a primarily modernist, aristotelian stance. Good education is seen as that which helps students to use their reasoning processes to determine the facts of a matter in the light of observation and the systematic ordering of data. So it is that the systematic approach of the scientific method has not only become the tool for discerning truth in biology or chemistry, but we have also developed the allied systems approach in geography and other disciplines. Any differing perspective often is viewed as mere conjecture or opinion when compared to the superiority of scientific, systematic processes in discovering truth.

Many modern Western educational strategists (as well as politicians and other commentators) take this perspective a step further. Since it is the relation of education to living in the real world that is important, practical, vocational and "life-skills" oriented courses must be given precedence in curriculum design and school timetables, with "less practical" subjects such as history and Latin having a diminishing priority. Postmodernity and platonic idealism are seen as "promoting a mindless relativism and turning schools away from teaching traditional knowledge" (Ozman & Crave, 2003, p. 76). Subject specialisation and streaming or tracking are viewed as appropriate organisational patterns for schools. From this perspective, the best measure of the success of a school is how well equipped its graduates are to enter the workforce (often called "the economy") or the degree to which its students receive an adequate foundation for tertiary education that will then equip them to enter the workforce at a later date. Hence we arrive at the contemporary commitment in the West to a concept of individualistic economic rationalism that controls many educational priorities—the idea that if something is good for the economy, then it is good, and schools should primarily focus their programs on the outcomes of preparing children to be effective economic producers and consumers. Sad confirmation was given of the veracity of this situation by Emeritus Professor Ivan Snook at the 2005 teacher education graduation ceremony at a government university in New Zealand when he commented that all that is now being asked of modern teachers is "… to prepare young people to be workers" (Snook, p. A5).

Impact on the Western mind and education

Socrates, Plato and Aristotle are the giants of Greek thought. Throughout subsequent periods of history, their ideas have remained as driving forces in shaping how Western people think. In each of the examples given at the beginning of this chapter, the formative influence of the Greeks in framing our thinking is clear.

Socrates, Plato and Aristotle are the giants of Greek thought. Throughout subsequent periods of history, their ideas have remained as driving forces in shaping how Western people think.

Plato laid the foundations for the enduring perspective that to know something is to conceive of it in the ideal world of the mind. We are also indebted to him for the unfortunate idea that this world is fundamentally inadequate and evil and that we can only find "true" truth in an ascetic escape into another realm. Neoplatonism's view of the divine as a distant, impersonal and inaccessible clockmaker-type god, together with neoplatonism's dualistic view of nature and grace or sacred and secular, still constrain and warp the way we think in the Western Christian church today. The Bible tells us a different story. Though our fall from grace through our forefather Adam has infected all of us with sin, the platonic mode of thought that this temporal body and world is somehow inherently evil finds no support in Scripture—otherwise the perfect Son of God could never have inhabited human form.

Finally, Plato gave us the concept of intellectual elitism discussed at the start of the chapter that is retained in the powerful intellectual-economic stratification of the 21st century and unhealthy priorities and patterns that result in education.

Aristotle brought our thinking patterns firmly back to earth, establishing the seeds for scientism which wrongly asserts that the only real knowing is that which can be understood through the senses and empirical analysis. Subsequent culture formers who followed in Aristotle's footsteps extended his ideas of logic and the superiority of the practical so that now it is a powerful building-block in economic rationalism to which education has been subordinated. In lamenting the primal sociopolitical place of economic rationalism in Western thinking and education, Brian Walsh in a lecture in Australia decried economic rationalism's insatiable desire for child sacrifice which leads politicians and educational decision-makers alike to align educational priorities with its greedy demands.

All of this should not lead us to be ignorant of the huge benefits which have come from these same Greek philosophers. Deductive reasoning, the pleasure of studying the world around us, the socratic questioning style, a love of learning, the values of humility, generosity, transparency and courage—these are all features of thinking and living that we see and admire in these ancient Greeks. And so we return to one of the primary purposes of this chapter—to recognise that the way that we think is not just the way things are, but is an often pagan, philosophically committed, cultural adaptation of ideas from long ago. Sadly, because these great Greek thinkers denied the truth of the one true God who created and sustains the world moment by moment by his word of power, they typically ended up falling into the same trap as the pagan Romans of Paul's day who took one aspect of God's creation and worshipped it in the place of the real Creator (Rom 1: 21–25).

A Christian response

Before concluding, we must begin one final and important exploration. Thus far, we have developed the idea that not only the content of our thinking, but also our thinking styles and processes themselves are not neutral but have been formed through traditions and processes steeped in the history of Western culture. This realisation by itself should be sufficient to produce a significant response in 21st century Christians. Although we are people of our age who have been influenced by our past, fundamentally we want to identify ourselves in all that we do (including our thinking) as people of the God of the Bible who live in the culturally rich but fallen context of the 21st century West. We are the people of God's gracious choosing, the children of Abraham for whom Christ died. We are those who seek to live in the light of the gospel narrative that we read in Scripture and who seek to celebrate the lordship of Jesus Christ (and not Plato or Aristotle) over all of creation—including the formative characteristics of why we think the way that we do today—as we prepare for the return of Jesus which "culminates in the restoration of the entire creation to its original greatness" (Bartholomew & Goheen, 2005, p. 12).

Even if Plato, for example, helped us to see some good things that exist in our thinking processes, for the Christian it is inadequate to accept them just because Plato said so. That which we decide is good and which informs our thinking must be the result of wrestling with God's order (not Plato's) in his creation, principally as revealed in the patterns and stories recorded in the Bible. Our final exploration then, is to suggest broad indicators as to how we can begin to acknowledge Jesus Christ as Lord in the formation of our thinking processes. The five contours outlined below are not exclusive or exhaustive. They merely provide a few touchstones that we might want to consider along the way.

1. Acknowledge that there is no neutrality

Every thought and every act is carried out in obedience or disobedience to God. There is no neutrality. Any statement presupposes a belief structure or thetical stance. Bringing every thought in subjection to Jesus Christ means making the deliberate choice to recognise non-neutrality and to recognise his lordship over our thinking processes.

2. Be relentless in critiquing our thinking

We need to know where our thinking patterns have come from. Although this chapter has briefly considered the influence of Greek thought, we also need to examine subsequent historical epochs and identify their impact on why we think the way we do. Only after identifying the problem can we then seek to put it right in a creaturely submission of our thinking patterns to the norms of the God whom we seek to serve.

3. See Christian thinking as a new way, not an amalgam of existing patterns

The Dutch philosopher Vollenhoven articulated the thetical-critical method (Kok, 1992), which has as its starting point a humble, self-critical and joyful commitment to a biblically authentic way of looking at the world, not just an uneasy extraction from secular perspectives that produces a slippery, unsatisfactory synthesis. In the light of this epistemological reformation, our God-honouring conceptual or thetical stance gives us a platform to evaluate other positions. As Paul did in Acts 17 in Athens, we will recognise truth wherever it is found, and will freely accept insights of secular writers—but only because these insights first of all have been critiqued and identified as legitimate components of a God-honouring way of seeing, being and thinking and thus become a part of a genuine, nonsynthetic Christian mind and worldview.

4. Recognise the authority of God's written word, the Bible, as foundational

Several useful Christian-oriented worldview courses have recently become available for Christian study groups to help us identify and live by a Christian way of being in the world. A dynamic distinctive of the worldview course written by Thompson (2005) is that it commences with an investigation of the Bible as foundational for Christian living. It is in holy Scripture that we find the stories, norms and principles to guide us in our search for right thinking patterns. As Greidanus (1982) has said, it is important to remind ourselves that our task is not to find ready-made answers in the Bible but to study reality in the light of biblical revelation. As Fowler puts it quite rightly: "The place of the Bible in our task of studying creation is not to give answers, but to guide us in our search for the answers, to be the light by whose illumination we will find the answers in the creation itself" (p. 7).

The lack of an acquaintance with the Bible that goes much beyond homilies and personal salvation morality is perhaps the biggest hindrance to the 21st century Christian community in the West in being able to develop and articulate a Christian mind. Serious, concerted effort in churches, study groups and Christian schools is needed in this regard if we are not going to be conformed to this world's ways of thinking but are to be transformed by the renewal of our minds, as we seek to serve as God's agents of shalom in our societies.

5. Comprehend and practise a biblically literate worldview

From the biblical basis of the preceding point, we can launch out and engage in the development of a Christian worldview. In a context where many Christians run like headless chickens between modernism on the one hand and postmodernism on the other, uncertain of where to cast their lot, a dynamic linkage of Vollenhoven's thetical-critical approach and the critical realism perspective of Lesslie Newbigin, Brian Walsh, Don Carson and others (and which is explored elsewhere in this book by Trevor Cooling and this author) provides a valuable philosophical framework. This fresh approach is termed reformed critical realism, and is examined at more length in another chapter in this book. It may help us give expression to a genuinely

Christian way of thinking so that how we think, what we think, and what we say and do as a consequence, can become humble celebrations of the lordship of Christ over all of his creation.

Conclusion

This chapter has firstly been devoted to establishing the fact that we think the way we do because of strong cultural influences. Secondly, some suggestions have been made about how Christians can critique and reform the way we think in order to reflect the biblical mindset to which we aspire. In closing, perhaps a couple of stories may help to illustrate these two points.

Good goal kicking in rugby

My good friend and esteemed colleague Ken Dickens was a rugby union player is his youth. In those days in the last century, Don Clark was a great fullback in New Zealand's famous All Black rugby team. Clark typified for Ken and every contemporary rugby player what effective goal kicking looked like. Clark would line himself up on the ball, pause, and then run straight in and kick the ball over the goalposts with the toe of his boot and lead his New Zealand team to yet another inevitable victory over the hapless Wallabies team from Australia. In those days, no-one thought to question Clark's style. The way he did it was the way good goal kicking was done. That's just the way it was.

Today, rugby goal kickers use a substantially different kicking style to Clark. Kickers run in onto the ball from an angle (called round the corner kicking), and most kick with the front side of their boots and not the tip. However much Clark is revered in the 21st century as one of the greats of rugby history, someone using Clark's kicking style today would be laughed out of the stadium.

How did this change come about? The answer is that at some point someone stopped assuming that the way Clark kicked was the way things were. Someone recognised (perhaps after observing ball kicking in soccer) that the Clark style was based on a set of assumptions about ball kicking that could be challenged and even replaced by a superior style based upon different assumptions.

Can you see the link between this analogy and why we think the way we do? To inhabit the mindfield in an authentic Christian manner means that we need to recognise, critique and biblically ground the formative influences that shape how we think. As we do this, our response to why we think the way we do will not be "because that's the way things are"; neither will it be because of an unconscious but idolatrous commitment to Greek beliefs or beliefs of any other pagan philosophical epoch. Instead, we will be able to shape the foundations of why we think the way we think, and formulate the educational processes that are a product of this thinking, as the fallen and humble yet genuine and dynamic reflections of the character and mind of God.

President Bush speaks at Calvin College

Calvin College is a reformed Christian liberal arts college in the US and, apparently at the initiative of White House personnel, the US President gave the commencement (graduation) address in May 2005 (bumping Nicholas Wolterstorff from the role in the process). Given Calvin's thetical-critical vision for its staff and students to be transformational in the public domain, critiquing all of life from a Christian worldview perspective, it was a controversial situation and not without fallout. President Bush received loud applause when he rose to the podium. His presence on campus was warmly supported by some but was disturbing to others. Aware of the extraordinary media attention that such an event attracted, one of the ways he was welcomed was in the form of a declaration placed in the public press by a number of the college's faculty and selectively reported in the secular media across America. Here is an extract from that declaration:

We the undersigned, respect your office and we join the college in welcoming you to our campus. Like you, we recognize the importance of religious commitment in American political life. We seek open and honest dialogue about the Christian faith and how it is best expressed in the political sphere. While recognizing God as sovereign over individuals and institutions alike, we understand that no single political position should be identified with God's will, and we are conscious that this applies to our own views as well as those of others. At the same time we see conflicts between our understanding of what Christians are called to do and many of the policies of your administration. (Calvin College, 2005)

Without commenting conclusively on the wisdom or otherwise of having the US President give the graduation address (I'm not even sure how one would one go about rejecting the president's offer), aspects of the declaration are a good example of thinking Christianly—it demonstrates the humble but dynamic cultural engagement of the reformed critical realist perspective that is advocated in this chapter.

Questions for discussion

1. How is dualism a reflection of a Greek mentality, and how does it hinder effective thinking and living by Christians?

2. What is elitism? What are its origins, how is it evident in our thinking in schools today, and what can we do about it?

3. Earlier in this chapter, Emeritus Professor Snook was quoted as suggesting that the mindset of modern Western culture is that the function of schooling is to do nothing more than prepare children for jobs.

   a. How is this a reflection of a Greek mentality?

   b. How does it lead to Brian Walsh's contention that schools are held hostage by economic rationalism and its insatiable appetite for child sacrifice?

   c. Describe some of the differences that would be evident in a Christian school where the mindset is based upon an alternative vision of challenging children with the celebration of the lordship of Christ over all creation.

4. Identify two ways in which specific policies and/or practices in your school or classroom have been shaped by Greek thinking. Critique these policies/practices and compare them to what a Christian worldview would look like in these areas.

5. Since Plato lived before the birth of Jesus Christ, how can we expect thinking patterns based on his ideas to reflect a biblical perspective?

6. If asking questions in the style of the socratic method owes its origins to Socrates, should Christians abandon this pedagogical technique because it was developed by a non-Christian?

   a. If so, what biblically informed approach should we think about and implement?

   b. If not, what acceptable justification do we have for adopting the socratic method as a mindset and practice in the Christian school?

7. Read the parable of the talents in Matthew 25:14–30. What different thinking patterns could the principles outlined in this parable give us for how we approach achievement rewards in the Christian school?

8. Develop a checklist that Christians could use to identify the presuppositions behind why we think the way that we do.

9. From a critical realist point of view, and in the post-Iraq political climate in the US, if you were an advisor to the Calvin College president, how and why would you have counselled when he was advised that President Bush was interested in giving the address at the College Commencement (Graduation) ceremony?

References

Bartholomew, C., & Goheen, M. (2005). *The drama of scripture: Finding our place in the biblical story.* Grand Rapids MI: Baker Academic.

Blamires, H. (1963). *The Christian mind.* London: SPCK.

Calvin College. (2005, May 21). Calvin commencement concludes. *News and Media Relations.* Retrieved May 22, 2005, from http://www.calvin.edu/news/releases/2004_05/commencement-concludes.htm

Goheen, M. (2004). The gospel and the idolatrous power of secular science. In J. Ireland, R. Edlin, & K. Dickens (Eds.), *Pointing the way: directions for Christian education in the new millennium* (pp. 33–54). Blacktown, Australia: National Institute for Christian Education.

Greidanus, S. (1985). The use of the Bible in Christian scholarship. *Christian Scholar's Review.* Retrieved April 20, 2005, from http://www.cccu.org/resourcecenter/resID.952,parentCatID.15 2/rc_detail.asp

Henderson, P. (2004). Aristotle: A man for our times. *Evidence, 9,* 53–56.

Jackson, P. (1992). Conceptions of curriculum and curriculum specialists. In W. Jackson (Ed.), *Handbook of research on curriculum* (pp. 10–25). New York: Macmillan.

Kanitz, L. (2005). Improving Christian worldview pedagogy: Going beyond mere Christianity. *Christian Higher Education, 4,* 99–108.

Kok, J. (1992). *Vollenhoven, scriptural philosophy, and Christian tradition.* Retrieved May 25, 2005, from http://home.wxs.nl/%7Ersw/nwe/vollenhoven/kok.html

Kok, J. (1998). *Patterns of the western mind: A reformed Christian perspective.* Souix Center, IA: Dordt College Press

Ozmon, H., & Craver, S. (2003). *Philosophical foundations of education* (7th ed.). Columbus OH: Merrill Prentice Hall.

Sire, J. (2000). *Habits of the mind: Intellectual life as a Christian calling.* Downers Grove, IL: InterVarsity Press.

Snook, I. (2005, May 16). Graduate teachers warned of strife. *New Zealand Herald*, p. A5.

Tarnas, R. (1991). *The passion of the western mind.* London: Pimlico.

Thompson, R. (2005). *A biblical introduction to worldview.* Auckland, New Zealand: Masters Publishing.

Chapter 5

Curiosity - vice or virtue for the Christian teacher?

Promoting faithfulness to scripture in teacher formation

Trevor Cooling

*Distance Learning Courses Leader
for The Stapleford Centre, Nottingham &
Secondary Education Adviser for the Diocese of Gloucester*

An earlier version of this chapter was delivered as a plenary paper at the conference *The Formation of the Christian Teacher* organised by the Stapleford Centre in January 2005. I am very grateful to delegates for helpful comments made then. Responsibility for the views expressed remains, of course, mine.

In the course of his career Trevor has been a secondary school teacher of science and religious education, a housemaster, Director of a Christian education charity and a Principal Lecturer in the University of Gloucestershire where he led the development of a distance learning degree in theology for Christian ministry. He has written widely on religious and Christian education. With his wife Margaret, he developed the concept cracking approach to teaching religious education in schools, which is influential throughout the UK. He has two sons and a foster daughter and five grandchildren.

Abstract

Most of those with responsibility for preparing Christian students for the ministry of teaching will agree that enabling them to be faithful to biblical teaching is a fundamentally important aim. In this chapter, it is suggested that two models of being faithful can be identified. The first emphasises faithful replication, the second emphasises theological contextualisation. Traditionally a replication model has been promoted by evangelicals, but in this article it is suggested that the contextualisation model is to be preferred. Building on this suggestion, it is argued that the virtue of theological curiosity should be promoted in the formation of Christian teachers.

Introduction

It was a Thursday afternoon in 1985 and I had just picked up my foster-daughter from her school. We pulled in to the petrol station to refuel in advance of our regular journey home. Three hundred yards away from the forecourt, the engine died. Three hours later a mechanic finally diagnosed the problem. The garage had sold me a full tank of water. The resulting repair meant the engine had to be thoroughly flushed through with petrol. All traces of the offending water had to be removed. Only then would the engine function properly.

I was reminded of this incident a couple of years ago when I was listening to a Christian educator speaking about teacher training. His view was that students had to be thoroughly deprogrammed so that all the influences that they absorbed from the secularised culture in which they lived were removed. Then they could be reprogrammed with biblical teaching. In the speaker's view

> *What virtues should be promoted as essential for the Christian ministry of teaching?*

this was an essential preliminary to any distinctively Christian teacher training. It seemed that he viewed his students in the same way I had viewed my car. Their minds and hearts needed flushing through to remove the contaminating water of secular thinking and to replace it with the petrol of correct Christian thinking.

These introductory thoughts are designed to introduce a very important question for those responsible for the formation of Christian teachers. What virtues should be promoted as essential for the Christian ministry of teaching? What are the characteristics of the Christian mind and character that we should be promoting? Before we can even begin designing a curriculum for a teacher education program, we have therefore to decide what are the attitudes, skills, knowledge and understanding we wish to promote through the process of forming Christian teachers.

An important assumption

Before embarking on my main argument, I want to highlight an assumption that I will make throughout the rest of this paper. In the world of academic theology there is a view that students should not prejudge the conclusions of their studies by approaching them from the perspective of a committed Christian faith. It is argued that academic theology in a modern university should be open to people of any tradition and faith, or none, and should not be premised on the assumption of commitment to any one of them.

Alister McGrath (e.g. 2001 & 2003) is a vocal critic of this view. As part of a withering attack on the idea that theology should be a neutral and objective activity, McGrath describes a visit he made to a former student who had shown great promise as a brilliant academic whilst at seminary before spending five years in pastoral ministry. This academically gifted student's conclusion was that the theological tomes that he used to revel in had nothing to say to the people he served in parish ministry or to himself as he sought to serve them (2003, p. 17). Utilising the ideas of Antonio Gramsci, McGrath's alternative is to invoke the concept of the organic theologian, who refuses to collude with traditional academic culture.

The organic theologian will see himself as working within the great historical Christian tradition, which he gladly makes his own. Even when he feels he must critique the contemporary expressions or applications of that tradition, he will do so from a deep sense of commitment to the community of faith and its distinctive ideas and values. He will not see his task as imposing alien ideas upon the community, but as being like the householder who brings out of his treasures "things new and old" (Matthew 13:52). His responsibility within the community is to explore and apply its tradition; outside the community, his task is to commend and defend its ideas and communicate them as effectively as possible. So where have all the Christian novelists and journalists gone? We need them now, perhaps as never before. On Gramsci's account, they fall into the category of "organic theologians" (2001, p. 152).

The issue is to do with the primary loyalty of the Christian theologian. Is it to the community of faith in the service of God or to the community of professional academics? The assumption made in this paper is that McGrath's vision of forming Christian teachers who are organic theologians is essentially correct. Furthermore,

I am assuming that the organic theologian will be committed to the ultimate authority of the Bible and to treating its teachings as normative in the life of the Christian. My presumption is, therefore, that being faithful to the teachings of the Bible is a primary calling for the Christian teacher.

Given this assumption, I want to ask a very specific question. To what degree is encouraging theological curiosity important in the formation of Christian teachers?

Curiosity and learning

A recent advertising campaign for washing detergent on roadside hoardings in England featured a child covered in paint. The text was: *It's not mess, it's curiosity.* The message was that curiosity is a good thing. The sub-text was that, for many people, curiosity is problematic because it creates mess. So how do Christian who aspire to being biblically faithful react to the concept of theological curiosity?

Being faithful to the teachings of the Bible is a primary calling for the Christian teacher.

In his seminal book on Christian adult education, John Hull's (1985) thesis is that curiosity is intimately linked with learning, because curiosity is a motivating factor in people wanting to know and understand more. His observation is that Christians are often not curious about those things that are closest to them, the taken-for-granted aspects of their lives. The result is that they stop learning about their faith. An analogy might be the difference between the young man wooing his sweetheart who is for ever curious about her and keen to learn more about her and the married man who, after 40 years, simply takes his wife for granted. Curiosity easily dies with familiarity. Hull's conclusion is that the same is true of Christian faith. He gives an intriguing example of elders from a Baptist church who were resisting the minister's wish to introduce a cross on the communion table on the grounds that they did not believe in symbols. So the minister took the elders into the church, sat them in a pew and invited them to gaze around:

at the massive central pulpit, at the rows of fixed pews and the gallery above, every pew facing towards the pulpit, upon which rested a Bible on a cushion. Below the pulpit was a communion table with a vase of flowers on it. It was as symbolic as it would be possible to create, but they had never noticed it (p. 55).

Despite worshipping amongst potent symbols, these elders had never been curious enough to notice them or ask themselves what they communicated to the congregation. Hull attributes Christians' lack of curiosity about their own faith to defensiveness, in that, as with the married man forced to look again at his relationship with his wife, asking probing questions about our faith will be painful and unsettling. Indeed, it may even be dangerous, opening a theological Pandora's Box. To avoid the risk of creating a theological mess, Hull (1985) believes that many Christians suppress their curiosity and defer to experts to tell them what is safe to think rather than grapple with challenging issues that the more curious notice in their faith (p. 135). In the face of theological ambiguity, he suggests that the common response is for Christian teaching to become petrified (in both senses of the word). Certainly, I have met Christian educationalists who will not ask open-ended questions in case learners speculate and give the wrong answer. Hull directs his criticisms at more conservative Christians, but recently Andrew Wright has identified the same problematic mindset in more liberal, radical and atheistic traditions of theology (2004, pp. 93, 155).

Christian curiosity—vice or virtue?

In the rest of this paper I intend to develop Hull's thesis. I will suggest that there are two theological traditions influential amongst those who aspire to being biblically faithful. These represent two poles of the spectrum of shared evangelical commitment to the Bible. By focusing on the poles, I am of course in danger of polarising and stereotyping and of suggesting a conflict that might not exist. Both traditions share a desire to be faithful to Scripture and hold that a Christian's responsibility is to discover the truth that is embedded in Scripture. Neither espouses the liberal view that humans create truth for themselves in response to the inspiration of Scripture. For both traditions, the ultimate authority is the mind of God that is revealed through the Bible. But, given this important qualification, the two poles do reflect two distinct approaches to biblical interpretation and generate very different responses to the idea of promoting theological curiosity.

1. The fix and transmit tradition: Literal or naïve realism

On the one hand is the fix and transmit tradition that sees the authoritative teaching of Scripture as having an unambiguous meaning that can be downloaded from the Bible (in PDF format?) and then transmitted to Christians irrespective of the cultural context of their generation. This is illustrated by an advert that I once saw for a Bible which claimed that this particular version needed no interpretation. It proclaimed itself as the revolutionary new translation that allowed the reader to understand immediately and exactly what the original writers meant.

As a young Christian I grew up within a tradition of teaching that largely accepted this view of the theological method. I was taught that my task was to accept the clear meaning of what the biblical writers taught and then copy it. Biblical teaching was applied down to the last detail. In my own personal experience in the 1970s this manifested itself in a focus on the length of boys' hair—with church leaders, on the basis of 1 Corinthians 11:14, providing biblical haircuts for wayward youth.

I have called this the fix and transmit tradition, because this way of thinking is characterised by the idea that it is possible to find an unambiguous statement of biblical teaching that can then be straightforwardly applied in the world of today. Emphasis is given to propositional truth that is expressed through dogmatic or systematic theology and on the careful transmission of that teaching from genera-tion to generation, sometimes through a catechism. In this view, the educational task is to reprogram secularised students with this right doctrine. They are then equipped to confront the errors of the world.

A significant feature of this tradition is its seeming acceptance of what I shall call literal realism, the idea that biblical truth is accessible in a clear and unambiguous fashion, which, once discerned, can be applied without problem. It is also referred to in the literature as naïve realism. An interesting example that I once came across was when a teacher told me that she was seeking to discern God's curriculum for schools by searching the Scriptures. Her idea that there was a ready-made curric-ulum embedded in Scripture that could be downloaded and then taught in any school reflected a literal realist approach to biblical interpretation.

The fix and transmit tradition approach to learning is generally to regard it as the transmission and accumulation of correct teaching. It operates on a top-up model of life-long learning, where the emphasis is on acquiring more correct doctrine. There is little emphasis on process and considerable suspicion of the constructivist approaches that are currently prevalent in theories of education. On this tradition, curiosity is generally seen as a vice, because it encourages students to think wrong thoughts and thereby puts them in danger of succumbing to heresy.

2. The contextualise and transform tradition: Critical realism

This approach is a response to literal realist approaches in that it wants to recognise the role of context and human interpretation in the discovery of truth. It shares the literal realist commitment to the idea that truth is correspondence to the way things are and is not, ultimately, a human creation, but it draws on postmodern insights concerning the embeddedness of every human in particular cultures and ways of thinking and is therefore less confident that human beings have direct and unambiguous access to that truth. It is therefore critical and not literal in its realism. Critical realism can be summarised as comprising three basic claims: that there is an authoritative reality existing independently of human perception, which means that the meaning of biblical text ultimately stands over and above humans and not the other way round; that human comprehension of that meaning involves subjective engagement and is, therefore, always someone's interpretation; and that the complexity and ambiguity of reality requires a degree of critical thinking since meaning cannot often be read from the biblical text by human beings in a straightforward manner. The goal of the critical realist is to identify scriptural truth so that it can be expressed appropriately in particular human contexts in ways that transform those contexts in a more Christian direction. Its aspiration is summed up by these words of the Sri Lankan theologian D. T. Niles:

The gospel is like a seed and you have to sow it. When you sow the seed of the gospel in Palestine, a plant that can be called Palestinian Christian grows. When you sow it in Rome, a plant of Roman Christian grows. You sow the gospel in Great Britain and you get British Christian. The seed of the gospel is brought to America and a plant grows of American Christian. Now, when missionaries came to our lands they brought not only the seed of the gospel, but also their own plant of Christian, flowerpot included! So what we have to do is to break the flowerpot, take out the seed of the gospel, sow it in our own cultural soil, and let our version of Christian grow (in King, Cooling, Cooling & Stanley, 2001, p. 8).

> *The gospel is like a seed and you have to sow it.*

In relation to faithfulness to biblical teaching, the contextualise and transform tradition makes a distinction between human interpretations of biblical teaching and biblical teaching itself. It has four main criticisms of the fix and transmit tradition that, in turn, lead to its embracing the importance of theological curiosity.

a. It claims to be timeless

The fix and transmit approach assumes it is possible to discern timeless truths from Scripture that are uninfluenced by the context of the interpreter and can then be transmitted to learners. Its critics, however, argue that a purported timeless truth is, in fact, a product of a particular time and place. For example, in his discussion of systematic theology, John Goldingay (2000) regards it as an approach that reflects a Greek way of thinking reinforced by the distinctive concerns of the medieval period and of the Enlightenment, which has become fixed and uncritically transmitted through the tradition.

However, adopting a critical realist understanding gives a very different picture. A theological critical realist believes that there are universal and authoritative truths to be discovered in the Bible and communicated, but that the process of interpreting and expressing them is not a simple process of reading literal meanings, is never complete and is always influenced by the context of the interpreter. There is a very important distinction between believing, as critical realists do, that scriptural truths are universal (so legitimately applicable to everyone at all times, but in ways that are contextually appropriate) and believing they are timeless (applied in the same way irrespective of historical or cultural context) as literal realists do. To express the universal in the midst of each particular context requires the cultivation of theological curiosity.

b. It assumes itself to be uncontroversial

This is a related criticism to the one above. The critic is concerned about the literal realist idea that once established our understanding of the truth never changes, that it is a once-for-all discovery. Literal realists are unlikely to admit that their conclusions might be controversial or even in need of reformulating.

However, the fact is that theological traditions develop and change. Critical realists would say that one reason for this is that biblical interpretation is an activity of fallible human beings who are embedded in a particular context. Christians need therefore to be aware of the possibility that they might have reached conclusions that reflect more their own situation and interests than biblical teaching. The theological support given in the past to apartheid by the Dutch Reformed Church in South Africa is a warning of a danger that all Christians face. One conclusion from this insight is that Christians need always be self-critical and open to the possibility of needing to correct their theological formulations if they are to remain biblically faithful.

The response of those inclined to literal realism is often to regard such curiosity as dangerous, creating theological mess. Critical realists would say, however, that if we are to be faithful to biblical teaching, we should not be trigger-happy with our heresy sharpshooter. There is a legitimate debate to be had about the reliability of traditional doctrinal formulations in terms of their faithfulness to biblical teaching and continuing curiosity about them is therefore appropriate.

c. It is unrelated to people's experience of life

Joel Green (2000) criticises the idea that biblical texts can be treated as "self-interpreting, semantically sealed meaning factories" (p. 31) as is usually assumed in literal realist approaches. In doing this, he is wishing to challenge the implicit assumption that there is a linear, automatic process in applying biblical teaching that starts with biblical studies, creates a biblical theology, turns this into systematic theology and then, finally, applies systematic theology to life. In his view the process simply doesn't work like that. Theological reflection is not a linear process that starts with an abstract truth and ends with an application of that truth in real life. Green's view is that, as contextual theologies like environmental theology and liberation theology illustrate, the process often starts with questions of application. New questions raised by new situations often reveal new (i.e. previously hidden) truths within Scripture.

If Green is right, this means that theological application must involve careful analysis of the context in which the theologian is seeking to apply biblical teaching, alongside and in dialogue with the study of biblical texts. It is therefore a circular rather than a linear process with the theologian toing-and-froing between the text and the context. Those involved in such a process will find that understanding the context properly raises

> *It seems to be true that students, in their future work, model the processes and methods by which they are taught in their training.*

questions that may never before have been asked of Scripture. To take a British example, every pupil in state schools must participate in an act of compulsory, broadly Christian worship every day. To discover what the Bible might teach about such an issue requires being very clear as to what are the fundamental questions to ask. They include: Can unbelievers truly worship? What is the nature of the God that is worshipped in such a context? Can worship be compulsory? The results of interrogating the biblical text with such demanding questions will probably be very different than if we assume some context-free, pre-packaged and abstracted biblical view of worship and simply seek to assert it. Such questioning will also prepare the ground for transforming the context. For many British Christians this leads them to question whether such a seemingly good thing as Christian worship in school might not actually need radical transformation if it is to be faithful to biblical teaching.

It seems to be true that students, in their future work, model the processes and methods by which they are taught in their training. If, in the formation of Christian teachers, we model a process that assumes that the most important part of the teaching task is formulating abstract theological truths, that is exactly what they will do in their own teaching ministry. The hard work of applying (or contextualising/ inculturation, to use the new terms) Christian truth will be given little attention. There is much to be learnt in this respect from Mark Noll's (1994) penetrating critique of the evangelical world's lack of seriousness in seeking to understand the world around it. Application of theological insights is a sophisticated and demanding task, into which Christians training for ministry need systematic and sustained induction. It cannot be done without cultivating theological curiosity.

d. It is not faithful to the nature of the Bible

The critics of literal realist approaches would say that they ignore the fact that the Bible is not a repository of timeless propositions that can be downloaded and arranged into a systematic theology, but is rather essentially a narrative. John Goldingay (2000) makes the observation that "narrative is by nature open-ended, allusive and capable of embracing questions and ambiguity" (p. 132). By implication he suggests that systematic or propositional theology is in contrast fixed and dogmatic or doctrinaire. Critical realist approaches are intimately linked to narrative approaches to Scripture, which allow for more openness in interpreting and applying the text and invite theological curiosity as a means of indwelling the text.

e. Concluding remark

So far it has been suggested that theological curiosity is welcomed in a critical realist approach to the reading of the Bible, but is considered potentially dangerous in literal realist approaches because it is thought to foster heresy. Critical realists promote theological curiosity because, in their view, it is a mindset that is more likely to remain faithful to the Bible. Theological curiosity encourages Christians to ask the questions that prevent them from slipping into the complacency of assuming that traditional interpretations are *necessarily* the correct ones. It alerts them to the need to be challenged by other views as a way of ensuring that their understanding of truth is as close to the reality of biblical meaning as they can get. It ensures that they never rest in the struggle to be faithful to Scripture as they seek to contextualise in and transform the world around them. It is as concerned about truth as a literal realist view, but more self-critical about its own ability to reach uncontroversial conclusions.

Critical realists are committed both to the discovery of truth and the fallibility and context-related nature of human interpretations. They will, therefore, be curious to keep examining and questioning their own beliefs in case they are in someway incorrect. They are therefore more serious in heeding warnings about uncritical absorption of the intellectual fashions of the world (see Wells, 1993 & Guinness, n.d. for examples). Critical realists are ever aware of the danger that their tradition might be an excuse for abusing Scripture in the service of their own selfish ends. Literal realists, however, are more confident that truth is unambiguous and accessible to humans and therefore are far less curious about their own faith. Once understood, it is regarded as fixed and uncontroversial. The danger is that their confidence in Scripture slides into over-confidence in human interpretation. They are, therefore, more prone to being unfaithful to biblical teaching even though their aspiration is exactly the opposite.

Why theological curiosity matters in teacher formation

To conclude, I will outline three reasons why I believe that we should be promoting critical realism, and the theological curiosity that derives from it, as a virtue in the formation of Christian teachers. I will propose that these three reasons illustrate that our capacity to undertake the Christian ministry of education is damaged if we don't promote theological curiosity.

Firstly, we need to heed the warning of Alan Jamieson's (2002) research on Christian leaders who abandon their vocation. In an important study of former leaders from evangelical, pentecostal and charismatic churches, Jamieson found that many of them had left their churches not because they had lost their faith, but because their churches gave them no support in seeking to relate and minister to a world that was intellectually and culturally a million miles away from that of these churches. In their own faith development, these former leaders were finding themselves driven to asking questions that arose out of their experience of ministry. They were thereby demonstrating the necessary curiosity for them to contextualise the gospel in the world with a view to transforming that world. However, this curiosity was perceived as threatening by their churches. The result was that these leaders left their churches, with a legacy for them of emotional and spiritual damage and for the church in the loss of creative and dynamic ministry. Evangelicals are usually adept at watching the front doors of their churches to ensure they bring in the newcomer. They are not so good at watching the back door, so as not to lose those whose desire to be biblically faithful leads them to challenge traditional theological formulations and patterns of thought.

My own experience of working with Christian teachers over many years resonates with Jamieson's findings. I remember particularly one teacher whose Christian life was in crisis because she had no theological framework for thinking about her role. She had to choose between the literal realist understanding offered by her church, which required her to subvert and fight her non-Christian colleagues in school, or the relativist agenda offered by the Religious Education (RE) profession, which undermined her faith in the universal and ever-relevant gospel. Both treated her curiosity to find another way as threatening (Cooling, 1993). The spiritual destruction of those in the frontline of Christian ministry is a shameful judgment on a Christian mindset that refuses to allow the curious to develop new forms of relevant ministry. If Christian teachers are to flourish, they need preparation in the skill of being theologically curious and support in managing the reaction that this might create in their church. Only in this way can we nurture a vibrant understanding of the Christian vocation of teaching.

Secondly, we need to take note of the exhortation in the recent report of the Church of England on the future of the church. In his opening remarks Bishop Graham Cray (2004) says:

One of the central features of this report is the recognition that the changing nature of our missionary context requires a new inculturation of the gospel within our society. The theology and practice of inculturation or contextualisation is well established in the world church, but has received little attention for mission in the West. We have drawn on this tradition as a major resource for the Church of England ... Inculturation is central to this report because it provides a principled basis for the costly crossing of cultural barriers and the planting of church into a changed social context. Church has to be planted not cloned. At the same time, any principle based on Christ's incarnation is inherently counter-cultural, in that it aims at faithful Christian discipleship within the new context, rather than cultural conformity (pp. xii–xiii).

As I have already suggested, effective inculturation requires theological curiosity. Sadly, an influential reaction of Christians to educational debates has been to revert to fix and transmit strategies. This reflects a colonial strategy that assumes that the church can simply export its traditional ways of operating into new cultures and is confrontational in its style if it meets resistance. But as the Archbishops' Council's report neatly express it, "the gospel can only be proclaimed in a culture, not at a culture" (Cray, 2004, p. 87).

A particularly poignant example of the fix and transmit approach is the way that many Christians in Britain cling to the concept of Christendom, the idea that Britain is constitutionally and in actuality a Christian country and that the state should therefore legislate to promote Christian ideals. Much of the Christian resistance to reforms in Religious Education and to the legal requirement for a daily act of worship in state schools in England has been based on the assumption that Christendom is a *biblically faithful concept* because it is *the traditional evangelical* way of understanding the church's relationship to state education. So any creative reinterpretations of that relationship in terms of mission in a plural or secular society are dismissed as heretical (see Cameron, 1995 for an example). Arguments for Christian influence in state education are therefore based on the idea that we should be nurturing all children in their historic and cultural faith rather than on the idea that we should be seeking to contextualise the gospel for students who are nurtured in the culture of the godless West. On the latter view, the task of teacher formation is to prepare our students for what Lesslie Newbigin (1989) has dubbed a missionary-encounter with the prevailing culture and not for the transmission of a universally shared Christian culture, as is the case with the Christendom model.

Thirdly, we need to take inspiration from the work of Christians who have sought to apply the principles of curious critical realism and contextualisation. In missionary quarters, the pioneering work of Vincent Donovan (1978) is often cited. As an educational example I would cite the work of the Charis Project (Smith, 1999). In this project the challenge was taken up to produce curriculum materials that demonstrated how Christian insights could make a difference to the teaching of subjects like mathematics and modern foreign languages. Traditionally Christians have either seen their faith as irrelevant to such subjects or they have sought to baptise them by adding Bible verses to the textbook. The danger of such approaches is either that they leave the basic assumptions that may be shaping the subject unchallenged or that the Christian teaching is syncretised with non-Christian ideas.

The genius of the Charis Project was that the project team realised that fresh and relevant expressions of Christian faith will not be generated by simply quoting Bible verses. They sought to examine the fundamental presuppositions of a subject and then to transform them from a Christian perspective in ways that were culturally relevant to the context of British schools. At that time, the particular need for cultural relevance was to demonstrate how subject teaching contributed to the spiritual and moral development of all pupils, irrespective of their personal faith background.

> *We need to take inspiration from the work of Christians who have sought to apply the principles of curious critical realism and contextualisation.*

To take the example of modern foreign languages, the team asked whether there are fundamental biblical themes that could shape the teaching of languages. Their answer was to utilise the biblical idea of hospitality to the stranger which "provides an ethical imperative for rethinking the basic objectives and emphases of foreign language education" (Smith & Carvill, 2000, p. xiii). As is illustrated in Smith's contribution in this book, they then proceeded to demonstrate how the teaching of foreign languages based on this fundamental principle transformed the subject from one that amounted to a trivial promotion of tourist values to one that promoted positive interaction between persons of different language and culture. It is not difficult to see the compelling nature of their approach, both for Christian and for secular people concerned with spiritual and moral development. In my view such innovative mission thinking, exhibiting creative faithfulness to Scripture, is much more likely to be achieved by those whose theological curiosity has been nurtured through exposure to a contextualise and transform, critical realist approach to their faith.

Conclusion

This chapter began with the story of my petrol tank being filled with water. I used this to illustrate the ideas of some Christian educationalists who feel the need to deprogram and then reprogram their students with Christian truth. I have suggested that such a view reflects a fix and transmit, or literal realist or naïve realist, approach to biblical interpretation. In contrast I have argued for a contextualise and transform, or critical realist, approach that nurtures theological curiosity. My reasons for preferring this are, firstly, that such an approach is ultimately more faithful to the Bible and, secondly, that it is more likely to achieve the mission goals of the church. I have proposed that it is this approach which more fully fulfils the shared aspirations of Bible-focused Christians.

In order to nurture theological curiosity, the emphasis in Christian formation for teaching will have to shift from the transmission of traditional ideas to the development of the skill of contextualisation of Christian truth. This means that those responsible for Christian teacher formation will have to shift from deprogramming and reprogramming their students (something they do to them) to equipping them with the ability to deconstruct and reconstruct their own thinking in the cause of being biblically faithful (something the students learn to do to themselves). Young teachers nurtured in this approach may well find themselves very surprised at how unfaithful the Christian community has been to Scripture in its traditional approaches. They may also be surprised at how many ideas there are in the non-Christian world of education that can make a positive contribution to Christian transformation. To adapt our car analogy, instead of looking to flush out the water of secular thinking with pure Christian petrol, they may often find that they can transform the polluting leaded petrol of secular thought with an improved unleaded Christian version.

In terms of a curriculum, I suggest that, in addition to traditional, and essential, subjects like Bible knowledge our students will also need to encounter areas of study like faith development, pluralism, contextualisation, epistemology, cultural studies, hermeneutics, missiology and the philosophy of ideas. Above all they will need to be encouraged to welcome the challenges of mission in a plural world and not to prefer the retreat into the Christian ghetto. We should aim to develop skilled cultural navigators (see Jackson 1997), not slogan transmitters. Our students will need to be open to the ambiguity that is generated by such encounters and to the possibility of new, biblically-faithful ideas emerging in new contexts. Simplistic answers never sit easily with the theologically curious.

Questions for discussion

1. How helpful is the author's distinction between the two traditions of interpretation? Can you recognise these two traditions in Christians that you know? How much are you influenced by either or both of them?

2. Does the Bible contain timeless truths that apply to all humans throughout history? How helpful is the author's distinction between timeless truths and universal truths?

Discuss from the perspectives of a critical realist and a literal realist the question "Does transmitting correct doctrine matter?"

3. Is it appropriate to promote theological curiosity in those who are training for Christian ministry of teaching?

4. Is describing teaching as a missionary encounter with secular culture a helpful way of thinking about it as a Christian ministry?

5. Can you give examples of where a Christian teacher has contextualised the Christian message in their school and thereby transformed it so that it is more biblically faithful?

References

Cray, G. (2004). Introduction. In Archbishops' Council, *Mission-shaped church: Church planting and fresh expressions of church in a changing context*. London: Church House.

Bartholomew, C. (1998). *Reading Ecclesiastes: Old Testament exegesis and hermeneutical theory*. Rome: Editrice Pontificio Istituto Biblico.

Bartholomew, C. & Goheen, M. (2004). *The drama of Scripture: Finding our place in the biblical story*. Grand Rapids, MI: Baker Books.

Cameron, N. M. De S. (1995 June). Review of a Christian vision for state education. *Light & Salt*, 7(1), pp. 18–20.

Cooling, T. (1993). Living as a Christian in the world of Religious Education. *Spectrum*.

Cooling, T. (1994). *A Christian vision for state education*. London: SPCK.

Donovan, V. (1978). *Christianity rediscovered*. London: SCM.

Goldingay, J. (2000). Biblical narrative and systematic theology. In J. Green & M. Turner (Eds.), *Between two horizons: Spanning New Testament studies and systematic theology* (pp. 123–142). Cambridge: Eerdmans.

Green, J. (2000). Scripture and theology: Uniting the two so long divided. In J. Green & M. Turner (Eds.), *Between two horizons: Spanning New Testament studies and systematic theology* (pp. 23–43). Cambridge: Eerdmans.

Holm, N. (2003, November). Teaching on the verandah. *Think Piece, 6*.

Hull, J. (1985). *What prevents Christian adults from learning?* London: SCM Press.

Jackson, R. (1997). *Religious education: An interpretive approach*. London: Hodder & Stoughton.

Jamieson, A. (2002). *A churchless faith*. London: SPCK.

King, J., Cooling T., Cooling, M. & Stanley, B. (2001). *Global perspectives on Christianity*. Norwich, England: RMEP.

McGrath, A. (2001). *The future of Christianity*. Oxford: Blackwell.

McGrath, A. (2003). Theology and the futures of evangelicalism. In C. Bartholomew, R. Parry & A. West. (Eds.), *The futures of evangelicalism: Issues and prospects* (pp. 15–39). Leicester, England: IVP.

Newbigin, L. (1989). *The gospel in a pluralist society*. London: SPCK.

Noll, M. (1994). *The scandal of the evangelical mind*. Grand Rapids, MI: Eerdmans.

Smith, D. I. (1999). Cross-curricular spiritual and moral development. *Journal of Christian Education*, 42(2), 27–34.

Smith, D. I. and Carvill, B. (2000). *The gift of the stranger: Faith, hospitality and foreign language learning*. Grand Rapids, MI: Eerdmans.

Smith, D. I. & Shortt, J. (2002). *The Bible and the task of teaching*. Nottingham, England: The Stapleford Centre.

Wells, D. (1993). *Whatever happened to truth: Or no place for evangelical theology*. Grand Rapids, MI: Eerdmans.

Wright, A. (2004). *Religion, education and post-modernity*. London: RoutledgeFalmer.

Wright, C. (1991). The authority of Scripture in an age of relativism. In M. Eden & D. Wells (Eds.), *The gospel in the modern world* (pp.31–48). Leicester, England: IVP.

Wright, N.T. (1993). *The New Testament and the people of God*. London: SPCK.

In pursuit of an authentic Christian paradigm:

The place of reformed critical realism

Chapter 6

Richard Edlin

Principal, National Institute for Christian Education

Richard Edlin is the principal of the National Institute for Christian Education (NICE), a government-accredited, degree-granting postgraduate teacher training organisation based in Sydney, Australia. Although Richard his wife, Annette, and their three adult children currently all live in Australia, the Edlins have travelled the world in their commitment to the cause of Christian education. Richard has written many books and articles on Christian Education, as well as producing videos and other ICT media on the subject. His experience includes over 30 years of teaching and administration in both secular and Christian educational contexts in both the developed and the developing world. His earned doctorate in teacher education is from the University of Alabama. In 2005, he was awarded a rare honorary doctorate from Kosin University in Busan, Korea, for his international contribution to Christian education.

Abstract

*This chapter is partially a technical reflection on and partially a further explora-
tion of a core theme from Cooling's preceding chapter on curiosity. Cooling is encouraging Christian teacher educators to consider a paradigm called critical realism as
a framework for engaging in biblically authentic teacher education. O'Toole also
advocates this position in his chapter on science. The purpose of this chapter is to indicate
the philosophical background of the concept
of secular critical realism, highlight its key
features, and show how the critical realism
of Cooling's chapter could more helpfully be
termed reformed critical realism. Reformed
critical realism is a distinctive perspective with
solid Christian roots which provides an attractive alternative to the polarities of postmodernity on the one hand and a re-emergent
modernity on the other. Though reformed
critical realism has strategic parallels with the
perspectives of Roy Bhaskar it is not a mere synthetic reformulation of Bhaskar's critical
realist theory. Reformed critical realism is a distinctive perspective that is reformed
in a theological and foundational sense and that deserves further investigation by
thoughtful Christians.*

> *Truth is viewed as a social construct that will have many forms, each as legitimate as the others.*

Introduction

Throughout the last few hundred years, modernism or modernity has been the
predominant cultural paradigm of the West. People lived as if the systematic,
logical application of the scientific method was the way to discover truth. It owed
its origins to Aristotle and the realists who came after him from the Renaissance
onwards, and was an optimistic view of the world, believing that this perspective
would inevitably lead to the betterment of all humankind.

Modernity is often regarded as having died with the dropping of the atomic bombs
on Japan in 1945. Hiroshima and Nagasaki demonstrated for all to see that logical
scientific enquiry was not necessarily going to lead inexorably to progress and the
betterment of humankind. The resulting post-war disenchantment with modernity
liberated the forces that led to the flowering of postmodernity. Postmodernity is a
powerful cultural paradigm in contemporary society. For the postmodernist, science
is a discredited god. There is no big story to live by any more. Truth is viewed as
a social construct that will have many forms, each as legitimate as the others. The

educational variant of this perspective is von Glasersfeld's radical constructivism which shapes much of contemporary educational theory and practice. Children are independent thinkers who do not discover meaning, but who actually create their own meaning in their learning activities. Concepts and methodology in English literature instruction in schools, for example, from its idolisation of the hermeneutic of suspicion (which in its place has real value), to the pastiche interrogation of books, provide obvious examples of postmodern or radical constructivist determinants in the classroom.

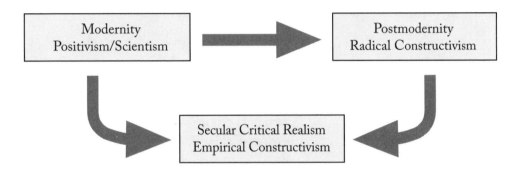

The above diagram provides a simplified illustration of the progression of secular ideas discussed in this chapter. For most of recent history, modernity or scientific positivism has been the predominant worldview paradigm. The latter half of the twentieth century saw the wholesale abandonment of modernity with postmodernity (in education called radical constructivism) taking its place as the principal paradigm. Subsequent disenchantment with postmodernity's unworkable rejection of external reality and truth which are intuitively acknowledged by most people, has seen the development of new paradigms such as empirical constructivism and secular critical realism in the public domain. Reformed critical realism is not shown on the diagram because, although it has parallels with secular critical realism, it is a distinctive philosophical perspective that is not a synthetic derivative of aspects of modernity and postmodernity. It is an earnest endeavour in its own right to faithfully apply the Scriptures in determining a philosophical paradigm for 21st century Christians.

Despite its insights, the fundamental dilemma with postmodernity is its transient view of truth and reality which does not ring true with the experience of many people. Most people don't want to believe the postmodern proclamation that they exist as powerless pawns in a nihilistic, purposeless belief vacuum. Conversely, there are things that they experience in the world such as love, humour and hope which they feel are inadequately valued and understood in reductionistic modernity. What are they to do? The worldview of modernity has failed, and the postmodern worldview seems just as inadequate.

It is at this point, really only in the last few years, that critical realism has emerged. It has recognisable links to both modernity and postmodernity, but explores a third way that is distinct from both (see the diagram above). Secular critical realism, with its acceptance of reality on the one hand and recognition of the limitations of individual perceptions of that reality on the other, is seen by its adherents as the saving alternative worldview paradigm for modern Western humanity:

> *The worldview of modernity has failed, and the postmodern worldview seems just as inadequate.*

Critical realism rescues us from the postmodernist nightmare and restores us to reality. We cannot manage without a concept of truth. There is (as most of us thought all along) a pre-existing external reality about which it is the job of science to tell us (Caldwell, 2003, p. 3).

Caldwell's comment typifies the enthusiastic response to critical realism in the secular faith community today. In my own doctoral studies a few years ago under Dr Rebecca Oxford, a renowned secular educator with globally recognised expertise in learning styles, the ability to reject radical constructivism (or full postmodernity) in favour of empirical constructivism provided her with a peer-acceptable platform from which to pursue her own research. Other respected educators also were glad to escape from the shackles of radical constructivism for this alternative worldview (albeit still non-Christian) that seemed to keep the best features of modernity without accepting the excesses of postmodernity.

Cooling explores the challenge for Christians in contemporary society, and particularly in education, of negotiating the current worldview mindfield in the search for patterns and descriptors that meet the basic goal of most evangelical, reformed believers: to adopt a way of thinking that is faithful to the Scriptures as God's revealed, infallible word and guide for all of life. Cooling suggests that the concept of critical realism is worthy of further investigation and possible re-formation and adoption by Bible-believing Christians as a means to achieving this goal.

Critical realism has a multi-flavoured history. Many philosophers and writers, both inside and outside a Christian worldview, use the term "critical realism" in a way that is different from the way Cooling uses it in his chapter. The purpose of these few comments therefore, is to delve into the roots of modern critical realism, looking at its various expressions first in the secular faith community and then in the Christian faith community. Next, the intention is to suggest how the understanding of critical realism espoused by Cooling, which we term reformed critical realism, is a perspective that reflects Vollenhoven's thetical-critical method. As such, it may well offer us a paradigm with the best possibility of approaching the Bible, God's written Word, with the deepest respect, and allowing the Holy Spirit to take the Scriptures and apply them as the touchstone and direction-giver for our celebration of the lordship of Christ over all creation.

Contemporary secular critical realism

Although critical realism's widespread contemporary appeal largely has to do with its suggestion of a credible alternative to modernity on the one hand and postmodernity on the other, the origins of the concept predate the full flowering of postmodernity.

Karl Popper

Decades before his death in 1994, Karl Popper railed against the concept that science was a neutral activity that would lead to the discovery and application of truth. For him, science, while useful in a tentative socratic way, was a process of trial and error, punctuated with myth and conjecture that leads us to a more accurate but value-laden understanding of the way things are.

The assertion of Popper that is central to contemporary critical realism is that truth is there to be discovered, but that our perceptions of that truth must always be held lightly as they are reached on the basis of less-than-objective and incomplete knowledge, being situated within a particular cultural context. In the same way, a child from New Zealand might think that hokey-pokey is the best flavoured ice-cream in the world, but one would have to assess that judgment to be very contextualised if in fact the child had never been to Canada and tasted chocolate chip-cookie dough ice-cream. The judgment, while considered true by the child, has to be viewed by others as being subjective due to the limited range of the child's knowledge and experience. Make what you like of the North American penchant for calling their national baseball competition the "world series"!

Roy Bhaskar

If Popper is a forefather of contemporary secular critical realism, then British philosopher Roy Bhaskar is its father. According to Verstegen (2000), others such as

Sellars, Lovejoy and Mandelbaum propounded the notion earlier in the twentieth century, but it is Bhaskar whom most contemporary secular critical realists consider to be the originator of many of their ideas. Considered to be a Marxist philosopher (Moore, 2003), Bhaskar was born in London in 1944 to an Indian father and English mother. Through his studies at Oxford and beyond he came to espouse a pattern of thinking or epistemological framework that avoided the excesses of modernism on the one hand and postmodernity on the other. Modernity's reductionistic rationalism suggests that absolute truth exists, and that we can know it absolutely. Postmodernity's irrationalism insists that there is no objective view of reality, but only individualistic perspectives that are the result of one's subjective experience. Bhaskar's critical realism claims that a reality independent of our sense experience does exist, but that our limited point of view constrains our understanding of that reality. Andrew Basden (2004) puts it this way:

Critical realism says that there exists a reality independent of our representation of it, but it acknowledges that our knowledge of reality is subject to all kinds of historical and other influences. It draws a clear distinction between reality and our knowledge of reality, and Bhaskar criticises much postmodernist work for failing to distinguish between them. It sees reality and our knowledge of reality as operating in two different dimensions (p. 1).

Liberal Christianity and critical realism

Christians today have responded to critical realism in many different ways. Significant writers such as J. P. Moreland (2004) view it as little short of a sell-out of the certainty of the gospel. Other critics of the perspective such as Travis Allen dismiss it because it is linked with N. T. Wright and the so-called new perspective on Paul. Still others link it with the critical-historical approach to biblical interpretation, the presuppositions of which diminish the position and authority of Scripture.

Another group of more liberal contemporaries who would lay claim to a genuine Christian profession (a claim rejected by many evangelicals) espouse critical realism. Richard Holloway (2000), one-time bishop of Edinburgh, claims to have a critical realist stance—though tendencies in his writings seem to appeal more to a unique brand of mystical positivism. Arthur Peacocke, renowned biochemist, Anglican vicar, and 2001 recipient of the Templeton Prize for Progress in Religion, also "describes his theologically liberal Christianity as critical realism" (*Christianity Today*, 2001). In his investigation of secular critical realism and theological critical realism, Shipway (2000) identifies another group of theologians such as Huyssteen and Barbour for whom critical realism has an appeal—though in this case some of them also appear to give human rationality an undue primacy.

Reformed critical realism

The reformed critical realism described by Cooling in his chapter in this book, and the position being suggested for consideration by this author, is related to but distinct from all of the forms of critical realism so far described. Other proponents of the form of critical realism suggested here include such diverse but respected evangelical Christian scholars as Don Carson, Lesslie Newbigin, Brian Walsh, Andrew Moore, Allister McGrath, Craig Bartholomew, Richard Middleton, and Mike Goheen—all of whom share the concern of many contemporary evangelical Christians to maintain the Scriptures in the very highest place in shaping our thinking and living, under the active influence of God's Holy Spirit. N. T. Wright also subscribes to this unique reformed take on critical realism, and his contribution in this area should not be ignored despite the controversy that rages in some circles about the new perspective on Paul (NPP).

Critical realism, Vollenhoven, and thetical-critical method

There are three significant components to reformed critical realism. They show that reformed critical realism is distinct from secular critical realism in that the starting faith commitment of secular critical realism remains the human mind whereas the starting point or presuppositional commitment of reformed critical realism is the existence, authority and involvement of a knowable God who has revealed himself through his Word including Jesus, and that all of life is lived out in obedience or disobedience to his authority. These three reformed critical realism components are as follows:

- First, the *a priori* commitment to commencing any discussion from a declared Christian worldview position.

- Second, the commitment to the sustainer-creator God who reveals himself in Jesus Christ and in his infallible written Word, the Bible which declares God's truth.

- Third, the recognition that we as fallible human beings only grasp a small portion of who God is, and that our understanding of God, his kingdom and his Word must be critiqued as the constructs of sinful people and not be mistaken for divine precepts.

A *priori* commitment to a Christian worldview: The contribution of D. H. T. Vollenhoven

Every comment reflects a point of view. Whether one is providing a definition or describing science as either a myth or the determiner of truth, one still is presenting a point of view. That point of view is the product of a person's presuppositions and particular view of reality. There is no neutrality. Even to say that one has no point of view at all about an issue is in itself a point of view. And our point of view, or religious commitment or worldview, determines how we see things, how we explain things, and what we choose to be significant or not significant to any particular conversation.

It is at this point that the thetical-critical method espoused by Vollenhoven becomes significant. Dirk Hendrik Theodoor Vollenhoven (1892–1978) was a Dutch Christian who was influenced by great thinkers such as Abraham Kuyper and Herman Bavinck —and also by contact with his university colleague and younger brother-in-law Herman Dooyeweerd. Although his thinking has only recently begun to be explored in the English-speaking world, it provides strategic philosophical support for reformed critical realism. Vollenhoven claimed that Christians should start their thinking from a deliberate commitment to genuine Scripture-based thinking. To commence from a synthesis of components taken from various strands of pagan thinking is to attempt the impossible because it will result in the corruption of biblical truth. A clever little piece from Pontificator (2004) puts it this way:

> *The hesitancy of contemporary Christians to humbly but boldly assert the biblical authenticity of their perspective in the public domain has disempowered the Christian church today.*

If our presuppositions automatically preclude us from saying, for example, that Jesus could not have understood himself as the divine son of God, we may well be excluding from our reconstruction the single most important fact about the historical Jesus and the interpretive key to understanding his person, words and actions (p. 2).

The hesitancy of contemporary Christians to humbly but boldly assert the biblical authenticity of their perspective in the public domain has disempowered the Christian church today. Though secular scholars accept as legitimate their peers expressing perspectives as being from a feminist position, or a socialist position or a postmodern perspective, Christians have been very reticent in claiming a space in the public sphere for a Christian perspective. Instead, we have typically preferred to hide our faith under a dualistic bushel and essentially live life using a pietistic paradigm in the Christian worshipping sanctuary on Sunday and the prevailing secular humanist one in the modern or postmodern faith community of the world around us for the rest of the week. According to Vollenhoven, our cognitive premises must be *reformed* so as to be a reflection or flowering of biblically shaped perspectives. Kok (1992) reports:

For Vollenhoven the term "reformation" implies first of all a turnabout, a conversion, in one's relation to God and his law, that is, in religion, such that everything, including our theoretical pursuits and educational projects, is seen in relation to God and, hence, as subjected to his will. At the same time, reformation for Vollenhoven also implies the active and ongoing element of reconsideration, revision, and reformulation (p. 13).

This is not to say that features of secular critical realism or other paradigms will not be found within reformed critical realism. Of course they will—but where this is the case, they will be there not because the reformed critical realist engaged in a potluck derby. But all truth is God's truth. The elements of secular critical realism that are evident in reformed critical realism exist there because an analysis of them confirms their rightful presence within a biblically authentic framework.

A comment should be made about the context of the word "reformed" as it is used in this chapter. It does not refer to a specific theological or denominational position, but it used to describe a worldview stance. Firstly, this worldview usage of the word reformed looks back to a commitment to the whole Bible, as was done by the great culture-shakers of the Reformation (see below). Secondly, reformed in this chapter refers to a worldview stance which projects forward into biblically faithful culture forming under the Lordship of Jesus Christ. Thus, as is argued in the introduction to this book, it is appropriate for Christians of any evangelical, denominational persuasion to retain their particular theological commitments but still espouse the reformed critical realism perspective that is advocated here.

The fidelity of Scripture

Vollenhoven, and reformed critical realists, take the highest view of Scripture. All Scripture is God-breathed and written by men who lived in real life contexts. This means that an understanding of the context of the Bible helps us to perceive the meaning that God has for us in his Word. Whilst we don't need a university degree to understand the Bible, it does not in some disembodied way "speak for itself". Much could be said about this matter, but it is interesting to note in passing that even the Bible itself engages in contextualised commentary on the stories it contains. For example, in chapter 4 of his gospel, the apostle John tells the story of Jesus' interaction with the Samaritan woman. Well aware that many of his readers would be Gentiles, John is careful to insert a contextual comment about Jews not having dealings with Samaritans, just in case Gentile readers misunderstood the significance and cultural context of the event.

The laudable but mistaken stance of modernist literalism in approaching the Bible and presupposing that it is contextless and speaks for itself in an objective way is an example of naïve realism. The theological version of naïve realism refuses to accept the real time and place setting of the Bible and can lead to a simplistic and distorted understanding of God's Word. The misunderstanding by naïve realists of the biblical concept of knowing, or their quandary about which of the various divergent forms of government that are presented in the biblical drama is the godly one (they all are contextualised forms that are faithful responses to over-riding biblical norms) are two examples. This stance is rejected by reformed critical realists.

> *The theological version of naïve realism refuses to accept the real time and place setting of the Bible.*

Reformed critical realists also reject postmodern approaches to the Bible. Postmodernists are often relativist social reconstructionists. They claim that the Bible is the thoughtful reconstruction of history by men who shaped their biblical storytelling to validate their preconceived views about God. Thus stories such as the virgin birth and the resurrection of Christ are dismissed as fanciful inventions by men who rewrote history to serve their own ends. It is on this matter that the huge differences become obvious between reformed critical realists who actually believe the Bible, and liberals like Peacocke and Holloway who claim a critical realist stance but who in reality emasculate and mythologise Scripture.

God did not ignore his world when sin entered it through Adam and subsequently impacted all of creation. He turned towards it in love and set out to restore it to himself through the substitutionary sacrifice of Jesus his Son. Consequently all of life (including the life of the mind) needs now to be lived in the light of the wonderful metanarrative of the Bible.

Reformed critical realists acknowledge that not only the Bible writers, but also we the 21st century readers, live in particular cultural and finite settings. Therefore, while we must be emphatic about the authority of Scripture, we should be careful to understand it in its context and should be much less dogmatic about the accuracy of our interpretations of it in contemporary society. Craig Keener's (1993) persuasive introductory essay to the IVP New Testament Historical Commentary is incisive in its clarity on this issue of the infallibility yet contextualised nature of the Bible. Duncan Roper's (2004) insights concerning norms and rules in the Bible are also very useful in this regard.

The finiteness of human knowing

In contrast to God's infinite wisdom and knowledge, the perspectives that we have as humans on thinking and the world are always finite and subject to error. God's comment (Jer 17:9) about the deceitfulness of the human heart, and the Psalmist's reflection on this same thought (Ps 139: 23–24), also remind us of the frailty of our own perceptions. Nevertheless, with the aid of the Holy Spirit to help us to understand the Bible as we read it in all its glorious fullness, we can live confidently and expectantly, yet humbly and open to correction, as we seek to take our place in God's grand kingdom story.

We affirm that there is a God-created truth and certainty in the universe which are revealed in God's Word. We will stand our ground and declare the true truth (to use Schaeffer's term) of Scripture, which is re-expressed in the great historical creeds of the faith. The fact that the miraculous stories of the Bible are beyond scientific explanation does not tempt us to deny their time and place reality. Once again, we join with David (Ps 139:6) in celebrating these extraordinary demonstrations of God's authority over his world—such knowledge is almost too wonderful; it is too lofty for us to attain. At the same time we also remember that the mundane and ordinary things of life also only occur because of God's sustaining hand. But we recognise that we perceive God's truth and certainties through our own culturally and socially affected spectacles. As reformed critical realists we therefore believe that all human knowledge should be held up as in some way incomplete and tentative despite the fact that we accept the need to act on that knowledge as though it is certain.

According to Don Carson (2001), quoting Stanton Jones, as critical realists

we believe there is a real world out there where it is possible to know and to know truly (hence realism), but we also believe that our theories and hypotheses about that world, and our religious presuppositions and beliefs about reality, color and shape our capacity to know that world (hence critical realism) (p. 14).

Carson, confessing that this stance of (reformed) critical realism is the paradigm that best encapsulates his own position, affirms that "no truth which human beings may articulate can ever be articulated in a culture-transcending way—but that does not mean that the truth thus articulated does not transcend culture" (p. 15).

Reformed critical realism celebrates the empowerment of Christians to revel in the authority of the Scriptures in a way that is liberated from the bondage of the unwarranted idolatrous positivism of modernism (naïve realism) on the one hand, and the individualistic uncertainty of postmodernism (nonrealism) on the other. As Paul said, "I am not ashamed, because I know whom I have believed, and am convinced that he is able to guard what I have entrusted to him for that day" (2 Tim 1:12).

Paul himself, right from within the pages of Scripture, provides us with a good example of reformed critical realism. Constantly in his travels and letters, he unpacked the story of Jesus and the resurrection by explaining the continuity of God's salvation history through the Old Testament and into the New Testament. Paul continually reflected on the enculturated nature of God's dealing with humankind throughout history and into the post-ascension period. This did not weaken Paul's message. Rather, it strengthened it. With fervent apostolic authority he was unswerving on matters central to the faith and called for a similar commitment from his fellow believers. However, on matters about which the Bible did not seem to speak clearly, although Paul advocated a particular position, he acknowledged individual conscience concerning these "disputable matters" (Rom 14). His basic contention was that in these contextually important but noncentral issues such as whether or not it was acceptable for Christians to eat food offered to idols, there needed to be a recognition of the personal nature of these beliefs. Paul advocated a plurality of practice and a liberty of individual conscience before God as long as the believers concerned had wrestled with the matter at hand and were ready to give a biblically consistent answer for the choices that they made. This is an example of the balanced approach of reformed critical realism.

Conclusion

Perhaps two stories might help illustrate the distinctives of each of the three forms of realism mentioned here and referred to in Cooling's chapter. It is vital that we be able to make these distinctions, as many fine Christians are trapped in the bypath meadow of naïve realism. Their transition to critical realism would allow them to both value the heritage of the Reformation and live in the light of a renewed and godly understanding of what the Bible actually is and says.

Parable of the umpires

Many writers, such as Carson (2001) and Jaichandran & Madhav (2003) have used Walter Truett Anderson's (1990) parable of the three umpires as a helpful handle for understanding critical realism's place in the continuum from naïve realism (similar to modernism) to nonrealism (similar to postmodernity). The story goes like this:

An old joke about three umpires summarizes the range of viewpoints. They are sitting around over a beer, and one says, "There's balls and there's strikes, and I call them the way they are". Another says, "There's balls and there's strikes, and I call 'em the way I see 'em". The third says, "There's balls and there's strikes, and they ain't nothin' until I call 'em" (p. 19).

The first umpire is a naïve realist. His way of seeing is correct and there is no other way to see it. The second umpire is a critical realist. He recognises that others might view the situation differently, but he's the umpire and he will make the call to the best of his ability. The third umpire is a nonrealist. Everything is as nothing until he gives it meaning. Although this story is helpful, readers should remember that the critical realism that it describes does not embody all of the core concepts of the thetical-critical method (it does not have an overt Christian presuppositional foundation) so that it still does not fully equate with the Christian position of reformed critical realism.

Parable of the three jumpers

The second story is a parable about three men standing before God. God tells all three of them to jump. The naïve realist asks "How high?" The nonrealist says "Why do I have to do what you tell me?" The reformed critical realist says "Yes, Lord, but do you mean "Jump over", "Jump up", "Jump down", or "Jump around?" In this story, the naïve realist immediately assumes that he has understood the question in the only way it can be understood. The problem is that if God was really asking the naïve realist to jump down or jump over, then his jumping up would actually be an act of disobedience. The nonrealist is uncertain about whether or not anyone has the right to arbitrarily demand that he jump, so he is left in an inactive, questioning quandary. The reformed critical realist, like the naïve realist, recognises God's authority and is keen to jump. However, he is uncertain that he adequately understands what is being asked of him so he seeks to know more before he acts, so that he can obediently jump the way God is wanting.

Perhaps one final way of demonstrating the distinctives of the three types of realism is to show the difference between them in a chart. David Naugle (2003) at Dallas Baptist University has constructed just such a table, an amended version of which is reproduced over the page.

Category	Naïve Realism or Literal Realism	Critical Realism	Nonrealism
Description	Certain certainty	Certain certainty Certain uncertainty	Certain uncertainty
Umpire illustration	"I call 'em as they are"	"I call 'em as I see 'em"	"They ain't notin' till I call 'em"
Response to God's command to jump	"How high?"	"Tell me what sort of jumping and I'll gladly do it."	"What right have you got to tell me to jump?"
What can we know?	Everything	Something	Nothing
Psychological stance	Idealism	Realism	Pessimism
Ethical stance	Confident, arrogant, contentious	Assured, humble, modest, fallible	Cynical, sceptical, despairing
Theological stance	Pharisaism	Pauline ("We see through a glass darkly") 1 Cor 13:12	Ecclesiastes
Worldview stance	Modernism, scientism, naturalism, foundationalism	Premodern, Christian theism	Postmodernism, nihilism
Rational stance	Too much confidence in science and autonomous human reason	Recognition of what reason can and cannot do	Too little confidence in divinely led human reason
Philosophical stance	Dogmatism	Realism	Skepticism, sophistry

Though all are faith commitments, reformed critical realism is unlike secular critical realism or liberal theological critical realism. Reformed critical realism is the application of Vollenhoven's thetical-critical perspective. It declares that all of life is lived out by human beings either in obedience or disobedience to God's laws. As Cooling suggests, reformed critical realists are very aware of the danger that their tradition might be used by some as an excuse for abusing Scripture in service of their own selfish ends. However, it remains an avowedly Christian paradigm. It acknowledges the foundational authority of the creator-sustainer God over every aspect of his creation, including people and their intellectual processes.

Despite the idolatrous view of science reflected by Caldwell in the quotation at the start of this chapter, his delightful welcome of critical realism onto the stage of human ideas should come as no surprise, given the fundamental bankruptcy of the other alternatives. We acknowledge the dangers that attend when a term such as critical realism with its deep Aristotelian roots is used to give definition to a biblically authentic idea—especially when so many pagan and pseudo-Christian scholars also lay claim to the concept. However, along with Carson, Cooling and many others, we maintain that a *reformed* concept of critical realism with its origins in Vollenhoven's insights, provides a startlingly different and biblically authentic alternative to modernity's naïve realism on the one hand and postmodernity's nonrealism on the other. Reformed critical realists recognise that while God's perfect ways are higher than our ways and his thoughts higher than our thoughts, we as sinful but redeemed image-bearers of God, guided by God's Word, can live joyful lives in service and worship, celebrating the lordship of Christ in everything.

In his visit to Athens (Acts 17) Paul did not hesitate to identify the useful insights of Greek philosophers as he sought to explain the Christian gospel in a way that resonated with his pagan audience. Similarly, it may well be that reformed critical realism, with its biblically authentic roots and concepts that resonate with the secular community, may well provide Christians with a biblically authentic place of residence in the world of ideas and it may also give us a recognisable platform from which to disciple others in the name of Jesus Christ.

Questions for discussion

1. List all the terms used in this chapter that are examples of jargon (specialist educational or philosophical terms). Allocate the terms to different members of your group and have your members explain and provide an example for each term.

2. Consider Caldwell's comment from earlier in the chapter and repeated below. How can it be that this comment both gives Christians an entrée into the public debate but yet is still idolatrous?

   Critical realism rescues us from the postmodernist nightmare and restores us to reality. We cannot manage without a concept of truth. There is (as most of us thought all along) a pre-existing external reality about which it is the job of science to tell us (Caldwell, *Philosophy Now*, 2003, p. 3).

3. Consider Pontificator's comment recorded below. How important is it for Christians to start from, and overtly champion, a biblically authentic set of presuppositions in our contributions to public discussion? How does this compare to Paul's technique on Mars Hill as recorded in Acts 17 where he quoted the Greeks' own philosophers to them in his attempt to woo them with the message of the gospel of Jesus Christ?

   If our presuppositions automatically preclude us from saying, for example, that Jesus could not have understood himself as the divine Son of God, we may well be excluding from our reconstruction the single most important fact about the historical Jesus and the interpretive key to understanding his person, words and actions (p. 2).

4. Identify a couple of features in your school/community (eg curriculum, management structure, buildings, key learning areas; recruitment and promotion etc.) that reflect a modernist perspective, and a couple of features that reflect a postmodernist perspective. Be specific. Suggest how and why these features might be different under a reformed critical realist paradigm.

5. Why might an evangelical Christian like J. P. Moreland object to (reformed) critical realism, and how could one respond to his objections?

6. Is there an apparent conflict between Vollenhoven's thetical-critical method which calls for distinctively Christian foundations for our thinking, and reformed critical realism which seems to use perspectives from Bhaskar's secular critical realism? Explain your response and suggest a way forward.

7. What other biblically authentic worldview paradigms, apart from critical realism, exist today that might be appropriate for Christians to consider?

References

Anderson, W. T. (1990). *Reality isn't what it used to be: Theatrical politics, ready to wear religion, global myths, primitive chic and other wonders of the postmodern world.* San Francisco: Harper & Row.

Barnhart, J. (1996). Karl Popper: Philosopher of critical realism. *The Humanist, 56*(4), 35–37.

Basden, A. (2004). *Bhaskar's critical realism: Comparison with Dooyeweerd.* Retrieved May 15, 2005, from http://www.isi.salford.ac.uk/dooy/ext/bhaskar.html

Caldwell, R. (2003). How to get real. *Philosophy Now, 42,* 1–6. Retrieved May 10, 2005, from http://www.philosophynow.org/issue42/42caldwell.htm

Carson, D. (2002). Maintaining scientific and Christian truths in a postmodern world. *Science and Christian Belief, 14*(2), 107–122. Retrieved May 10, 2005, from http://www.cis.org.uk/scb/articles/carson.htm

Holloway, R. (2000, 11 March). *Charge to the Synod of the Diocese of Edinburgh.* Paper presented at the meeting of the Diocese of Edinburgh. Retrieved May 14, 2005, from http://andromedia.rutgers.edu/~lcrew/holloway02.html

Jaichandran, R., & Madhav, B. (2003). Pentecostal spirituality in a postmodern world. *Asian Journal of Pentecostal Studies, 6*(1), 39–61.

Keener, C. (ed.). (1993). *The IVP Bible background commentary of the New Testament.* Downers Grove, IL: InterVarsity Press.

Kok, J. (1992). *Vollenhoven, scriptural philosophy, and Christian tradition.* Retrieved May 25, 2005, from http://home.planet.nl/~srw/nwe/vollenhoven/kok.html

Middleton, R., & Walsh, B. (1995). *Truth is stranger than it used to be: Biblical faith in a postmodern age.* Downers Grove, IL: InterVarsity Press.

Moore, A. (2003). *Realism and Christian faith: God, grammar and meaning.* Cambridge: Cambridge University Press.

Moreland, J. P. (2004). *Truth, contemporary philosophy, and postmodern truth.* Retrieved May 8, 2005, from http://www.str.org/free/points/truth.htm

Naugle, D. (2003). *Epistemology, objectivity, and subjectivity.* Retrieved May 12, 2005, from http://www.dbu.edu/naugle/institute_handouts.htm

Peterson, D. (Ed.). (1999). *Witness to the world: Papers from the second Oak Hill College Annual School of Theology.* Carlisle, United Kingdom: Paternoster.

Pontificator. (2004, April 11). *Will the real Jesus please stand up.* Retrieved May 10, 2005, from http://pontifications.classicalanglican.net/index.php?p=87

Roper, D. (2004). Using the Bible faithfully: Norms, rules and the word of God. In J. Ireland, R. J. Edlin, & K. Dickens (Eds.), *Pointing the way: Directions for Christian education in a new millennium* (pp. 131–154). Blacktown, NSW: National Institute for Christian Education.

Shipway, B. (2000). Critical realism and theological critical realism: Opportunities for dialogue? *Alethia, 3*(2), 29–33.

Verstegen, I. (2000). *Bhaskar and American critical realism.* Retrieved May 18, 2005, from http://www.raggedclaws.com/criticalrealism/archive/iverstegen_bhaskar

Wilson, J. (2001, 3 December). *Examining Peacocke's Plumage.* Retrieved May 15, 2005, from http://www.christianitytoday.com/ct/2001/111/11.0.html

Chapter 7

Church and the Christian School

Ken Dickens

Senior Lecturer, National Institute for Christian Education

Ken has been a teacher for 30 years. He has taught in all sections of schooling and has spent equal time in state schools and Christian schools. During his time in the latter, Ken was involved in leading two schools in New South Wales. For the past five years Ken has been Senior Lecturer of the National Institute for Christian Education. His academic interests include the theological and philosophical basis of Christian education and leadership. His current doctoral research through the University of New South Wales concerns the relationship between theology and worldview in the vision and practice of Christian parent-controlled schools and Anglican schools. Ken preaches in his local church and is a regular speaker at conferences. He is married to Jennie and they have four children, three of whom have grown up and left home and one is in high school still living at home with them in the Blue Mountains of NSW.

Abstract

This chapter seeks to explore the relationship between the church and the Christian school. It begins with a discussion of what is meant by church. From this context, it then seeks to find a legitimate place for the Christian school. The dichotomy of either making too little or too much of a distinction between the two is discussed. The major part of the chapter is devoted to issues that affect both the church and the Christian school and issues that each has with the other. It concludes with recommendations for Christians who are involved with Christian schools to act with integrity and sensitivity within their local churches.

> *In some churches it is a mark of orthodoxy to have your children in a Christian school... in others, it is an indication of a lack of commitment to evangelism.*

In some churches it is a mark of orthodoxy to have your children in a Christian school. In others, it is an indication of a lack of commitment to evangelism. In many churches it is divisive to discuss schooling. Some churches run schools. Many denominations run schools. Some Christians within these churches and denominations think they should and others think that they shouldn't. It's all very confusing! Christian schools say that they want to honour Christ in the schooling process—an aspiration that one would expect to resonate with church. But it is not always the case. Parents choosing this form of schooling are surprised that fellow Christians often do not share their conviction and are even critical of their decision. Sometimes it is the leaders of the church who are most critical.

There are many complex reasons for churches reacting differently to Christian schools and even more complex reasons for the often experienced tension between church and school. Some of these reasons will be discussed later in the chapter but first it is important to talk about what church is.

Concepts of church

My interest in church preceded my interest in Christian schools and I am tempted to say that it is more important. This may concern some in our heritage who strongly contend for parity of sovereignty. I have great respect for this position.

Suffice it to say, church is a prior commitment and it is a commitment that concerns all Christians at all times, as opposed to school, which affects only some and for some time.

Understanding church is a fundamental endeavour and should precede any discussion of Christian education. Church is at the heart of God's purposes for his people and for his world. Much of the New Testament is devoted to this subject. The church is integrally tied up with the person of Christ. It is variously described in metaphors such as Christ's bride, the body of Christ and the household of God.

There is not space in this chapter to engage in a comprehensive ecclesiology. A brief glance at the subject, however, will show that evangelicals have some differing views on the issue. An example can be clearly seen in the excellent if slightly dated publication from Moore College entitled, *Church, worship and local congregation* (Webb, 1987). The centrepiece of this book of essays is the one by Broughton Knox, who insists that church is the local congregation—a community of the Holy Spirit for the purpose of fellowship with Jesus and each other.

Another contributor, Graham Cole, concurs with this notion but raises the problems associated with an inward-looking mindset that may come from such a position. He helpfully suggests that we put too much weight on the word "church" and that we need to use other broader biblical terms such as "kingdom of God" and "people of God". This not only reminds us of our missional stance towards the world but it also maintains the integrity of church as congregation.

Bill Lawton makes another contribution. He suggests that looking at what the Bible means by church is not the whole picture. We need to understand the situation historically and sociologically and see the development of church as a legitimate thing as long as it is faithful to the gospel. This position warns against a naïve primitivism and reminds us that forms and expressions can legitimately change over time and cultures. This, however, does not negate the need for Christians in every age and culture to discern the biblical essence of church—the basic norms.

Church in the New Testament is people meeting together with Christ. It was best described in William Tyndale's translation as "congregation". The church is the people who meet as Christ's bride, body and household. This local expression is representative of all God's people who are gathered around Christ in time and eternity. However, despite the deeply communal aspect of its nature in the New Testament, we continue to understand and define church by other metaphors and confuse it with other things.

Not denomination

Most commonly, we confuse church with denomination. We refer, for instance, to the Uniting Church or Anglican Church rather than the Uniting or Anglican denomination and in so doing see church as a complex, centralised institution rather than a gathering of believers. There is nothing inherently wrong with denominations or with like-minded churches linking together for mutual support but that concept ought not to define church. Neither should it interfere with the biblical functioning of church (Knox 1987).

Not institution

Even when we think about church in its local context, we often think about its structure, programs and leadership rather than the people who make up church. Every group needs structure and organisation but the emphasis ought to be on the organisation serving the community not the other way around. Stuart Fowler (1994) made this point in reference to school communities. It seems the case is even stronger to consider church as community rather than as primarily organisation. The leaders of churches need to see themselves as shepherds not executives or entrepreneurs.

Paul teaches in Ephesians that within the fellowship and teaching of the local congregation, the believers will be prepared and built up for works of service. Some of these ministries will be within the church while other ministries will be exercised in the wider community. In all cases, these ministries will be carried out by the people of God, in building the kingdom of God. This kingdom is concerned with the whole of creation and stretches across the whole gamut of human experience. The people of God are active in the world for the kingdom of God. Christians who are being built up in their local fellowships will serve in the world. Sometimes they will set up organisations to do specific things. These organisations do not need to be seen as part of the church's ministry. Neither do they need church endorsement. Christians involved thus in kingdom work will look to their local congregation for support and encouragement.

Church and Christian organisations

A Christian school then is an organisation established by part of the people of God for the kingdom of God. The organisation will be for a specific purpose with a specific character. As has been suggested earlier, one aspect of the character of school will be the subordination of organisation to community. But how can one know what the character of this organisation should be when the Bible does not speak specifically regarding this thing called school? There are entities that the Bible does specifically talk about. We have been discussing the biblical concept of church. The Bible also talks about family and the state. Some things are ordained by God and other things are developed by people as a response to our God-ordained cultural mandate. This development is carried out with either regard or disregard to creational and biblical norms. It goes without saying that Christian people ought to develop schools with a full regard to the sovereignty of God over all of creation.

But this idea is by no means universally accepted among Christians. For many the business for Christians is church, and school is a neutral, cultural entity that has a set structure with which we have no right to interfere.

School is no less under the sovereignty and interest of God than church unless the "all things" of Colossians 1 somehow doesn't include those things which have been developed by people. Space will not allow here for a biblical theory of school. Suffice it to say that it behoves Christians involved in the endeavour to start with the gospel of Jesus and with gospel-focused eyes to look at the biblical narrative as well as the creation. Then, they seek to consider "How would God have us teach our children?" Many of the things God says about families would be relevant, but a Christian school is not the same as a family. Much of what God says about the government may apply, but Christian schooling is not a task of government. Many of the things God says about church would fit, but a Christian school is not the same as church. A school is a separate entity which is the responsibility of parents; it has some characteristics of church but with government implications. It is with this separateness and similarity regarding church and Christian school that this chapter is concerned.

> *A school is a separate entity which is the responsibility of parents; it has some characteristics of church but with government implications.*

The defining difference between church and school

There are so many features of a Christian school that are like church. They are both covenant communities. They both submit to biblical authority. They are both concerned with discipleship. They both uphold the primacy of relationships. They are both concerned for the glory of God. They both proclaim the centrality of the gospel. They both recognise giftedness of their members. They both promote service. They both aspire to holiness of their people. They both engage in evangelism. They both see conversions. They both recognise godly servant-leadership … just to name a few! So what is the difference? The difference lies in the basic task for each community. The basic task for the church as a gathering of believers is encouragement by mutual edification through God's Word and Spirit. The basic task for school is the disclosure to children and teenagers of the world and their place in it. Each would be involved in the other's task but each has its own basic task.

What about the church school?

Given the understanding of church that has been presented in this chapter, the church school doesn't exist. That which we know as a church school is either a denominational school or a school organised by people from a local congregation. Whatever it is, the distinction between it and a Christian school is maintained by both parties. It can be seen in the criticisms that they have of each other. Paradoxically, church schools make a stronger distinction between church and school. Advocates of Christian schools accuse these schools of pushing the distinction to the extent of setting up a dualism between church-related Christian studies and other academic studies. On the other hand advocates of church schools accuse Christian schools of confusing school with church and not sufficiently separating their distinct purposes. Given that both kinds of school are seeking to advance God's kingdom, two implications are apparent. One is that each kind of school needs to learn how to be more self-critical. The other is that we need to learn how to be gracious in our approach to each other.

Issues for church and school

Christian schools and churches are concerned with the kingdom of God and with the people of God. The kingdom has not yet been consummated and the people of God have not yet been glorified. Like all relationships, there are some tensions, and one purpose of this chapter is to air some of these tensions in the hope that greater understanding will be achieved. Before we consider some of these tensions, we need to consider some issues that churches and Christian schools share. I am not referring to the characteristics mentioned before and to which both aspire. I am referring to issues that cling to churches and Christian schools as we seek to accommodate ourselves to the culture in which we are immersed.

Michael Frost (2002) has lamented that the contemporary church is "attractional, hierarchical and dualistic" (p. 16). The issue of dualism continues to be a problem for schools but perhaps it is a bigger problem for churches. This will be discussed later in the chapter. The other issues—those of being attractional and hierarchical—are very relevant to schools as well as churches. In our enthusiasm for growth we look to the market. Rather than focusing on being faithful within our communities and gracious to those outside, we are more concerned with what attracts the potential buyer. We design our program to get them in the door. Growth is usually indicative of life and in itself a good thing. The issue for a number of people is the methods we use to promote growth. David Wells (1993) has written an excellent critique of the church growth movement. Much of what he has to say is just as applicable to the Christian school. Nancy Pearcey (2004) looks at the uncritical acceptance of business methodology by Christian organisations, especially in their advertising and marketing. The irony is that the most powerful evangelistic tool is the local church embodying the gospel and functioning as the body of Christ. The most powerful promotional tool for a Christian school is the demonstration that it is going about its business of nurturing children.

> *The hierarchical school emphasises the need for individuals to conform to the institutional character of the school.*

Churches and schools can so easily become consumerist. The consumer most likely to keep the institution going will come from the middle class so both the church and school are in danger of being captive to the values of that socioeconomic group. Not only will this make it difficult for us to include the people with whom Jesus most identified (the poor and dispossessed), but the conservatism of values inherent to our middle-class culture can effectively blunt the radical demands of the gospel.

What of hierarchical leadership? It depends who you talk to. There is a group which bemoans the postmodern egalitarian attitude of the young in our churches and schools, while others perceive a heaviness of control under the guise of biblical authority. The issue is more complex and has to do with how we see our churches and schools and the leaders who lead them. If we see them primarily as institutions to be protected and promoted rather than communities to be nurtured, then we can expect a leadership of control and the accompanying destructive effects not only on the communities but the people who lead. Dawn (2002) makes this point powerfully:

There is unleashed among the principalities in this society a ruthless, self-prolifer-
ating, all-consuming institutional process which assaults, dispirits, defeats, and destroys
human life even among, and primarily among, those persons in positions of institutional
leadership (p. 76).

Stronks and Blomberg (1994), quoting Kirkpatrick, distinguish between three kinds of school communities. The *contractual school* emphasises individuals coming together to achieve their own ends. The *hierarchical school* emphasises the need for individuals to conform to the institutional character of the school. Christians aware of the dangers of individualism often embrace this model as the one that upholds community. Many schools and churches become hierarchical for good reasons. However, they achieve conformity more often than community. In a *covenant community*, commitment to God, each other and the communal task is emphasised. The community and the individuals, who comprise the community, are respected. The other models use community to achieve another end either for the institution or the individual. Are Christian schools and churches functioning as covenant communities? In eschewing the individualism of contemporary contractual communities, too many of our schools and churches maintain a hierarchical community style and do not fully embrace the joys and dangers of living in covenant relationship.

Having discussed problems that are shared by churches and Christian schools, we will now move to issues which they have with each other.

Issues that church has with the Christian school

There are doubtless many issues that churches and Christians within churches have with Christian schools. I have chosen three to discuss because I think they are the most common.

The first issue is where the Christian school is seen as a rival to the church, vying for commitment from its members. This concern is very understandable. I have known teachers in Christian schools to consider their commitment to the Christian school so great that they dropped out of church. I would suggest that this is not on! Conversely I have seen Christians continue to maintain all their ministries in a local church while trying to maintain a spiritually demanding ministry in a Christian school. This is not wise either!

Christian schools need to recognise that their staff and parents have other responsibilities and impose extra commitment expectations carefully and sparingly. The

involvement of Christian school people in their local church is important. Similarly, churches need to recognise that many of its members have significant ministries outside the congregation. This should be a cause for rejoicing not competing if indeed these ministries are for the kingdom. It is worth noting also that the Christian school does not have the monopoly on these outside ministries.

The second issue that the church has with Christian schools is that they are divisive. This occurs at the level of the parents and the students. Enthusiasts for Christian education have, at times, insinuated that other parents are wrong in not sending their children to a Christian school. This has caused a moratorium on discussion regarding education in many churches. Christian parents have the right and responsibility to choose the education for their children. And we make different choices based on a number of factors. It is not appropriate for others to impose their views on parents making these decisions. It is, however, entirely appropriate for people in fellowship to discuss a whole range of issues in a nonjudgmental manner. Indeed it is entirely inappropriate not to share important information with our brothers and sisters. It is time the moratorium was lifted and it is imperative that both advocates and critics of Christian schools speak without arrogance or judgment.

> *In some cases Christian students whose parents do not enrol them in a Christian school can feel abandoned by their Christian peers who leave for a Christian school.*

The young people in the church feel the tension when the majority of their peers attend a particular school. Sometimes this school will be a Christian school; at other times it will be a state school. The minority group always has the potential to feel on the outer. The answer is not to have all children attending the same school but to deal with the potential inadvertent division in a specific, pastoral way. It also behoves Christian schools to encourage their students to maintain unity in their church communities and not allow their enrolment in the school to cause any hint of superiority.

The problem also occurs in the context of the school. In some cases Christian students whose parents do not enrol them in a Christian school can feel abandoned by their Christian peers who leave for a Christian school. This is a real issue and there are no easy answers. The reality is that with choice in schooling friends will be separated because of the choice for all kinds of schools, not just Christian schools. One of the factors in parents making their decision may be the impact on friends. But there are many other factors that need to be considered as well. Perhaps this issue demonstrates the enormity of the decision about schooling.

The third issue of concern that has been often raised by church members in relation to Christian schools is that they are unprofessional. This is a tough one and strongly linked, I would suggest, to the issue of dualism, which will be discussed in the next section. Have there been examples of unprofessionalism exhibited in Christian schools? Of course there have. Christian schools are a comparatively new entity. In our immaturity, we haven't always done things well. In our zeal to include a biblical perspective we have been guilty of trivialising the Scriptures by making them fit our curriculum designs. This has been recognised and some profound thinking is being done in the area of applying the Bible authentically to education. British scholars John Shortt and David Smith (2002) have advanced our thinking in their book, *The Bible and the task of teaching*. The Australian scholar Rod Thompson (2004) addressed this issue in his doctoral research and has written in *Pointing the way: Directions for Christian education in the new millennium* from this research. These insights have great implications for how Christians read and apply the Bible to all areas of life.

> *To put it bluntly, Christians find it hard to trust other Christians to do education properly from a biblical perspective.*

Criticism of Christian schools does have a basis in real situations. It also has a basis in thinking that is dualistic. To put it bluntly, Christians find it hard to trust other Christians to do education properly from a biblical perspective. A dualistic mind cannot conceive of the two going together, not realising that education always takes place within a religious perspective of some kind. There is a suspicion by some that we will spoil education by trying to bring the gospel into it. There is also another element to this criticism. Not only is there a suspicion that we will inevitably teach academic disciplines badly, but there is also a judgment by some that we teach the Bible badly. There is a suggestion by some that trained theologians should teach the Bible and teachers should teach other stuff. Without discounting the great benefit of theological training, Christian teachers need to be growing in their ability to teach the Bible and they should look to their pastors to help them.

Issues that the Christian schools have with churches

This issue of dualism is the main concern that proponents of Christian schools have with churches. Not only does this affect the way members of churches view Christian schooling, but it is also a problem affecting the way churches view the world. It is not overstating the case to say that the greatest contribution that the Christian school movement can make towards the kingdom of God is to confront the issue of dualism. To limit the church to concern with the spiritual is to limit the sovereignty of God. All of life is spiritual and God is interested in all of life. That is not to say that the church does everything. Its essence is fellowship. But within this fellowship living all of life to the glory of God needs to be promoted and celebrated. It is a truncated view of the gospel to see life in terms of winning souls to Christ who in turn win other souls to Christ while we wait for heaven. Making disciples involves an all-of-life discipleship. Walsh and Middleton's book, *The transforming vision* (1984) helps us to understand dualism and its effects.

The second concern in regard to the church's relationship with Christian schools is the paucity of understanding of the issues involved. Education continues to be seen as a neutral endeavour. It seems that Christians are the last ones to know that it is driven by powerful religious forces. Why should the church be interested in something which after all, in some minds, is just a hobby-horse for a few? Apart from the fact that the few need encouragement for the kingdom work in which they are engaged, education is a major national concern. Churches need to be involved in the discussion regarding the nature of education. It is a battle-ground for the gospel. To come alongside schools for the purpose of evangelism is fine but to take the "thought [of education] captive to make it obey Christ" (2 Cor 10:5) is even better. For too long Christians have left school education as a secular concern. With the renewed interest in education generally and the recent proliferation of denominational schools, it is timely to have informed discussion on the issues surrounding education within the fellowship of the local church.

The third issue is one of double standards displayed by some in churches. A strong argument against Christian schools has been the perceived retreat from the opportunity of witness in the public schools. I have great sympathy with this argument. As one who spent half of my teaching life in public schools, I know the opportunities and in God's grace I took them fully. There will always be Christian teachers, parents and students in public schools and God will use them for his glory. I left because I wanted to be involved in the redeeming of education rather than evangelism within a conflicting paradigm. Many will continue to serve God by staying. This is not the issue. The thing that undermines the argument is that many of the people who denounce Christian schools' damage to the witness in public schools end up enrolling their children in denominational schools—not for the sake of witness nor even for the sake of Christian nurture but for the sake of perceived academic advantage.

The way ahead

I have written this chapter in the hope of building bridges between people in churches opposed to Christian schools and people in churches enamoured with Christian schools. I have set church and school up as distinct and sometimes opposing entities because, in the first place, this is the way it is and, in the second place, this is the way it sometimes feels. To be consistent with my own argument, I cannot define church as institution or by its leaders. It is simply people within churches who disagree on the subject of education. The perception is that there is a tension between church and school.

As people committed to Christ, our first priority is to be committed to a local congregation.

I want to acknowledge this tension in the hope that it can be resolved, and address my concluding remarks to people in churches who are committed to Christian education. The kingdom of God is bigger than our local churches and bigger than our Christian schools. The central things that unify the people of God have nothing to do with our decisions on where to send our children for schooling.

As people committed to Christ, our first priority is to be committed to a local congregation. Our commitment to this congregation needs to be responsible. Being responsible doesn't mean doing everything that is asked of us. It does mean striving to maintain the unity in Christ with our brothers and sisters.

Maintaining unity does not mean remaining silent on issues that need airing. But we should raise these with gentleness and humility. Seek to have the issues related to education and schooling put on the agenda for open and loving discussion. Seek to have other important issues discussed and be interested in issues about which we may be ignorant. Seek to enlarge the recognition of the lordship of Christ over all creation and seek to enlarge the recognition of the scope of the gospel that concerns the reconciliation of all things.

Finally, respect the right of brothers and sisters to disagree about disputable matters. Despite our passion about Christian education we affirm that it remains a disputable matter.

Questions for discussion

1. There are many connotations today to the word "church". How helpful is it to stress a narrow biblical definition?

2. What are the problems and benefits of inviting local pastors in to exercise a ministry in the Christian school?

3. What are the problems and benefits of the Christian school principal preaching in local churches about Christian education?

4. What would you say to the claim that the Bible encourages dualism with verses such as "set your minds on things above …" (Col 3:2) and "my kingdom is not of this world …" (John 18:36)?

References

Cole, G. (1987). The doctrine of the church: Towards conceptual clarification. In B. Webb (Ed.), *The church, worship and the local congregation* (pp. 3–18). Sydney, NSW: Lancer Books.

Dawn, M. (2001). *Powers, weakness and the tabernacling with God*. Grand Rapids, MI: Eerdmans.

Fowler, S. (1994, June). *The practice of community in learning and teaching*. Paper presented at the Scholarly Conference for Christian Teacher Educators, Sydney.

Frost, M. (2002, May). Flaws in the church's DNA. *Alive Magazine*, (p. 16–17).

Knox, D. B. (1987). The biblical concept of fellowship. In B. Webb (Ed.), *The church, worship and the local congregation* (pp. 59–82). Sydney, NSW: Lancer Books.

Lawton, W. (1987). A response to Broughton Knox's paper. In B. Webb (Ed.), *The church, worship and the local congregation* (pp. 83–92). Sydney, NSW: Lancer Books.

Pearcey, N. (2004). *Total truth*. Wheaton, IL: Crossway Books.

Smith, D. I & Shortt, J. (2002). *The Bible and the task of teaching*. Stapleford, Nottingham: Stapleford Centre.

Stronks, G. & Blomberg, D, (Eds.). (1993). *A vision with a task*. Grand Rapids, MI: Baker Books.

Thompson, R. (2004). Genesis and Jesus and a Christian worldview. In J. Ireland, R. Edlin, & K. Dickens (Eds.), *Pointing the way: Directions for Christian education in the new millennium* (pp. 155–174). Blacktown, NSW: National Institute for Christian Education.

Walsh, B. J. & Middleton, J. R. (1984). *The transforming vision*. Downers Grove, IL: InterVarsity Press.

Webb, B. (Ed.). (1987). *The church, worship and the local congregation*. Sydney, NSW: Lancer Books.

Wells, D. (1993). *No place for truth*. Grand Rapids, MI: Eerdmans.

Chapter 8

Where the rubber meets the road:

Christian education in a young teacher's classroom

Coralie Harris

Teacher, Southern Highland Christian School

Coralie Harris is currently teaching in the Infants Department at Southern Highlands Christian School in New South Wales, Australia. She completed her BA, DipEd at Macquarie University in 2001, which included units taught by lecturers from the National Institute for Christian Education (NICE). She is now working part-time on completing a Masters degree in Christian education with NICE. Coralie has been married to Carl for three years, and they have a Pomeranian named Toffee. She is a prolific reader and loves to renovate old furniture and watch the garden grow, while pondering the bigger issues of life.

Abstract

As Christian educators we seek to teach our students about their maker, the world and their task in life. How we do this is a matter for questioning. Though our desire may be well founded, too often we rely on inherited methods in the classroom that undermine the very things we aim to teach. The following thoughts are the result of an attempt to analyse classroom practice and instigate changes to make classroom routines and learning sessions more God-honouring. The challenge before us is to continually and critically reflect on the what and the how of our teaching, analyse the underlying worldview and consciously reject it in favour of a biblical worldview perspective.

In the course of life, everything we do reflects a core belief, of which we may or may not be aware. Every action conveys adherence to one principle or another; from the way we greet our friends to the way we look after the environment, to the way we teach and educate. To participate in the education process in any capacity, one must be able to define what one believes to be essential to education. The New South Wales Department of Education and Training (NSW DET) (2004) states the key priority of public schools is "to provide children and young people with the foundations for lifelong learning so that they become literate, numerate, well-educated citizens with the capabilities and confidence to make a positive contribution to our society". By contrast, Christian schools would state something like "Christian education must ensure that students learn about the world and their places and tasks in it from a biblical worldview" (Edlin 2004, p. 2). These are vastly different definitions, and without going into an analysis of the undergirding worldviews of these two statements, it is sufficient to say that, given the many conflicting worldviews promoted in society, we need to analyse what we do in the classroom to ensure that we convey the worldview that we profess. As Walsh & Middleton (1984) write, "to do scholarship Christianly, then, is to consciously allow our faith to direct our studies" (p.172).

> *In the course of life, everything we do reflects a core belief, of which we may or may not be aware.*

Classroom flexibility

Based on my reflections on the journalling exercise conducted as part of study with the National Institute for Christian Education (NICE), and honest conversations with colleagues, I made some observations about my teaching style. My teaching style seems to be characterised by flexibility, an emphasis on developing relationships and communication and the use of a variety of work styles (indoors/outdoors, desks/floor, individual/group, active/passive). I consciously work on giving good reasons for decisions. I think it is important to spend time at the beginning of a lesson outlining goals so that the students have a purpose as they work. I value routine, but do not hesitate to change it whenever something unplanned, yet important, comes up. For instance, a discussion in devotion time could take the entire first lesson. In this instance I wouldn't discontinue the conversation for the sake of keeping routine. Similarly, the students may be unsettled, so I will change the lesson (not necessarily the planned outcome) in order to meet the given need. I have also noted that I quite commonly plan the outcome to be met (particularly in phonics lessons), but not the means, so that I may facilitate but leave the choice of method to the students.

The English program and working in community

As I reflected on my English program I attempted to analyse what I conveyed regarding the nature of education to the students. I came to the conclusion that the program, particularly the structure of reading groups, did not take a genuinely holistic approach. As Pearcey (2004) writes, Christians "take great pains to make sure their message is biblical, but … never think to ask whether their methods are biblical" (p.34).

I believe that if, as Strom (1989, p. 112) writes, "we are to serve the Lord in everything we do and reflect dependence on him, in thinking and doing", this needs to be reflected in our teaching. Everything we do in the classroom needs to demonstrate our relationship with him. Practising this means that the students can observe that teachers don't have the monopoly on knowledge and wisdom. Rather, we rely on the Lord for wisdom in giving instructions and in decision-making, and can share the process with the students. In this I have found that they can help each other and give answers also. "Christian education treats children with the dignity of beings made in the image of God" (Colson & Pearcey, 1999, p.201). As beings made in the image of God, we need to develop not only the academic aspect of the students, but their spiritual, social and emotional facets as well.

In my original English program, the academic aspect of education was over-emphasised. I believe this presented a somewhat dualistic view of education, as academia was seen to be important but the other aspects of the children didn't rate as high a mention. That's certainly not what I would have professed to believe, but it is what was conveyed in practice. In an effort to convey that academic, spiritual, social and emotional development are all important, the group-style English teaching system was changed to a partner system, where partners were chosen specifically by the teacher to complement each other's skill set. Advanced readers were partnered with students who struggled with reading but who were good at cooperative work, and students with good comprehension skills, or sentence building skills, were paired up with students possessing complementary skills. Before the partner system began, time was spent explaining why the system was being changed and getting the students to offer ideas and opinions. Students also spent time analysing their own and others' visible skills and gifts, and discussing how skills could be matched up to good effect. Students were then taught how best to help their partners, by asking questions and prompting without giving away the answers.

Upon reflection, students made statements such as: "I help him with the reading, and he helps me do a proper sentence answer"; "I found out that my partner is good at helping me concentrate", and "my partner reminds me to put in capital letters and full stops, and I help him answer the questions". This demonstrates that the children gained an appreciation for the different skills sets that they had. Additionally, the better readers in the class were more challenged in the attempt to develop their social skills than they would have been by simply advancing their reading skills. The system also built up the confidence of the students who didn't read so well, as they were affirmed as being good at something else. I believe that the students truly learnt that school is about more than just being able to complete the work; it is about how you do it. This perspective, in the end, was much more biblically sound. "We are all special" was not only verbally conveyed to the children but also practically acknowledged in day-to-day classroom activities.

Homework and a Christian worldview

Changes also took place in my criteria for decent excuses for late homework as I had to reflect on what I conveyed about education through homework expectations. I know that I aim to convey that I see education as a whole-of-life undertaking, not just something that is conducted at school. However, I realise that sometimes I don't reflect this. For example, a parent came in to speak to me about her child not having homework ready on time as the family was going through a rough patch at home, and therefore the homework hadn't been completed. I judged that to be completely reasonable and went out of my way to watch out for her child in all areas of school life. In another scenario, occurring at the same time, I was intolerant of homework being incomplete and made a student finish it off at school, as the parent had not communicated with me as to the reason. I found out later that the family had been moving house at the time, but even so, I emphasised to the student, "You should have been able to complete it anyway" as I felt that as it was not an emotional problem relocating was not an adequate excuse. Upon reflection, I believe that this presents a divided view of life, in that dramatic events, which have emotional implications, are seen as more important than exciting/stimulating events, which perhaps have social implications. This seems to be compartmentalising life when, as Strom (1989) suggests, "all of life is inter-related" and "there is always more than one way of seeing anything" (p.112). I should perhaps have tried to either adapt the homework to suit her, or excused her and asked her what she had learnt from moving house. She may have been learning how best to serve her parents in a busy and potentially stressful situation.

So, what do we convey through the setting of homework regarding the nature of education? Hopefully, we are flexible enough to factor in the varying home situations and the variety of events that occur in a child's home life throughout the year, so they understand that we are not regarding ourselves as the only important educational input in children's lives at any given time. For, in regarding ourselves in this singular way, we are conveying the message that education only occurs through school and school-related activities. The Christian school is a part of the whole community of faith and needs to participate as part of this community, not as though it is of sole importance. We must "bear one another's burdens and so fulfil the law of Christ" (Gal 6:2). For it is only in community that Christians, and therefore Christian schools, can stand strong (Walsh & Middleton, 1984). If we regard ourselves as the only means of education and of absolute importance, we are not working from a Christian worldview at all but rather supporting the dualistic view of life, which weakens the potential impact of the school.

> *The Christian school is a part of the whole community of faith and needs to participate as part of this community, not as though it is of sole importance.*

Student motivation and gifts

Another area of reflection and change centres on the question "What do I convey about education in the way I motivate the students?" In reasoning with students about their motivation, we should be able to talk about working as a response to God's love, not to achieve anything for pride or esteem or to compare against others. We are all made special, just the way we are meant to be, and should use our minds to the best of our ability in response (Strom, 1989).

I know that I believe that students should do their best because they should use the gifts that God has given them, but I have promoted a different worldview in the classroom on occasion. A couple of months ago, I had a conversation with a student about his lack of motivation and the resulting poor work. Our conversation ran along the lines of "Do you think this is your best work?" "No." "OK, why isn't it?" "Because I don't want to do it." "How are you going to learn to read or write if you don't practise?" "Dunno…" So I tried a different tack. "What sort of job do you want to do when you grow up?" "Dunno", and after a few job suggestions which elicited a similar response I asked, "Do you want to be a garbage collector?" "No!" "Well then, you have to learn to read and write and since I am your teacher this year, you need to do the activities I set for you." This conversation had its desired effect and the student proceeded to improve his standard of work. However, I wonder now if it was a wise line of argument as this student could rightfully walk away with the impression that education is about learning at school in order to get a high paying and high status job. This is clearly an economic rationalist argument. In my teaching, I desire for equal emphasis to be placed upon all areas of study as "every square inch of life is God's. He declared it is all good and he gave it to us to explore, rule and enjoy. It is a false question to ask whether preaching or ploughing is more pleasing to God" (Strom, 1989, p.112). Now, instead of the "do it, and do it well, or you will never learn and you will end up being a garbage collector!" approach, I maintain the emphasis on using the gifts that God has given us to the best of our ability. I also give examples from the Bible, such as explaining the parable of the talents (Matt 25:14–30). This was not a complete change, as I would say this to students anyway, but the difference is that I would now never (consciously) resort to an economic rationalist argument simply to add weight to what I was trying to say.

Students from non-Christian backgrounds

It is difficult, as I found recently, when you talk to a student who doesn't have much of a relationship with God, and doesn't really care about the way God made him. The temptation is strong to revert to secular motivation when the biblical perspective doesn't seem to pack enough punch. Once again, this is conveying to the student a false view of what education is about. If I were to revert to secular motivation, this would convey that education was solely about academic standards and achievement. As Strom states, "every thought and act is religious, because everything expresses a basic heart commitment. We are either God's servants, or his enemies. Even rebels remain in God's image. So all of us live in varying degrees of consistency with what we were meant to be" (Strom, 1989, p.112). Rather than me being concerned for his spiritual/emotional well-being, I am singularly focused on the academic to the disadvantage of his whole self. I need to acknowledge that "the world is no longer exactly how it was meant to be. In each situation, we must wrestle with the physical, social and personal effects of sin". I need to "think through the broad pattern of creation, fall and re-creation" (Strom, 1989, p.112) and both teach and minister to this child from this perspective, recognising his fallen state and encouraging him with the redemption to come. Not only is he encouraged, but I am encouraged also by the hope I have knowing that the Holy Spirit works where the Word is being proclaimed and acted upon.

Conclusion

In order to maintain maximum effectiveness in the integration of a Christian worldview in teaching practice, a number of strategies can be implemented. Firstly, follow-up lessons with the students will be conducted analysing what they thought of the changes, what worked and what didn't work. Also, reflective discussions regarding what they learnt about themselves and their partner will be conducted. Secondly, in the actual programming process, I will endeavour to write in not only the necessary academic development but also the social, emotional and physical developmental goals, as a reminder of this holistic approach. Also, conversations with colleagues are an integral part of the reflecting and brainstorming process. Honest appraisal and new suggestions are welcomed and given due thought. Finally, I find continued reading on relevant topics beneficial as it assists me to understand and be aware of the differing worldviews and also serves as a reminder that these issues need to be continually addressed.

Christian education "is not just an introspective activity. It exists to equip young people to share God's dynamic message of hope and peace in Christ, in every vocation and activity, with a lost and forlorn generation" (Edlin, 2004, p.3). Education is not simply a way to shape students into positive contributors in society; it is the means by which we challenge students to "celebrate the lordship of Jesus Christ over all of creation" (Edlin, 2004, p.2). As Christian teachers, we must reflect on and define our worldview, and teach accordingly. We need to "clearly understand, teach, and live a radical, biblical worldview perspective" (Edlin, 2004, p.3).

Questions for discussion

1. What do you hope that, in your teaching, you convey to be the meaning of education?

2. How do the goals that you set in the classroom reflect your worldview?

3. Give an example of how your relationship with Christ influences the way you run your classroom.

4. What practical steps can you take to ensure that your classroom practice reflects a biblical worldview perspective?

5. How do you motivate students and what is your biblically authentic foundation for this practice?

6. Discuss the difficulties involved in practising a biblical worldview perspective in the classroom, when other perspectives overrule elsewhere.

7. How do you deal with students from non-Christian backgrounds and why?

8. Explain the place of homework in the life of the Christian school.

References

Colson, C & Pearcey, N. (1999). *How now shall we live?* London: Marshall Pickering.

Edlin, R. J. (2004). Why Christian schools? In J.Ireland, R.Edlin & K.Dickens (Eds.), *Pointing the way: Directions for Christian education in a new millennium.* Sydney: National Institute for Christian Education.

New South Wales Department of Education and Training. *About public schools.* [On-line] Retrieved November 19, 2004, from http://www.det.nsw.edu.au/aboutus/public.htm

Pearcey, N. (2004). *Total truth: Liberating Christianity from its cultural captivity.* Wheaton IL: Crossway Books.

Strom, M. (1989). *Days are coming.* Sydney: Hodder and Stoughton.

Walsh, B. J. & Middleton, J. R. (1984). *The transforming vision: Shaping a Christian world view.* Downers Grove, IL: Inter Varsity Press.

Chapter 9

Does God dwell in the detail?

How faith affects (language) teaching processes

David I. Smith

Director, Kuyers Institute for Christian Teaching and Learning; Associate Professor of German, Calvin College, Grand Rapids, MI, USA

David I. Smith is the Director of the Kuyers Institute for Christian Teaching and Learning (www.pedagogy.net) and Associate Professor of German at Calvin College, Grand Rapids, Michigan, USA. He also serves as coeditor of the *Journal of Education and Christian Belief* and editor of the *Journal of Christian and Foreign Languages.* His recent publications include *The Bible and the task of teaching* (with John Shortt) and *The gift of the stranger: Faith, hospitality and foreign language learning* (with Barbara Carvill).

Abstract

This chapter addresses the gap that often exists between the broad description of a Christian worldview or Christian educational principles and the day-to-day detail of teaching particular curriculum areas in particular classrooms. The assumption that big worldview categories or general Christian principles translate straight-forwardly down into pedagogical work in different curriculum areas is questioned. Different teaching areas have their own cultures to which Christian belief may relate in varied ways. This process is illustrated with examples of how the culture of second and foreign language education can resist or be influenced by Christian approaches to teaching and learning. The images of language education as hospitality to the stranger and of teaching as the provision of a home are explored in relation to the question of how to teach Christianly.

The Christian gospel came to Iceland in the tenth century and immediately led to tensions between those who accepted the new religion and those who resisted it. Stephen Neill (1986) describes the *Althing* (the great gathering of local assemblies) of the year 1004:

> *Different teaching areas have their own cultures to which Christian belief may relate in varied ways.*

The heathen men summoned a great gathering, and there they agreed to sacrifice two men out of each Quarter and call upon the heathen gods that they would not suffer Christendom to spread over the land. But Hialte and Gizor had another meeting of Christian men, and agreed that they too would have human sacrifices as many as the heathen. They spoke thus: "The heathen sacrifice the worst men and cast them over the rocks or cliffs, but we will choose the best of men and call it a gift of victory to our Lord Jesus Christ, and we will bind ourselves to live better and more sinlessly than before, and Gizor and I will offer ourselves as the gift of victory of our Quarter" (pp. 91–92).

I mention this episode because it colourfully captures an element of integrative Christian visions of education which appealed to me as soon as I encountered them. When I began teaching, I had come across a view that went something like this: Christian teachers can best witness to their secular colleagues by showing excellence in their work. Being a Christian teacher simply means being a good Christian and a good teacher—not so much teaching any differently as teaching *well*. "Whatever your hand finds to do, do it with all your might" as Scripture puts it (Eccl 9:10). Doing everything as working for the Lord, we should commend the gospel by associating it with educational excellence. Hialte and Gizor display something of this spirit. If the heathen offer human sacrifices, then we will offer them too—just as many as they offer. If they offer the worst people, then we will outdo them and offer our best people. In doing so we will be offering a gift of victory to Christ.

At the same time, our medieval Icelandic brothers show pointedly why such a call to excellence is insufficient, even dangerous. If we stopped reading halfway through their declaration, we would probably find little to admire—Christians excelling by offering human sacrifices? But they go on to change the terms. The heathen will sacrifice by throwing folk off cliffs; they, in contrast, will sacrifice by binding themselves to live more sinlessly. In order to excel in a Christian way, Hialte and Gizor carry out a daring redefinition of the practice concerned, one enabled by the language of the New Testament. They will offer *living* sacrifices, an image perhaps so familiar to us that we forget its strangeness (cf. Rom. 12:1). Without this redefinition they would have found themselves achieving excellence at the wrong thing, being just as good as the heathen at something that should not be happening at all, or at best should be happening in a radically different way. This thought should inject a healthy sense of unease into our strivings for educational excellence.

The reading over many years of many books and articles on Christian worldview and Christian approaches to education has given me some answers to questions that had perturbed me. It also has saddled me, however, with a bigger and more permanent question. That question has to do with how the great truths of the Christian faith relate to the daily grind, the everyday detail of my work as a teacher. The grand affirmations, sweeping frameworks and fervent visions for faith-filled educational practice have often helped, but they have also often frustrated. Studying work on the nature of a Christian worldview taught me that it was possible to think from out of the heart of faith, but the road from such broad vistas to teaching German to 12-year-olds first thing on a Monday morning somehow still seemed long and dusty.

The big picture and the daily detail

As I began, early in my career, to read whatever I could lay my hands on that dealt with the role of faith in education, I soon encountered writings (especially from the reformed tradition) that insisted that Christian education should *not* simply be regular education done better, but rather education reworked on a Christian basis. This insistence comes out in talk of a Christian worldview, a Christian philosophy of education, a Christian mind, biblical foundations for education or the integration of faith and learning. Behind such language I detect the healthy unease to which

I just referred, the desire not to be caught up in the pursuit of an unexamined excellence. Instead, there is a desire to know whether we are pursuing the right project in the first place, to know what particular kind of excellence will really channel grace, life and peace. It was this unease, with its accompanying desire, that captured my attention as I entered teaching, leaving me permanently delighted and burdened with the question of how I could teach not only well but Christianly.

For anyone who has dwelt at any length on Paul's breathtaking vision in Colossians 1 of all things—things visible or invisible, things in heaven or on earth, all kinds of powers and authorities—reconciled to God through the cross of Christ, this is an inspiring desire. I soon found, however, that it can also be a deeply frustrating one. The big vision was exciting but tantalisingly unspecific. I knew that I needed to become more humble, patient and kind, and that was challenging enough, but what it meant in particular for teaching German to beginners was far, far from obvious. I found myself somewhat in the position of the musicians in a poem by Austrian poet Ernst Jandl (1981) entitled "Das fanatische orchester", or "The fanatical orchestra" (p. 60). In Jandl's poem, the conductor raises his baton, and in response the musicians swing their instruments into the air. He taps his baton on the edge of his music stand and they smash their instruments on the floor. He wipes sweat from his brow and they mime a battle with raging floods of water. And so it goes on. At first glance the musicians' behaviour seems wild, out of control, but it soon becomes clear that they are in fact fanatically trying to obey; every slight gesture from the conductor brings forth actions from the orchestra that correspond to it in some way. The strangeness of the musicians' behaviour comes not from disobedience but rather from desiring to obey without understanding *how* to obey. They cannot discern which of the conductor's motions are significant and in what way. This is where exhortations to teach Christianly left me for a while as a foreign language teacher. I had a healthy desire to obey but no clear idea of exactly what that meant I should *do*. Several factors contributed to the difficulty.

In the first place, I found that recent Christian educational discussion has been rather selective. Discussions of how creation and evolution should be handled in science teaching, or of what to teach about sex were not hard to come by. But I taught foreign languages, and such themes were not part of my task. It was not unusual to find books claiming to give a Christian survey of the whole curriculum but either dealing with foreign language learning in a couple of sentences or passing it over in silence. Today, Christian teaching in different subject areas still receives widely varying levels of stimulation or support for Christian reflection, and this remains a serious issue if the Christian community cares about the growth and fruitfulness of all of its teachers. To make matters worse, the Bible seemed equally uninterested. The only mention I could find in the Bible of any practice characteristic of the foreign language classroom was the pronunciation test in Judges 12. When the Gileadites got the upper hand in their fight against the men of Ephraim and captured the fords of the Jordan, they asked every survivor who passed that way to say "Shibboleth". Those whose faulty pronunciation revealed them as being from Ephraim were promptly slain. This was not exactly a promising basis for a biblical approach to foreign language education. Apart from anything else, it would probably not do much for enrolment.

As I began to read more widely and attend conferences of Christian educators, I soon heard that the answer was to develop a Christian worldview. Yet what I heard and read was often very general in focus—a Christian view of life, the universe and everything. My task was more specific. I was teaching foreign languages to teenagers in a compulsory, mixed-ability secondary school context. What I heard seemed to imply that if we could just get clear on the outlines of a Christian worldview, applications to specific issues would simply follow. What I found was that even when I had done more than the average amount of reading about the nature of a Christian worldview, the connection with teaching German adjective endings to 14-year-olds on a Monday morning still seemed murky to say the least. To avoid misunderstanding I should add at once that I found worldview discussions invaluable, but they still seemed to lack purchase on the daily grind of lesson plans and learning tasks. It seemed as if the most natural impulse of Christians when they set aside time to look Christianly at their work was not to examine concrete pedagogical issues, but rather to write mission statements. I often felt that even though God occupied the moral and conceptual high ground (and this was no mean thing in itself), the devil retained a firm hold on his traditional residence among the details.

> *It seemed as if the most natural impulse of Christians when they set aside time to look Christianly at their work was not to examine concrete pedagogical issues, but rather to write mission statements.*

Subject cultures and curriculum change

Now part of my problem was (and is) still having a lot to learn, but it is also worth considering the parallel between the project of Christian education and other efforts at curricular redefinition and reform. The one I know best is the recent discussion in Britain concerning the place of spiritual development in the school curriculum. In the late 1970s Her Majesty's Inspectorate (1977), the body then overseeing educational standards, tried to counter perceived fragmentation in a discipline-based curriculum by identifying eight areas of experience that should be addressed across the whole curriculum. These included the spiritual area of experience, an inclusion that helped to spark decades of debate. The relationship between religion and spirituality remains a subject of hot discussion to this day; suffice it to say for present purposes that talk of spiritual development in British education means something broader and more ambiguous than what Christians might mean by the term, but that spiritual development as understood by Christians is potentially included (Smith, 1999). In 1988 the idea that teachers should address the spiritual development of learners across the curriculum became a legal requirement, and the heat was turned up in 1992 when schools began to be inspected on this basis (see *Education Reform Act 1988* and Gilliat, 1996). There have since been regular conferences and a large number of publications on the topic.

Nevertheless, there is evidence that the effects in actual school classrooms have been decidedly patchy and gradual. Regarding the eight areas of experience, inspectors found early on that there was a tendency for schools to simply align the areas with the existing disciplinary distinctions, assigning the aesthetic to the art classroom, the spiritual to the religious education teacher and so on (see Department of Education and Science/Welsh Office, 1983). In other words, the common pattern was to pour the new ideas into the existing educational moulds, thereby largely neutralising their impact. Some words of Jesus about new wine and existing wineskins come to mind. A quarter-century later, there had been some progress (Office for Standards in Education, 2000), but still the idea of addressing the spiritual development of learners across the curriculum has been far more readily grasped and applied in some subject areas than in others. There has been a corresponding unevenness in the quantity and quality of published guidance. In some areas of the curriculum virtually no concrete guidance has been made available.

A significant part of the problem has been the existing subcultures of teachers working in different subject areas. Teaching a particular discipline draws a teacher into a particular set of issues, conversations and professional traditions. It accustoms a teacher not only to a particular branch of knowledge but also to a finite range of teaching techniques, student expectations and accepted standards of success. There are certain kinds of discussion that do and do not take place in the related professional journals. In short, the culture of post-elementary education is made up of complex subject or departmental subcultures (see, for example, Siskin, 1991). Education is not a seamless entity, to be converted at a single stroke. Conferences on spiritual development are still largely attended by specialists in religious education, citizenship education or personal and social education. Teachers in areas such as art or English literature have had a relatively easy task relating to talk of the spiritual in learning. In the field of foreign language learning there has been little response (for an overview of published guidance, see Smith, 2002). Learning goals have been predominantly pragmatic since the 1970s, focused on the acquisition of basic communicative skills to enable practical transactions to take place on trips abroad. Moreover, for several decades and until quite recently the dominant way of talking about teaching among foreign language educators has been in terms of teaching method or teaching methodology. A method in modern times tends to mean a procedure that is repeatable without variation in different times and places or by different people, is under careful control and will guarantee particular outcomes if followed correctly. It is not a concept with much room for the spiritual (Smith, 2000a, 2000b). In these ways and others, the existing subculture of foreign language education was not receptive to talk of the spiritual, and the professional publications read by foreign language teachers have left spiritual development undiscussed in spite of its statutory status in the British education system.

It is not hard to see that this kind of dynamic poses challenges to attempts to secure an integrally Christian education by first articulating a Christian worldview and then applying it in a trickle-down manner. Education is not a single vessel into which a Christian worldview can be poured from above. It is often more like a loose network of tribes, each possessing its own subculture which will by turns resonate with and resist the gospel in its own particular ways. Achieving the kind of Christian transformation indicated at the outset of this essay has to involve a lot of detailed dialogue with the natives. In the following pages I want to illustrate this kind of dialogue as I have experienced it in the context of foreign language learning. I will focus on particular examples but will try to suggest some broader implications for the project of Christian education as I go along.

An example: foreign language education as hospitality

I mentioned earlier that I found general descriptions of a reformed Christian worldview helpful, but only up to a point. Worldview books commonly talk in terms of creation, fall, redemption and final consummation (e.g. Walsh &

Middleton, 1984 and Wolters, 1985). The world in all of its dimensions is originally created and enjoyed by a loving God, caught up in the consequences of human disobedience and open to a process of redemption achieved through the death and resurrection of Christ and now proceeding to its final completion. Now these truths surely do have implications for teaching and learning, but notice that they are global truths. They have in view the world as a whole with all of its peoples. Foreign language education, on the other hand, has begun to move away from a view of language as either abstract grammatical structure or generalised communication skills and toward an interest in the interplay of language and culture and the dynamics of cross-cultural encounter. I was therefore particularly interested in how we should approach local differences in language and culture. The immediate issue was not whether language per se was created, but how speakers of one language should approach learning another; not whether people in general are fallen or redeemed, but how to approach differences between particular cultures. Here the broad categories start to become more slippery: How, for instance, shall I accurately discern the traces of sin in another culture when I am in some measure looking through the eyes of my own culture, which is no more pristine than theirs? The big truths of creation, fall, redemption and consummation do provide a larger context for such questions. I felt, however, a need for something more fine-grained.

How, for instance, shall I accurately discern the traces of sin in another culture when I am in some measure looking through the eyes of my own culture, which is no more pristine than theirs?

It was this kind of dissatisfaction that led Barbara Carvill and me to dwell on the biblical theme of hospitality to the alien (Smith & Carvill, 2000). I will summarise briefly the biblical material. There are numerous places in the early books of the Old Testament where the Israelites are reminded that their community arose out of the foundational experience of being aliens in a foreign land among speakers of an unfamiliar tongue. Reflect on this, they are told, and be sure that you remember it when you encounter aliens in your land. The various statements of this reach a climax in Leviticus 19. Verse 18 of this chapter was later included by Jesus in his summary of the law: It says, "Love your neighbour as yourself". That sounds right, we might reply, but who is my neighbour? Leviticus 19 replies a few verses later with a slight reformulation. Verse 34 reads, "Love [the alien] as yourself".

Loving the stranger as oneself appears to be a paradigm case of loving one's neighbour as oneself, a task which stands close to the heart of our human calling. We find the connection again in Luke 10:25–37, where a scribe comes to Jesus and asks him to interpret Leviticus 19:18: Who is my neighbour anyway? In response, Jesus tells the parable of the Good Samaritan, and instead of answering the scribe's question he concludes with a crafty multiple-choice question of his own in which all the most desirable responses have been eliminated in advance. The scribe (like many Christian readers) probably expected the answer to be, "Your neighbour is the person in need, the man lying wounded by the roadside". Jesus excludes this answer by the form of his question: "Which of these three do you think was a neighbour to the man who fell into the hands of robbers?" (v.36). Now we are down to three choices but the priest and the Levite are hardly compelling candidates for the title. The answer is the one who had mercy on him, the Samaritan. Note that of the four initial possibilities, three were Jews, while one was an alien—a Samaritan, ethnically different, mistrusted, avoided. Once again the neighbour turns up in the guise of the stranger, and we are told, "Go and do likewise"—emulate this foreign neighbour who himself loved a stranger, a Jew.

The point is driven home even more sharply in Matthew 25:31–46. Here again the question of what must be done to inherit eternal life looms large (v.46; cf. Luke 10:25). The divine king is seen separating the sheep from the goats, the righteous from the unrighteous. The righteous are told:

I was hungry and you gave me something to eat, I was thirsty and you gave me something to drink, I was a stranger and you invited me in, I needed clothes and you clothed me, I was sick and you looked after me, I was in prison and you came to visit me … [W]hatever you did for one of the least of these brothers of mine, you did for me (Matt 25: 35, 40).

The unrighteous are those who failed to do these things. Again, the kind of welcome given or not given to the stranger is presented as one of the marks of discipleship, one of the signs of responsiveness to God—or the absence thereof.

In a seminal article Barbara Carvill (1991) suggested that foreign language education in the Christian context should be seen as a preparation for exercising hospitality to the stranger and for being a good stranger when visiting overseas. This is intended literally; that is to say, students should be well prepared to receive foreigners who visit or settle in their area and to be sensitive travellers abroad. However, it is not just intended literally. Hospitality to the stranger is also offered as a basic image for the process of learning a foreign language. Learning a foreign language is not simply mastering words and structures, but making a space within oneself for what comes from another culture, and interacting with it in love.

Against this backdrop I began to notice that the reasons commonly given for learning another language were usually couched in terms not of love for the stranger but rather of love for the self. If I learn another language, I will become more employable, or I will earn more money, or I will be able to have better vacations or I will be a more educated person. It also became easier to notice how many of the dialogues practised in many course materials were concerned with getting services while abroad, and how rare it was for communicative functions such as forgiving, encouraging or consoling to be practised. I began to increase the amount of biographical material from the target culture in my courses in place of the consumer-oriented texts that filled the textbook, wanting my students to make space in their lives for Germans or French people who were fully human, who chose, hoped, wept and struggled as well as shopped, went on holiday and booked place tickets (Smith & Dobson, 1999). In these and other ways, all still very incomplete and in progress, the shift to thinking about my teaching through the lens of hospitality to the stranger began to change what I taught. The image connected with existing concerns in my field, in particular the interest in cross-cultural communication, and at the same time it challenged other parts of the subculture, in particular the emphasis on pragmatic goals and the tendency to think of communication skills outside of any ethical context (Johnston, 2003 contains a recent discussion of this point).

Now note something important. Hospitality to the stranger is, I believe, an important theme for educators to reflect on insofar as they deal with other languages and cultures, for it addresses specifically our relationship to those who are outside our cultural grouping. Moreover, it seems to occupy a position of some importance in Scripture: It appears repeatedly in the books of the law, again when Jesus offers and illustrates his summary of the law and once more in Jesus' depiction of the final judgment, surely all theologically significant junctures. Nevertheless, this theme is not given much attention in most of the general descriptions of a Christian worldview that I have read. This suggests to me that broad worldview categories are often more like the edge pieces of a jigsaw than the foundation of a building. Even if they have been correctly identified as edge pieces, they leave a lot of unexplored space and may not yet depict some important parts of the picture. Exploring that space may require us to augment our broader understanding of the Christian worldview. Working our way out from the particular, as well as in from the frame, may lead to new emphases, and these may have something important to say to the whole. The idea that welcome to the stranger is one of God's yardsticks for judging whether what we are doing is Christian has implications not only for the foreign language classroom but also for various other areas of the curriculum and for the educational institution as a whole.

So far so good. But we are still some way from that Monday morning grammar lesson. And here is the point at which many would suspect that the trail runs cold. Teaching literature confronts us with the issues of life; teaching culture can attune us to the fruits or absence of faith; teaching advanced language classes allows us to discuss deep human issues; but surely grammar is grammar. How could there be a Christian approach to adjective endings? This doubt is strengthened by the professional subculture mentioned above, which has seen the act of teaching a language as primarily a question of finding the most efficient method, the one that works regardless of such irrelevant local factors as the teacher's or the learner's spirituality. In recent years this emphasis has been giving way to greater attention to the various local factors that affect learning, particularly in ecological approaches to research in language education (see Kramsch, 2002 and Leather & van Dam, 2003), but method-talk has long been well entrenched in the field and gives way only gradually. Once we are accustomed to thinking of the act of teaching as a "routine of efficiency" (Ong, 1958, pp. 225, 232), the idea that there would be a way of doing it more *Christianly* begins to sound faintly absurd well in advance of any more detailed discussion.

Let me suggest, then, another change of image. Instead of seeing teaching as method or technique, a technology practised upon the learner, let us adopt an image from thirteenth-century France. In his history of the concept of schooling, Hamilton (1989, pp. 39–40) mentions in passing that the boys who studied at the nascent University of Paris were accommodated in hospices. These hospices, in which boys both learnt and lived under a communal rule, were known, among other names, as pedagogies. Here is an image to frame what follows: *A pedagogy is a home*, a holistic environment in which learners undergo both intellectual and spiritual formation according to a common rule. Being raised in a different home may (though not with technological efficiency or predictability) lead to developing a different character.

Pedagogy as a home

Let me give you a quick tour of two homes to illustrate what I mean. To return to the grammatical issue I mentioned in passing, suppose that two high school teachers wish to teach the correct use of adjectives in German. One teacher draws inspiration from Gertrude Moskowitz's manual of teaching techniques, *Caring and sharing in the foreign language classroom*. Two of Moskowitz's activities have been chosen. The first is employed to practise the use of adjectives in personal description. Each student is asked to imagine that he or she is going to give a speech before a group of people, either a public lecture or an after-dinner speech. The person who is to chair the event is a stranger and does not know the speaker. The speaker is therefore called and asked to draft a suitably glowing self-description to be used for the introduction. Students are told that "they don't have to be modest but should point out all of the terrific things about themselves and be honest" (Moskowitz, 1978, p. 82). The prepared introductions are brought to class, and each student is introduced by a partner using the prepared introduction. In another activity, encouraging practice of comparative forms, the teacher brings a recording of various sounds: birds singing, bells ringing, applause, rain on a roof, and so on. Students are asked to relax, listen to the sounds and note their feelings. Afterwards they can discuss their feelings with the whole group—"the birdsong made me feel happier than the bells" (pp. 180–181). For each of these activities, the linguistic forms needed are modelled appropriately by the teacher, but student utterances are not directly corrected.

Our second teacher is working with the *Charis Deutsch* materials, and has again chosen two activities. In the first, students are presented with various adjectives that could be used to describe character: honest, determined, foolish, serious, etc. After familiarisation with the vocabulary, they are asked to draw a circle around words that others have used to describe them, a rectangle around those that they would use to describe themselves and a triangle around any that represent aspirations. The sorted vocabulary is then inserted into a provided framework that enables students to construct a poem about their identity. Finally, they read a brief account of the life of Dietrich Bonhoeffer and read "Wer bin ich?" (Who am I?), a poem written in prison towards the close of World War 2 (Bethge, Bonhoeffer, Feil, & Gremmels, 1998). In the poem Bonhoeffer first reflects on others' praise of his courage and calm in prison and then contrasts this with his own inner sense of distress and weariness. He finally leaves the question of who he really is in God's hands. In a second activity, one that practises comparative forms, students have listened to a recording in which golfer Bernhard Langer discusses his priorities in life, and have completed comprehension activities. They are then given nine boxes arranged in a diamond pattern. Below them are nine words which are to be cut out: *sports, food, money, education, love, television, family, friends, faith*. Students work in pairs, with model sentences provided as cues. One partner places a word on the grid, saying, for example, "Food is the most important". The partner responds with another word, perhaps moving the first: "No, I think love is more important than food". They continue until they have negotiated a shared hierarchy of values.

These two teachers are teaching the same point of grammar and may well be using many of the same words. Yet each is building a different pedagogical home. Moskowitz (1978), the creator of the activities used in the first classroom, states openly that she wishes to bring learners to realise that "we all know what we need and what is right for us. We just have to tune into ourselves to find the answers. We are our own gurus" (p. 188). Her techniques are, I think, often creative and interesting; however, they consistently have learners talking primarily about themselves and their own feelings. No place is given to any challenge from voices from the target culture. Moskowitz's pedagogy consistently excludes any expression of negative qualities or feelings, and self-denial is explicitly rejected as an unacceptable attitude (pp. 2, 25). The two activities described above are aptly titled "Me power" and "I hear happiness". Another humanistic theorist of language teaching, Beverly Galyean (1979), captures the central emphasis well in her dictum that humanistic pedagogy "views all learning as learning about oneself" (p. 122). There is a commitment to emotional sensitivity and self-exploration, but humility or hospitality to the stranger do not appear to be on the agenda.

The textbook used by the second teacher comes from a Christian curriculum project, one concerned with spiritual and moral development across the school curriculum. There are some surface similarities between the activities described and those found in humanistic pedagogy, but there are also significant differences. The Bonhoeffer poem is explicitly suspicious of the public praise that the "Me power" exercise courts, and challenges learners to reflect upon the discrepancy between others' compliments, their own character ideals and the realities of their present inner experience. The comparative exercise is drawn from a longer sequence that asks students to reflect on their commitments (not merely their feelings) and how these affect their priorities in life. The underlying aim is to challenge students to face spiritual issues through encountering them in the lives of members of the target culture and then discussing them with their peers.

> *The underlying aim is to challenge students to face spiritual issues through encountering them in the lives of members of the target culture and then discussing them with their peers.*

It should be noted here that I intend no inflated claims for the formative effects of a single learning activity (though on occasion these should not be underestimated). Rather, I have in mind a classroom in which one or the other of these approaches consistently frames the learning agenda. Each offers a way of teaching the same grammatical forms, and on that level each will probably be successful. However, each also seeks to form students in particular ways that go beyond the linguistic. Any pedagogy, if practised consistently over a period of time, includes an element of spiritual formation.

Notice that I have not tried to meet scepticism as to whether there could be a Christian approach to teaching grammar by embarking upon a theology of grammar. This brings me to another observation concerning Christian education more generally. The faith–learning integration movement has produced fine work along the lines of developing a Christian understanding of the subject matter of the various disciplines. In this regard, see, for example, Marsden (1997). In this context it is perhaps understandable that discussions of whether there can be a Christian approach to language teaching or to maths teaching (substitute the unlikely discipline of your choice) can end up revolving unhelpfully around the question of whether there can be a Christian mathematics or a Christian grammar. What gets neglected in this kind of discussion is the fact that once maths or grammar enter the pedagogical home, they are not just maths or grammar any more. They are caught up in that complex web of human interactions which we call education. Think of an egg getting taken up into a cake; a theology of eggs would only get us so far if what we wanted to know about was the flavour of the cake. It seems entirely conceivable that an impeccably worked-out Christian view of science or history or foreign languages could be taught in a way that is pedagogically uninspiring or even with a pedagogy whose ethos runs counter to the very Christian convictions that have been espoused. A Christian view of each subject is a fine and necessary thing, but it should not be too quickly confused with a Christian approach to *teaching* that subject.

Jerome Bruner (1996) has put the matter this way:

Any choice of pedagogical practice implies a conception of the learner and may, in time, be adopted by him or her as the appropriate way of thinking about the learning process. For a choice of pedagogy inevitably communicates a conception of the learning process and the learner. Pedagogy is never innocent. It is a medium that carries its own message (p. 63).

Bruner's formulation not only reiterates the value-laden nature of pedagogy; it also highlights a central reason why all this is important, namely that a pedagogy may lead learners to see learning in particular ways. I will try to illustrate this point further by describing an episode from my own classroom when I was teaching in a secondary school in England (see also Smith, 1997).

Attending to learners' perceptions of pedagogy

One morning I was teaching French to 14-year-olds. We were practising for the oral examination at the end of the course. This involved rehearsing a range of personal questions such as: Where do you live? How old are you? What do your parents do? One student was having difficulty remembering the word for an obscure parental occupation, which was a common problem. Whatever the topic, there would always be some students who wanted to say things not covered within the vocabulary I wanted them to learn. Somehow there were always awkward students who instead of owning cats and wanting to be fire fighters kept pink-kneed tarantulas and wanted to be freshwater biologists, despite the fact that those words were not in the textbook and would not be on the exam.

On that day I responded in the usual way, a way learnt from colleagues. I suggested that for present purposes the student supply the name of any occupation that came to mind; after all, the external examiner would not really be interested in what this pupil's parent actually did for a living. He or she would just want to hear a correct French phrase in order to evaluate it for complexity, accuracy and pronunciation. My response echoed a broader pattern of advice I had picked up as part of the professional wisdom of my discipline. If, for instance, students were asked to design family trees in the target language, beginning learners with particularly complex families were advised to simplify the facts for the purposes of the exercise, so that they would not overburden themselves with unfamiliar words. Such suggestions had never seemed problematic to me before; wasn't language practice (rather than self-disclosure) the main purpose of what we were doing?

On this particular day I began to feel uncomfortable with my response. I began to wonder whether the ethics of communication did matter even in language practice. Should I as a Christian advise students to simplify and change the facts if truth or accuracy were inconvenient? Wouldn't it be more in tune with my Christian convictions to teach students to wrestle with the language they were learning until they could express themselves with integrity?

When I shared these thoughts with colleagues, things grew more complicated. My fellow teachers did not agree with me; in fact, it would probably be more accurate to say that they thought I was stupid. They had several arguments, two of which seemed important. In the first place, they said, I was confusing artificial practice exercises with real communication. What we did in the classroom, they argued, was just role-play for the purposes of learning; to expect learners to tell the truth was to apply an inappropriate standard. In any case, they went on, I had no right to expect my students to honestly divulge personal information in the classroom if they preferred not to do so. What if they didn't want to tell me what their father did? What if their father was in prison?

All this seemed to make sense, and for a while I thought they were probably right. As I kept thinking about it, however, I became less convinced. The first objection seemed wide of the mark for at least two reasons.

For one thing, we claimed in our schools to be following a communicative approach to language teaching. This meant, among other things, that when students used language in the classroom, their speech was to be as authentic as possible—as far as possible it should be rehearsal for and then practice of real communication, and not just manipulation of language out of context. We made extensive use of information gap activities, activities in which two or more students are each given part of the information needed to solve a problem, so that they really have to communicate with each other in the new language to get the problem solved. Wasn't there, then, something inconsistent about appealing to the artificial character of our role-play activities as soon as an ethical issue was raised? If we were trying to get our students to practise genuine communication, did we really want them to pay no attention to the ethics of their utterances in the classroom? After all, what attitudes toward communicating with real live strangers did we want to foster? Does telling the truth only matter when we are talking to members of our own language group? Furthermore, if we regularly implied to pupils that the content of what they said did not matter, were we not sending clear messages that, in spite of our communicative ideals, we were not really interested in what they had to say?

> *Does telling the truth only matter when we are talking to members of our own language group?*

These worries were strengthened when I began to listen to my students. I began to notice that, however sophisticated our distinctions between communication, rehearsal and role-play, student perceptions were much more down-to-earth: they tended to focus on the content of an utterance rather than on its form. For instance, if I asked 11-year-olds to do a class survey about pets, it was not uncommon for some of them to do it in English and proudly present me with the results. I thought we were rehearsing phrases; they thought they were doing a survey to find out about pet ownership. I found a parallel example in an article by researchers who observed an elementary school teacher trying to teach her learners about how laws get made (Clayden, Desforges, & Mills, 1994). The teacher had created an elaborate simulation in which the learners were marooned on a desert island and had to build a community, eventually engaging in discussion about what rules they would have for their community. Toward the end of the simulation, one of the researchers asked a student what she had been learning. She responded that their teacher had been teaching them what to do if they got stranded on a desert island. As with my pet surveys, the teacher's understanding of what was happening and the learners' perceptions of what was going on were two very different things.

This came to have a direct bearing on my concern about truth-telling. I found with various groups of learners who had been advised to practise flexibility with the facts that, before long, one student or another, especially between the ages of 11 and 13, would come up with the question "It's okay to lie in French, isn't it?" If I told students through the way I taught that the content of personal communications was not particularly important, their simple conclusion was that it was okay to lie in the new language. It was all very well for me to have fine distinctions between role-play and real communication, but what if the students perceived themselves as lying? And isn't attending to the perceptions of learners an essential factor in finding out what our pedagogy actually achieves? In the end, I came to find my colleagues' first objection unsatisfactory.

The other objection I found more persuasive. With the family circumstances of learners seeming to become more complex as the years passed, what right did I as their French teacher have to ask them to talk in front of their peers about what their parents did, where or whether they went on holiday or what their house was like? What if their family's inability to afford a holiday became a ground for ridicule at the hands of materialistically minded fellow learners? I was reminded of an incident a couple of years earlier, when I was training to become a language teacher. I had been given a standard oral test to administer to a class of 11-year-olds. It contained a sequence of personal questions including "Do you have any brothers or sisters?" When I put this question to one of my students, she burst into tears. Thinking that she was just stressed by the test situation, I tried to be encouraging, and found out too late that her brother had been killed in an accident just a few days earlier. That memory made me quite willing to wonder how a concern for truth could be coupled with the need to protect learners from intrusive, painful or embarrassing questions.

I began to experiment. My first idea was, in retrospect, stupid. I tried announcing to students that our course materials would involve classroom talk about personal matters, and that if there was any area about which anyone would rather not be asked, they should let me know so that I could avoid it. This, as I quickly realised, was virtually equivalent to saying to the students, "If any of you have embarrassing family secrets, please tell the teacher after class".

Two other strategies proved more viable. I decided to be much more explicit about what was going on in a given language activity. If, for instance, I asked them to write about their family, I now told them they could choose one of two genres. They could elect to do a piece of creative writing about a fictitious family and make up all the details. Alternatively, they could choose to write about themselves, in which case I asked them to work at finding the vocabulary and expressions they needed to give an accurate, truthful picture. Both kinds of writing would be given credit in the same way; the choice was up to the learners. In this way I tried to remove the ambiguity concerning when we were engaging in personal communication, which required integrity, and when we were playing with language.

In addition, I supplemented the content of my syllabus. I began to teach my students strategies for politely deflecting unwelcome questions, a communicative skill which had not been dealt with in our language course before. In response, some students began using phrases such as "I'm afraid that's none of your business" with gleeful enthusiasm!

This process probably took at least a year. It was an interactive process in which my beliefs and values, my ongoing experience of a particular teaching situation, a set of assumptions and teaching practices characteristic of a particular area of the curriculum, my wider reading and understanding of communicative teaching methods, the advice and objections of colleagues and the responses of my students all contributed. The interaction of these factors led to a series of modifications in the way I approached my teaching, and to an ongoing sense that I needed to rethink what I was doing. My Christian beliefs did not provide me with teaching strategies in advance, but they did stake out an area of concern within which my classroom practice could develop and change. Linguist Alan Maley (1982) once commented that the learner is not a pint pot to be filled, but rather a home brewery kit in which teacher input ferments. Something similar seems to be true about the input of Christian faith into the teaching situation.

The particular and the general

In conclusion, let me draw some threads together. I see a need in Christian educational discussion for more work which engages Christians in detail with the particular subculture, the peculiar pedagogical texture of particular curricular areas. General accounts of a Christian worldview and a Christian view of education remain essential, but if the movement is only from the general to the particular, then implementation will always be patchy, our understanding will be less rich and there will always be the danger that the noble sentiments of our mission statements have little genuine purchase on the daily grind. Reflection from within a particular curriculum area can enrich and extend our grasp of what a Christian worldview might be. This does not only mean that we need a Christian view of each discipline; we need Christian work in more areas that focuses on the *pedagogy* and not just on the *content* of particular subject areas. This requires us to become both sensitive to and critical of the varied pedagogical subcultures that make up education; if broad articulations of our mission are not in touch with an ongoing engagement with such subcultures, they may end up detached from much of what we actually do from day to day. Our yearning for the big picture needs to be balanced by disciplined attentiveness to the particular, to what is really happening in our classrooms.

All of this leaves me glad for the unease which I described at the outset, and for the frustration to which it can lead. I pray that both will prosper among Christian educators. The unease, if we keep it alive, can keep us from settling for a pedagogy that is not being renewed in the light of the gospel; and the frustration, if we let it lead us to engagement, can show us where we still have work to do. Both are part of a process which begins to look remarkably like sanctification, that continuous renewing of our hearts, minds and actions which applies to our lives as teachers, at least as much as it applies to the other areas of our lives. Keeping it at the forefront of our attention as Christian educators could threaten the devil's hold on the detail and turn the daily grind into the daily arena where salvation is worked out with fear and trembling.

Questions for discussion

1. Have you experienced frustrations when trying to relate big-picture discussions of Christian education to the practicalities of teaching? What issues have been left unaddressed by those accounts?

2. In your context, which areas of the curriculum have received most attention in relation to questions about how to teach Christianly? Which areas have been neglected? Does this chapter suggest any fresh ways of approaching the neglected areas?

3. If you teach a particular curriculum area, what is the culture of that curriculum area like? What things are talked about most and least, what are the key terms and concepts in relation to teaching? What aspects of this culture make it hard to make connections with Christian belief?

4. The chapter suggests that we can think of pedagogy as a home. How would you describe (in as much detail as possible) the kind of home that gets constructed in your classroom as you teach? What parts of it leave you dissatisfied?

5. What have you learned about the effects of your teaching by attending closely to what learners are doing and saying? Are there fresh ways in which you could be attentive to the ways in which they are responding to your teaching?

6. The chapter discusses how students in language classrooms are faced with choices concerning when to be truthful. What ethical demands do the teaching and learning processes in your classroom place on students? How do you explicitly help students to navigate those demands?

References

Baker, D., Dobson, S., Gillingham, H., Heywood, K., Smith, D., & Worth, C. (1998). *Charis Deutsch: Einheiten 6–10*. Nottingham, England The Stapleford Centre.

Bethge, E., Bonhoeffer, D., Feil, E., & Gremmels, C. (1998). *Widerstand und Ergebung: Briefe und Aufzeichnungen aus der Haft*. Gütersloh: Chr. Kaiser Verlag.

Bruner, J. (1996). *The culture of education*. Cambridge, MA: Harvard University Press.

Carvill, B. (1991). Foreign language education: A Christian calling. *Christian Educators Journal, 30*(3), 29–30.

Clayden, E., Desforges, & C., Mills, C. (1994). Authentic activity and learning. *British Journal of Educational Studies, 42*, 163–173.

Department of Education and Science/Welsh Office. (1983). *Curriculum 11–16: Towards a statement of entitlement. Curricular reappraisal in action*. London: Her Majesty's Stationery Office.

Education Reform Act 1988. London: Her Majesty's Stationery Office.

Galyean, B. (1979). A confluent approach to curriculum design. *Foreign Language Annals, 12*, 121–128.

Gilliat, P. (1996). Spiritual education and public policy 1944–1994. In R. Best (Ed.), *Education, spirituality, and the whole child* (pp. 161–172). London: Cassell.

Hamilton, D. (1989). *Towards a theory of schooling*. Basingstoke: Falmer Press.

Her Majesty's Inspectorate. (1977). *Curriculum 11–16: Working papers by HM Inspectorate: A contribution to current debate*. London: Her Majesty's Stationery Office.

Jandl, E. (1981). *Die bearbeitung der mütze: Gedichte*. Darmstadt, Germany: Luchterhand.

Johnston, B. (2003). *Values in English language teaching*. Mahwah, NJ: Lawrence Erlbaum.

Kramsch, C. (Ed.). (2002). *Language acquisition and language socialization: Ecological perspectives*. New York: Continuum.

Leather, J., & van Dam, J. (Eds.). (2003). *The ecology of language acquisition*. Dordrecht, Holland: Kluwer.

Marsden, G. M. (1997). *The outrageous idea of Christian scholarship*. New York: Oxford University Press.

Maley, A. (1982). Exquisite corpses, men of glass and Oulipo: Harnessing the irrational to language learning. In P. Early (Ed.), *ELT documents 113—humanistic approaches: An empirical view*. London: The British Council.

Moskowitz, G. (1978). *Caring and sharing in the foreign language class: A sourcebook on humanistic techniques*. Cambridge, MA: Newbury House.

Neill, S. (1986). *A history of Christian missions* (2nd ed.). Harmondsworth, England: Penguin.

Office for Standards in Education. (2000). *The annual report of Her Majesty's Chief Inspector of Schools: Standards and quality in education 1998/99*. London: Her Majesty's Stationery Office.

Ong, W. J. (1958). *Ramus, method, and the decay of dialogue: From the art of discourse to the art of reason.* Cambridge, MA: Harvard University Press.

Siskin, L. S. (1991). Departments as different worlds: Subject subcultures in secondary schools. *Educational Administration Quarterly, 27*(2), 134–160.

Smith, D. (1997). Communication and integrity: Moral development and modern languages. *Language Learning Journal, 15,* 31–38.

Smith, D. (1999). *Making sense of spiritual development.* Nottingham, England: The Stapleford Centre.

Smith, D. (2000a). Faith and method in foreign language pedagogy. *Journal of Christian and Foreign Languages 1*(1), 7–25.

Smith, D. (2000b). Spirituality and teaching methods: Uneasy bedfellows? In R. Best (Ed.), *Educating for spiritual, moral, social and cultural development* (pp. 52–67). London: Cassell.

Smith, D. I. (2002). Spiritual development in the language classroom: Interpreting the national curriculum. *Language Learning Journal, 26,* 36–42.

Smith, D. I., & Carvill, B. (2000). *The gift of the stranger: Faith, hospitality, and foreign language learning.* Grand Rapids, MI: Eerdmans.

Smith, D., & Dobson, S. (1999). Modern languages. In S. Bigger & E. Brown (Eds.), *Spiritual, moral, social and cultural education: Exploring values in the curriculum* (pp. 98–108). London: David Fulton.

Walsh, B. J., & Middleton, J. R. (1984). *The transforming vision: Shaping a Christian worldview.* Downers Grove, IL: InterVarsity Press.

Wolters, A. M. (1985). *Creation regained: Biblical basics for a reformational worldview.* Grand Rapids, MI: Eerdmans.

Chapter 10

Resilience and religious factors in Christian schools:

What do students think?

Jeanette D. Woods

Head of Flinders Christian Community College, Tyabb Campus

Jeanette has taught in Australia and overseas in government, church and Christian schools. Over the years she has taught English, geography, Indonesian, personal development and psychology in secondary schools, home schooled her own children while serving as a missionary in Indonesia, taught literacy to village women, lectured in Old Testament (in Indonesian) in a Bible school in West Papua and created courses in theological English in Central Java. She now heads up an independent Christian college of 800 students on the Mornington Peninsula, Victoria. A graduate of Melbourne University (BA, DipEd), Adelaide Bible Institute and Melbourne College of Divinity (BD), she graduated in 2004 with MEd with the National Institute of Christian Education. She is married to a pastor and has three married children and three grandchildren and likes to read, write and garden in her "spare" time.

Abstract

This article comprises the main impressions and findings from a qualitative research project that focused on the significance of religious factors in the development of resilience in secondary students in a Christian school. Qualitative research was used to explore whether the participants perceived these factors as assisting the growth of their own resilience, and to expand our understanding of how the students defined aspects of these protective factors. The central questions in resilience research concern why some young people appear to thrive in spite of difficulties while others appear to be at risk of negative outcomes in their lives. Religious factors have been identified as one cluster in the demonstrated protective factors in the development of resilience, and the project used surveys and interviews to explore the issues surrounding these factors. The participants generally had a positive perception of how these factors contributed to their resilience, with the most significant contributors being family and friends and their communities at school and in church.

Why do some people bounce back from disaster while others succumb to bitterness and despair?

Introduction to the project

Why do some people bounce back from disaster while others succumb to bitterness and despair? Why do some children from supportive homes struggle in life while other children grow up without much support and turn out to be strong and purposeful? The elusive factor is called *resilience* and how and to what degree it develops in people has become the focus of a growing body of research.

Resilience has been defined as the ability to bounce back or recover and overcome difficult and adverse circumstances and life events (North Central Regional Educational Library, 1994). The pithy and currently popular definition by a contemporary Australian writer is, "The happy knack of being able to bungee jump through the pitfalls of life" (Fuller, 1998, p. 75). Resilience research has involved international studies among youth in a range of social contexts, which have followed cohorts of young people who have been born into families in situations with extremely high risk factors through their developmental stages. The studies consistently showed that about one third of all young people born into these potentially risky families do in fact manage to meet the challenges of their lives positively (North Central Regional Educational Library, 1994).

Research in resilience has emerged from both studies concerning mental health and well-being (Moore and Halle, 1999) and studies on connectedness (Kessler, 2000). This has led to the identification of lists of risk and protective factors, the latter of which are seen to cluster in domains such as community, school, family and individual (Fuller, 1998; Howard and Johnson, 2000). From the long lists of protective factors that have been identified from the study of these domains has emerged a group of religious factors, sometimes referred to as spirituality. One of the first researchers to highlight the link between spirituality and resilience was Massey (1999), who defined spirituality as a "positive sense of life purpose, a sense of one's life meaning, and a sense of hope for one's future" (p. 1), and his study was one of the first to actually quantify the link. There seems to be a connection between spirituality or religion and positive development, although the dynamics underlying the association are not yet well researched. Religion appears to be a deterrent for risk-taking behaviours and is positively associated with decreased psychological distress. Religion supports coping through a sense of meaning, stimulating hope, offering a sense of control, a healthy lifestyle and a sense of divine support (Wagener, Furrow, King, Leffert & Benson, 2002).

Australian researchers, such as Witham (2001) and Fisher (1999, 2000a, 2001), have furthered research in this area, exploring connectedness and student well-being with respect to spirituality. Fisher (2000b) has shown that Australian students give different responses to standard measures compared to American students, often reacting negatively to questions about God. Thus studies which have shown spirituality to be a significant protective factor for American students have not thus far been duplicated in Australia.

In Victoria, 1500 Year 11 students were surveyed in the *Connect* project. They rated religion and spirituality tenth in their list of protective factors, although only 41% felt that religion and spiritual beliefs applied to them (Fuller, McGraw & Goodyear, 1998). Clearly there is room for exploration into the definition of spirituality. One initiative in this area of research is a project on youth spirituality by the Christian Research Association (2002) called *The Spirit of Gen Y*. This project is predicated on well-being research and is exploring spirituality, worldviews, values and commitments. Early impressions from the exploratory interviews have indicated that there are two major ways in which religion is functioning for students: as access to God and as a source of values (Hughes, 2004).

My project sought to use qualitative research to explore whether students in Christian secondary schools who had Christian faith perceived the religious factors in their lives as assisting the growth of their own resilience. The factors to be explored included those in the connectedness cluster, such as spirituality, religiousness as demonstrated in religious activities, influence of friends and families, teachers as role models, mentors and religious teaching, and activities in Christian school and church programs. As an educator in Christian schools for 18 years I wanted to understand how our schools contribute to the growth of resilience in our students, and in particular, how the students perceive the significance of those factors in their lives.

God did not promise an escape from trauma and difficulty, but that he would comfort and strengthen his people in the midst of their struggles.

We know that the Bible teaches that Christians have been given power to respond effectively to challenges and stressful circumstances (2 Tim 1:7). They can draw support from other Christians and the faith community, and can adopt a positive outlook in the face of adversity (2 Cor 4:8–12). Christians have God's promises, made real in the form of his Son, Jesus, who experienced suffering on behalf of humanity (1 Peter 2:24) and whose Spirit is right with them in the pain of their own lives (John 17:16). God did not promise an escape from trauma and difficulty, but that he would comfort and strengthen his people in the midst of their struggles (Matt 28:20). For those young people who are prepared to commit their lives to Jesus and to live for him, whatever the cost, God's promises can mean hope and a new purpose for living their lives for God and others. The Holy Spirit will be the teacher in the process of transformation and give discernment in the growth and change. Yet in spite of these promises of God-given resilience, and encouraging contexts such as families, Christian schools and church youth groups, some Christian young people struggle while others flourish.

The project was run over a year and as a preliminary stage 56 students in Year 9 and 10 in a Christian school completed a survey designed to explore their own perceptions of their levels of coping, their feelings and beliefs and the presence and effectiveness of religious protective factors in their lives. From these responses, 16 participants were chosen for the second stage of the research, which involved a semistructured interview developed from the themes that emerged from the survey.

Stage 1: Survey

An introductory question in the survey elicited some interesting information in answer to the question: "For you to have a good life, how important are the following factors?" The participants were asked to give each statement a rating from 1 to 10, with 1 = not at all important and 10 = extremely important. These were the mean ratings:

Factors for a good life:

1	Having a loving, supportive family	9.0
2	Being in a loving marriage	8.3
3	Opportunities to use my gifts and talents	8.1
4	Feeling safe from danger	7.6
5	Being able to do things that help other people	7.5
6	Being able to do things that make me feel good	7.5
7	Achieving high grades at school	7.0
8	Being approved of by my friends	6.7
9	Having a secure, well-paid job	6.6
10	Finding ways to look after the environment	5.7

Of note is that the two highest means, having a loving and supportive family (factor 1) and being in a loving marriage (factor 2), indicate that this group of 15–16-year-olds holds quite traditional values when asked to consider what would give them a good life. Their families are clearly important to them—in fact, the most important thing—in spite of their need to become independent of them. They also aspire to satisfying marriages, in spite of the low rate of success of marriages in society. These two factors are very relational, and are placed well ahead of personal factors such as opportunities (factor 3) and personal security (factor 4). The need for safety is rated highly, perhaps reflecting the fear of terrorism and global catastrophe that has become a feature of the lives of this group of young people. The responses to this question provided a context for the later responses of the participants, indicating what they perceived to be important for their own well-being and quality of life.

The survey generated two scores for each participant. The first of these, a coping score, was designed to give some indication of the participants' perception of their own level of coping as measured by statements concerning feelings about life in general and school in particular. Scores ranged from 0 to 12 (out of a possible 12), with a mean of 7.32 or 61%.

There were two interesting comparisons for coping scores. When coping scores were collated and averaged for all male participants, then compared with coping scores for all female participants, there was a difference between the genders. Out of a possible score of 12, the mean for males was 8.5, while the mean for females was 6.2, 17% lower. Eighty-four per cent of males scored 6 or more out of 12, while the remainder all scored 5. Only 65% of females scored 6 or more out of 12, with the remaining scores ranging from 0 to 5. A much higher percentage of males in the project felt that their levels of coping were at least satisfactory. Fewer females felt that they were coping, and those who felt they were not ranged downwards to more extreme scores in the very low range. It is worth noting here, however, that cultural values may have influenced the responses. It is probably more acceptable for females to admit weakness, while males are expected to be able to cope, and are therefore less willing to admit weakness.

When coping scores were collated and averaged for all participants according to their place in the family (with eldest meaning first born and including two twins, youngest meaning last born and including two twins and middle meaning all other children) and compared as percentages of the possible score of 12, there were differences between these means. The mean for eldest children's coping scores was 70%; for youngest children, 62%; and for middle children, 47%.

The purpose of the other score, the protective factors score, was to identify factors perceived by the participants as contributing to their resilience, especially those that could be seen as religious factors. Scores ranged from 0 to 18 (out of a possible 21), with a mean of 12.92 or 62%.

These scores were correlated and provided helpful information for the selection of interviewees for the next stage, along with other data on opinions, beliefs, experiences, family situation, friends, church and activities.

One of the most interesting outcomes of the survey was the extra material volunteered by 68% participants when asked if they wished to expand on their spiritual experiences. The following is a sample of the replies, grouped into some categories. (9/10 indicates year level and M/F indicates gender).

Dramatic

Jesus Christ gave me a midnight surprise a while ago. I saw him flashing a torch at the wall outside of my bedroom door. A second later I looked and he disappeared. I looked out the window and saw him walking down the road. (10F)

When I was little I saw an image of Jesus when I had a lot of fear in my life. I'm not sure if that is considered spiritual however. (9F)

Healing

I have had a few spiritual experiences in my life. One of them was I was sick one day at school and one of my teachers prayed for me. I went home and went to bed for an hour. I got up and felt great. As my teacher was praying for me I felt warmth through his hands. (He had his hands on me.) (10M)

I went on a missionary trip to the Philippines and prayed for people and they were healed. (9F)

Prayers answered

There are times when I feel that God is truly present in my life, times when I feel close to him. I find comfort and strength through prayer and his word. Most of the time I enjoy being around my friends although I love my family heaps. I have had suicidal thoughts before but it's not a regular thing. (10F)

Personally when I am going through rough circumstances in life I know prayer helps me and it has in the past. Sometimes the answers are immediate and other times delayed. (10M)

Because when I pray, God comes and helps you. He really does. (9M)

Feelings

When I'm alone, I feel connected sometimes. (9M)

There was a guest speaker at assembly and I felt touched by his words. (9M)

When I worship God—mostly during singing at school or church—I am touched deeply with his love which sometimes really makes me cry, as if I can feel his pain for souls. (9F)

Spiritual gifts

At youth group we were being prayed for so we would get baptised in the Holy Spirit and in turn speak tongues. (10M)

At Hillsong I was baptised in the Holy Spirit and at Youth [group] I got baptised in the Holy Spirit and received the gift of tongues. (9F)

General

It just meant a lot to me when my friends got to know who God really is, and when that started to happen they started to believe heavily in God and started praying and reading the Bible. They also started a journal. (9F)

I have been filled in the spirit and about 2 years ago God really convicted me of the way I was living, and now I'm 100% for Jesus. (9M)

Stage 2: Interviews

The next stage involved using a semistructured interview plan to talk to 16 participants. The information gained from the surveys showed that the statements eliciting the strongest agreement concerned the help received from friends, prayer, devotions, their religious beliefs, guest speakers, reading the Bible, ministers' opinions, teachers as role models and youth groups. Finding students at the right time in a busy school and then trying to record uninterrupted interviews in a quiet place was quite a challenge, but the students were wonderfully candid and articulate and many hours of recorded data were collected and transcribed. The data was then entered into NUD*IST (Qualitative Solutions and Research, 2003), a software program for managing and supporting the analysis of qualitative data. This article can only highlight some of the most important reflections that emerged from this material. The material is directly quoted from the interviews, with the number indicating which of the 16 participants is being quoted.

The majority of the interviewees identified school-related pressures as their main hassles, including the pressure of work and being teased or bullied.

At school, it's like reading and stuff. Like I get behind in every subject and I have to catch up with everything. At home ... nobody can help me at home because both my parents don't know English properly. (4)

I don't know. Probably work at school ... schoolwork, but sometimes getting it finished, and just basically getting it all finished in time. I struggle with that a lot because I have got so many extracurricular activities. (5)

Kids think you are not good enough sometimes and also they like bagging you a lot. Just different things, like if you can't do something and they laugh at you because they can do it. Some sports and some schoolwork. I have had some people say they are better than me when maybe they are, but still it's not a nice thing to hear. (10)

Getting picked on a bit ... Mainly at school, it doesn't happen too often. Mainly words. (12)

In addition, anxieties about the future, friends and relationships were a concern.

One of the main things I think about every day is my future and where I am going to be in my future because I am scared I will end up somewhere where I don't want to be and I am scared that I am going to die and not be successful at something. (3)

I worry a lot about what I am going to do because I am not naturally smart at all, and I am not really good at anything in particular, so I don't have any ambitions or anything. If I do, it's like impossible ones, so ... (8)

Mainly with friends ... the fact that ... because I am like an in-between person ... like I am friendly with both sides and especially when they are fighting, so, yeah ... (2)

There was interesting discussion about the preferred word—religious or spiritual? By far the most interviewees liked spiritual better, understanding it to mean particularly enthusiastic, while religious was associated with being weird or negative and just following the rules. All but one student attributed the origin of their spirituality to their parents.

Although not one participant knew the meaning of the word resilient, after some explanation they were able to contribute the following comments on the connection between their spirituality and their resilience, or response to difficulties and challenges.

I ask God to help me sometimes and ... like I pray and then hopefully I will ... normally I come back with renewed strength and then I just continue to ignore them or help ... there's this other boy that ... so, yeah, I ask God to help me because I can't do it by myself most of the time. (1)

> *The majority of the interviewees identified school-related pressures as their main hassles, including the pressure of work and being teased or bullied.*

Well I just pray to Jesus and say, "Can you help me there? I really need your help and I need the strength to get on" and so eventually he helps me and then I get on with it. (5)

There's a verse in Romans 5 or 8, or something like that, and it says "all things work together for those who love God" and that's one of my favourite verses because if something goes wrong, I know that someone will come along or I will read something and it will boost my ... what's the word, I can't remember what it was ... it will help me to bounce back. (6)

If I feel anxious ... I have got this thing at home on the fridge that says if you're anxious, let it be with God, do not worry, never worry, never get nervous or anything, just always leave it with God. I try to always trust my worries in God ... They used to always tease me about that sort of stuff. You could get down by that, and I tried to bounce back ... resilient ... and I think I got better faith out of it. I think that just helped my faith so much because I could just ... every day when they were bagging you, you put your trust in God with it, and I think that's how I became resilient. (9)

These young people found praying easier than reading the Bible, and some who laid claim to their spirituality helping them did not read the Bible at all. Those who said they did read the Bible were helped in different ways:

I get in touch with God and learning … like when you are reading the Bible you are reading things that God did and it helps you get to understand them more … (1)

It helps me. Some verses in the Bible cheer me up, some of them make you feel more sad … (4)

Most participants claimed that they had received answers to prayer, and several said that they prayed about their hassles and problems. Others prayed when they felt depressed or had decisions to make or for healing.

Does he answer your prayers?

Yes, most of them, in different ways to what I think but they always end up being better. (2)

Do you pray regularly?

I don't know … many times a day. (2)

If you have a problem … you are having one of these relationship problems, do you pray about it?

Yes. I pray about everything. (2)

Yes, prayer is one of the most important things in my life really … I have a diary and I write in that and there's prayers in that just because I feel those … and then praying is really big for me because I know that God is listening all the time, he knows what I am feeling, so … and he's been through worse. (6)

It feels like him listening to me … because Jesus is everywhere and he listens to you, everything that you say, and he's listening to me now and everything. When I pray it feels like he is holding my hand and just telling me, "Yep, that's good" … Praying, that's probably the best thing I can do. (7)

For those of us involved in Christian schooling, some of the observations about the school, teachers and Christian activities at schools are of interest. Teachers were seen as important models, but not the people they would choose to share with in the first instance.

Christian school:

Here you have freedom. You can listen to God and learn more than learning at home, you can even learn in school time, so that helps me. (4)

Definitely my friends … because most of them are all Christians, and I am not afraid to talk about God in a Christian school. (5)

I just feel … if I went to any other school, like a school that wasn't Christian, I don't think I would be like how I am. I don't think I would believe in God or believe in anything. I don't think I would have any belief. I wouldn't be going to church … It has been good, I mean, it's like a privilege to go to this school as well. I love the people here. (7)

Teachers:

They will put in a Christian point of view. Say if we are learning about something that is totally way off track, then they will help bring it into focus … They are happy and they are always willing to help if you need it, which are pretty much the main things that you need. (2)

> *I just feel … if I went to any other school, like a school that wasn't Christian, I don't think I would be like how I am.*

What do teachers do to contribute to your resilience that we were talking about? What do they contribute perhaps that friends don't?

Probably the fact that they are a lot older, they are able to say, well look we have been through stuff too and we have managed to get out and look where we are. (2)

And what makes them a good model?

Their attitude towards the students, I think. They will help you, things like that. They are open to do that and they don't think "I am the teacher, so just be quiet", things like that. (5)

Their spirituality … does that make a difference?

I think so. The methods in which they probably punish students, methods in which they talk, I suppose, the way they teach, things like that, I suppose … Christian teachers might understand it a bit more, understand the struggles. (5)

It's just great. They're not just teachers. They're looking out for you, they're looking out for your life and just you as a person. (16)

Guest speakers and devotions:

The teachers read the Bible it's like "wow" … it's really uplifting. Every morning it's devotions, like "wow". (7)

Some teachers they just read it and then they just finish with a quick prayer and that's it. Some of the other teachers take time and say, "What do you think this is saying? What do you get out of it?" and things like that, and then prayer points, and share what happens. (5)

Yes, sometimes it is really, really good, I really enjoy them and walk away going, "That was good, I really liked that" ... most speakers are comedians up there. They are comedians and they know how to get the audience to laugh and they interact with the audience and all that ... and what they say ... because of the interaction and how funny they are, you get more out of what they say because you actually listen for longer and it is not as boring. (3)

Last week it was one of the students and he was really, really good. His message was about being more on fire for God. He was very inspiring because the way he was talking, he was making it sound really fun and stuff. (6)

The last one actually that spoke was a student at the school, a Year 11 boy, and he was really powerful. Everyone just came out of there ... like "wow". He made me wake up and realise stuff. (8)

There was agreement that being real was important for devotions and assemblies, closely followed by being funny!

When asked who helped them the most with good advice and support, family members were cited about as often as friends, with older sisters rating a special mention. Then came church and youth group leaders, teachers, older students and coaches.

Friends, however, are really important to this age group and most agreed that they needed them to help them through.

I have heaps of really, really good friends there who are helping a lot, and I can just go to them whenever I need to and talk ... As for my friends, they are all Christians that I have got at the moment, so that's really good compared to some non-Christians as friends. (2)

Close friends, basically, more close friends ... everybody says it to me ... one person that I know ... she knows me inside out, literally inside out, we know each other's thoughts, we are that type of best friends. (3)

Probably my friends in youth group. Probably around 4 or 5 (friends). (We) talk about spiritual things ... One of my old best friends, I talk to him about things. (11)

Conclusions

These were the main trends that emerged from the survey and interviews with these students:

- The young people who participated in this research, and particularly the ones who were interviewed, generally had a positive perception of how their religiousness contributes to their resilience. For most of the participants, some or all of the religious factors that were addressed were judged as helpful in the daily battle to cope with the vicissitudes of life.

- Parents, siblings, peers, church and Christian school all seemed to have had roles in contributing to this religiousness. This influence varied, but all were acknowledged as being significant.

- Families were important to these young people, even given the strong perceived influence of peer groups. In particular, families were the source of the family religiousness that is then processed in adolescence before becoming a personal choice. Parents, for most of these Christian young people, were still people with whom they could share personal issues and problems.

- Parents played an important role in effective support to these young people, which was a factor contributing to their ability to cope with the demands of school.

- Friends were seen as the next most important influence, not so much as people with whom to discuss issues of faith, but as peers with shared values. This like-mindedness seemed to create a secure context for mutual support and a sense of connectedness, which are both contributors to resilience.

> *Families were important to these young people, even given the strong perceived influence of peer groups.*

- The participants acknowledged the benefits derived from being educated in a Christian school, and understood that their school experience helped them in their responses to daily challenges. Many of these characteristics, however, were not unique to a Christian school: Good friends, kind and fair teachers, inspirational speakers.

- Being in a Christian school brought them into contact with other young people and families with Christian faith and similar expressions of their religiousness.

This provided social interaction with other like-minded adolescents and was seen as a strengthening factor in the development of resilience.

- Most of those interviewed had experienced some form of bullying or teasing at school, some of them in a previous school. Responses to this problem ranged through dealing with it themselves, talking to supportive family members or speaking with a teacher or level coordinator. Those who said that their spirituality helped their resilience were speaking about their problems in general, and can be assumed to have included the bullying as one of their difficulties.

- Christian teachers were acknowledged as the source of direct and helpful religious teaching and fair discipline. They were chiefly described as role models, but for a small group of the students interviewed they functioned as mentors and friends (particularly when parents or church were not such strong supports for them). Another group had spoken to one teacher in particular about personal problems. The characteristics of those teachers who functioned as mentors were those of any good and relational teacher, not only of Christian teachers.

- Devotions and guest speakers at assemblies in this Christian school were perceived very positively and felt to be helpful in everyday life. The students' perceptions of the best devotions and speakers were generally related to their style of speaking (interesting, interactive and humorous) rather than to the Christian content of their messages or devotions.

- With respect to church involvement, the most significant influence was acknowledged to be from youth group as an activity, and youth group leaders as mentors. Involvement in youth group was another example of valued relationships within the context of those with shared faith and values, and shared activities that enhanced the sense of connectedness or belonging.

- Although all the participants were regular church attenders, there were varied perceptions of the degree to which they were influenced and/or helped by their pastors. Actual church attendance on its own was not seen to build resilience.

- Many of the participants found opportunities to contribute voluntarily as leaders through music and children's groups in community service and other activities. They found these activities helped them to feel useful and connected, which some understood to contribute to their level of resilience. These activities rated more highly than involvement in sporting and interest groups, but the activities were not exclusively religious. The exception was those who led Bible study groups for younger children.

- Personal religiousness was expressed more often as prayer than as Bible reading, and 88% participants believed that their own spirituality or religiousness contributed to their resilience. This was regardless of whether their Coping Score was high or low.

Practical implications for communities

For families

Although many Christian families may feel that their influence over their adolescent children declines as they move through secondary school, they should not underestimate the importance of the passing on the faith to their children before they reach this stage. Deuteronomy 6:7 instructs parents to "Impress [the commandments] on your children. Talk about them when you sit at home and when you walk along the road, when you lie down and when you get up". These young people acknowledged that their parents and families were the main source of their spirituality.

As well as parents, siblings can be very significant members of the support network for a young person. In the research, older sisters emerged as key players in the family dynamics, being seen as empathetic and mature, and with some wisdom that comes of being a little older. Young people would do well to work through the early childhood issues of sibling rivalry and try not only to build mature relationships but also to be available to other siblings to talk through the resilience issues that are particular to their family circumstances.

Furthermore, parents should continue to look for opportunities for ongoing communication with their children. Even though peers become important in adolescence, parents can still be an important part of the network which resilient young people call on when things are difficult. Their intimate understanding of their children combined with the spiritual maturity of being older Christians gives them a significant role in the ongoing development of resilience.

Schools

From the information gathered in this project, it is clear that a Christian school can provide a context for the religious factors that are acknowledged to contribute towards resilience. Principals should not underestimate the importance of employing Christian teachers, whose practice of faith can be a strong example for students. While their students are more likely to look to these teachers as role models than confidants, there are some young people who indicated their desire to develop a closer relationship with their teachers but felt they were too busy.

Teachers are to be encouraged to be sensitive to the needs of those students in particular who may not have other supportive adults in their lives and are looking for mentors in their teachers. Where the budget allows, time given to teachers to intentionalise building relationships with students could enhance resilience for some students. Some schools do this by appointing "Student Support Teachers" in addition to Level Coordinators.

Most Christian schools start the day with some form of devotional activity, but would do well to examine the style and content of these devotions. Given the positive response of most students to this activity, it behoves teachers to give adequate attention to preparation, and not to deliver it on the run. Teachers should also be encouraged to ask questions, use an interactive style and add information or personal experiences as part of their regular devotions, as this approach was perceived as being relevant and useful when compared to just reading the Bible without comment and praying.

Schools should also be encouraged to know that visiting speakers to the school are well appreciated by the students, and their messages can be instrumental in building resilience. It is worth the effort to find lively, biblical speakers, but they need to be warm, friendly, interactive and humorous! It is also recommended that some students be given the opportunity to address their peers on suitable occasions; there appeared to be real inspiration in being encouraged by a fellow student.

Christian schools are sometimes criticised for creating an overprotective hot-house environment that does not prepare students for the so-called real world. Presumably it is then predicted that these young people will not be as resilient as they should be when they make the transition to secular study or employment. In fact, this research should encourage the proponents of Christian education to continue to invest in the resilience-building factors indicated in this project, whether or not they are peculiar to Christian schools.

Churches

Churches looking to build resilience in their young people would do well to invest in their youth group ministry—in particular in training young leaders. Many of the participants in this study attribute part of their ability to weather adversity and to bounce back to the influence and support of their youth group leaders. While church attendance was not felt to contribute directly to their resilience, it is clear that belonging to a church is an important connection to activities and friends that do.

Leaders of churches who understand the influence of these activities, and their youth leaders in particular, will ensure that young people are drawn into these groups and mentored by those older young people who are seen to be still in touch with the youth culture, yet have matured in their faith. These relationships can contribute enormously to the resilience of youth who can so easily become vulnerable at this age.

It would seem also that if encouraging involvement in other activities such as children's clubs and musical teams builds self-esteem and a sense of belonging, church leaders would do well to intentionalise this, rather than merely hope it will happen. Programs to recruit and train youth of secondary school age could be vital in giving them opportunities to do something for other people, and to feel needed. The biblical teaching on serving others in the midst of personal struggles can bring a new perspective to those issues for young people of faith. On the evidence of the material in this project, there is a need to teach that there is more to a person's life than one's own needs and relationship with God—giving to others is at the heart of the gospel message.

Churches looking to build resilience in their young people would do well to invest in their youth group ministry.

As in educational decisions, parents have an important role in encouraging church involvement; this study would suggest that it might be ultimately more important to provide transport to a youth group activity that is less outwardly religious, than to insist on church service attendance, even though that is naturally to be encouraged. The social support which is provided in the community of faith should not be underestimated as a source of strength, healing and encouragement in difficult times. Young people who remain connected to the community of faith through these periods have more opportunity to learn and grow in their own faith, strengthening them for the inevitable storms they will encounter in their lives.

Churches also have an important role in providing a sound teaching program for their young people. The lack of interest in systematic reading of the Bible compared to prayer may not reflect lack of teaching programs but rather a lack of interest in what is actually provided. The preference for more spontaneous prayer over the discipline of studying the Bible could be a symptom of the prevailing culture, which emphasises feeling good and doing what feels easier. There is a challenge for those who have opportunities with young people to engage them in serious Bible study which will expose them to the full teaching of the Scriptures, including the theology of suffering (1 Pet 4:12–19), the character building which comes from endurance (2 Tim 2:1–3), and the strength and resilience which God gives to those who persevere through the hard times, knowing that in their weakness, God makes them strong (2 Cor 12:10).

Qualitative research often raises more questions than it answers, and, in general, the findings of this research do not support the claim of a clear relationship between the presence of religious factors in the life of a secondary student in a Christian school and the degree to which those students feel that they are coping with adversity. What emerged clearly is that the students themselves feel that many of the religious factors addressed in the research do help them deal with their difficulties and that supportive families, friends, schools and churches were valued by the students and all play a part in building resilience. Some issues that need to be explored now are whether religious protective factors are protective because they are religious and the distinctiveness of the connectedness factor for those with Christian faith, the relative significance of each factor and the nature of the relationships between the intersecting communities of which these students are a part—including our Christian schools.

"For God has not given us a spirit of fear, but a spirit of power, love and a sound mind" (2 Tim 1:7). *"We have been given power to respond effectively to stressful circumstances, love to connect with the people of God and to serve others, and a sound mind to adopt healthy habits of thinking about ourselves and the setbacks we all face. These are the gifts of faith as we all face the inevitable earthquakes in our lives"* (Brown, 2001, p. 3).

Questions for discussion

1. How do we define resilience from a Christian worldview?

2. If a student shows signs of not coping at school, how do we counsel him/her?

3. How do teachers make morning devotions interesting, relevant and biblical?

4. What are the characteristics of effective Christian mentors for young people?

5. How can schools and churches address the lack of interest in systematic reading of the Bible by young people?

6. What can be done to strengthen the links between the significant communities in a student's life—the school, the home and the church?

References

Brown, N. (2001). Bouncing back: Resilience in the Christian life. Retrieved March 12, 2002, from http://www.spu.edu/depts/uc/response/spring2kl/bouncing_back.html

Christian Research Association. (2002). *Spirit of Gen Y.* Retrieved April 17, 2003, from http://www.cra.org.au/topics

Fisher, J. W. (1999). Helps to fostering students' spiritual health. *International Journal of Children's Spirituality, 4*(1), 29–49.

Fisher, J. W. (2000a). Being human, becoming whole: Understanding spiritual health and wellbeing. *Journal of Christian Education, 43*(3) 37–52.

Fisher, J. W. (2000b). Assessing students' spiritual wellbeing as a basis for pastoral care. A paper presented at the First International Conference on Children's Spirituality. University College Chichester, UK, July 9–12, 2000.

Fisher, J. W. (2001). The nature of spiritual wellbeing and the curriculum: some educators' views. *Journal of Christian Education, 44*(1), 47–57.

Fuller, A. (1998). *From surviving to thriving: Promoting mental health in young people.* Melbourne: Australian Council for Educational Research.

Fuller, A. McGraw, K. & Goodyear, M. (1998). *The mind of youth: Resilience—connect project.* Retrieved August 17, 2002, from http://www.sofweb.vic.edu/wellbeing/druged/pdfs/MindYouth.pdf

Howard, S. & Johnson, B. (2000). Young adolescents displaying resilient and non-resilient behaviour: Insights from a qualitative study. Can schools make a difference? Retrieved August 17, 2002, from http://www.aare.edu.au/00pap/how00387htm

Hughes, P. (2004). The spirit of Generation Y: Some initial impressions. Pointer 14(2), 1–5.

Kessler, R. (2000). The soul of education. Alexandra, VA: ASCD.

Massey, S. D. (1999). A study of the relationship between resilience and spirituality among high risk youth. Doctoral thesis, University of Minnesota. Retrieved May 25, 2002, from http://www. youthandreligion.org/resources/ref_comparative.html

Moore, K. A. & Halle, T. G. (1999). Preventing problems vs. promoting the positive. Communitarian Network, July 1999. Retrieved March 23, 2002, from http://www.gwu.edu/~ccps/Moore.html

North Central Regional Library. (1994). Resilience research: How can it help city schools? Retrieved March 12, 2002, from http://www.ncrel.org/sdrs/cityschl/city1_1b.htm

Qualitative Solutions and Research (QSR). (2003). NUD*IST V6 Bundoora, VIC.

Wagener, L. M., Furrow, J., King, P. E., Leffert, N. & Benson, P. (2002). Religion and developmental resources. Unpublished dissertation, Fuller Theological Seminary, Fielding Institute and Search Institute, CA.

Witham, T. (2001). Nurturing spirituality in children and young people by developing resilience. Journal of Christian Education, 44(1), 39–45.

Chapter 11

Delighting in God's good gift of sports and competition

Michael Goheen

Geneva Professor of Worldview and Religious Studies,
Trinity Western University

An earlier version of this chapter was delivered as a keynote address at the Christian Society for Kinesiology and Leisure Studies Annual Conference held at Redeemer University College, Ancaster Ontario, 5 June 2003.

Mike Goheen is the Geneva Professor of Worldview and Religious Studies at Trinity Western University in Langley, British Columbia, Canada. Previously he has worked as an academic at Redeemer University College, Calvin Seminary, Dordt College and has pastored several churches. Mike is married to Marnie for 26 years. They have four adult 'children' ranging in age from 19-25. He has authored a number of journal articles, book chapters and books including *As the Father Has Sent Me, I Am Sending You: J.E. Lesslie Newbigin's Missionary Ecclesiology* which was largely a result of his doctoral studies at the University of Utrecht and, more recently he co-authored with Craig Bartholomew *The Drama of Scripture: Finding Our Place in the Biblical Story*. He speaks regularly around the world on worldview, theology, and mission and has on several occasions been a popular speaker at Christian education conferences in Australia.

Abstract

This chapter discusses the relationship between sporting activities and competition. The basic contention is that competition, as an integral part of sport is not essentially evil as some Christians believe, but can be a valid, exciting and appropriate celebration of legitimate human functioning within God's created order. It is a reflection of our image bearing of God and of humanity's creation mandate. It also helps us to learn how to overcome obstacles. Sport is essentially a cooperative activity and should be enjoyed for itself rather than used as an end to achieve other goals such as evangelism. The article acknowledges the severe impact of sin in the idolatrous way some forces in modern culture worship sport and champion competition at any cost. Nevertheless, properly perceived, the paper argues for the legitimacy of appropriate competitive sport for Christians as a satisfying, upbuilding and God-glorifying kingdom activity.

Introduction

My growing up years, especially my time in secondary school, were consumed with sports and athletics. They assumed an idolatrous role in my life. I was not living as a follower of Christ and I served the god of sport. One of my goals in secondary school was to be the best athlete in the school. That goal was accomplished I guess. I enjoyed success in at least five different sports and in my senior year I was chosen as the athlete of the year. But that accomplishment also set into motion something else that would eventually take my life in a different direction. I began to see the vanity of it all. Seeing my picture hanging in the halls of my school, the honour accorded to the athlete of the year, made me realise that in ten years students would probably be mocking my haircut—shoulder length hair in keeping with the times!—in the same way we ridiculed the crewcuts of the 1960s. (This did happen, by the way, when my youngest sister attended the same school ten years later!) The recognition and honour accorded me from athletic success was certainly not something that would last; it was here today, gone tomorrow. As I stood at the threshold of the rest of my life the question 'what now?' began to arise in my mind. Would I pursue wealth, fame, what next? And what if I accomplished my goals again, would the satisfaction of that prove to be as fleeting and short-lived as success in athletics?

> *I was not living as a follower of Christ and I served the god of sport.*

Several years later I was converted to Christ and my life changed. But the gospel which I embraced was a narrow, even world-negating gospel concerned primarily if not exclusively with a new relationship to God. Sports, athletics and competition had little place for the committed follower of Jesus Christ in my understanding. Sacred activities such as prayer, worship, evangelism, and so forth were what really mattered. All other activities were secular—inferior, wasteful, and frivolous at best. I succumbed to what Shirl Hoffman (1994) calls a "degraded view of sport" (p. 139). He quotes an editorial in the evangelical magazine *Christianity Today* as illustrative of this attitude: "Among the various things we can relax with, athletics are low on the scale of demonstrable religious significance" (as cited in Hoffman, 1994, p. 139).

I still remember the joy of discovery when less than ten years later I came to understand a much wider view of the gospel and fuller understanding of the Bible's teaching on creation. The gospel was a gospel *of the kingdom.* That is, God is restoring his rule over the whole creation. It came through the reading of a number of books but it was especially Al Wolters' (1985) *Creation regained.* More specifically with respect to athletics an article entitled 'Sports and Athletics: Playing to the Glory of God' in the book *At work and play* (Frey, Ingram, McWhertor, & Romanowski. 1986) liberated me from my diminished view of sport. Seeing Jesus Christ as Creator and Lord, and understanding the gospel as a gospel of the kingdom opened up a new and liberating understanding. I was able to understand sports, athletics and competition as gifts of God in creation to be richly enjoyed with thanksgiving.

A few years ago I saw a movie entitled *City of Angels.* In this movie Nicholas Cage plays a disembodied angel who falls in love with a woman. He finds out that it is possible for him to fall from heaven and become a human being. He takes the plunge. There is a five or ten minute section in the movie when now as a man with a physical body, he begins to discover many of the delights of creation. He slowly savours the moments taking delight and joy in the simplest pleasures. He tastes the sweetness of fruit for the first time; he lingers as he smells the pleasant aroma of perfume; he pauses to enjoy the sensation of hot water in the shower; he delights in the embrace of a woman. He takes the time to soak in the joy and delight of these new experiences. Sadly he enjoys the gifts of creation but does not acknowledge the Giver. Yet I was rebuked as I realised how easy it was for me to take for granted the many gifts of God's creation or to simply enjoy them with little thought of the Giver.

As Christians our thinking must always begin with the gospel. John 3:16 may be a good starting point: God loved his creation so much he sent his Son to salvage it through his death. God pronounced his creation "very good" in the beginning. He continued to love it even after sin twisted and deformed it. As creatures we have been given a rich and diverse life and each part is to be received as a gift from God's hand. Paul says: "For everything God created is good, and nothing is to be rejected if it is received with thanksgiving" (I Tim 4:4). The contemporary testimony of the Christian Reformed Church entitled *Our world belongs to God* (Christian Reformed Church, 1986) puts it this way: "We serve Christ by thankfully receiving our life as a gift from his hand" (par. 46). God is good, the creation he fashioned is good, and he delights to give us many things to enjoy, and he wants our thankful and loving response.

> *God is good, the creation he fashioned is good, and he delights to give us many things to enjoy, and he wants our thankful and loving response.*

This can be illustrated from my experience as a father. In the last four or five years I have travelled often. One of the favourite and delightful parts of my life is returning home. We all sit together as a family and I tell them about my trip. Part of that experience is to give them gifts I have purchased for them in my travels. As a father I delight to give these gifts to my children. I relish their pleasure in the gift, take pleasure when they joyfully thank me for them, and tell me that they love me. So it is with God! As a father he delights to enrich the lives of his children with manifold good gifts in his creation. He delights for us to discover and enjoy them, to turn to him in thanksgiving and gratitude, and tell him that we love him. I believe this to be an essential dynamic in what it means to be God's child. This is, I think, at the heart of God's creational intent for humanity from the beginning.

I submit that sports and competition must be included as those good gifts that God has given to us. It delighted God to give them; he created the potential in the creation for humanity to discover, develop, and enjoy them. He delights when we receive them as gifts, honour him in our use of them, and thank him for them. The ascetic and dualistic spirituality of my early years as a Christian that diminished sports, while cloaked as zealous commitment, was in fact simply ingratitude for one of God's good gifts. It also denied God the pleasure he has in giving and the delight he experiences when his children find joy in his goodness. The movie *Chariots of Fire* has it right. Eric Liddell said "God made me fast. When I run I feel his pleasure. . . . it's not just fun. To win is to honour him."

Once, after I offered a seminar on worldview, I was approached by a physical education teacher who asked me how what I had just said shaped his subject. I asked him if he was an athlete. He replied that he was. I then asked him "What is it about sports, athletics and competition that delights you?" He was able to quickly and joyfully rattle off a number of things. I suggested to him that as a Christian physical education teacher an important part of his calling was to foster in his students an attitude of delight and thanksgiving that joyfully acknowledges sports, athletics and competition as good gifts of God. I also asked him how sin had corrupted this good gift and how Christians might again embody God's good design over against this corruption. Again he had good answers. I suggested that if he could develop this in his students he would be a good and faithful servant. I want in the rest of this paper to reflect especially on the first issue, that is, sports and competition as good gifts of God.

The foundation of sport in creation

The whole area of sports, athletics and competition is rooted in creation in two ways. First, it is rooted in how God has created us as human beings. Second, it is rooted in the calling he gave us in the beginning to enrich our lives.

Sport and competition find their source in who we are as God's image. God has created us in his image with a diversity of functions and abilities. In my relatively brief exposure to literature on sports and leisure I have seen a number of proposals, both explicit and implicit, about what aspect of our humanity athletics can be grounded in. The two that make most sense to me are the social and imaginative.

God has made us to be social creatures, to develop and enjoy a diversity of relationships that enrich our lives. Out of this soil have grown various ways human beings enjoy one another in social intercourse, including play, leisure, and competitive interaction.

God has also made us to be imaginative creatures. As Bart Giammatti (1989) put it, sport is "part of our artistic and imaginative impulse" (p. 38) or as Arthur Holmes (1981) wrote, part of our "aesthetic potential" (p. 47). We are able to creatively construct imaginary worlds into which we enter for a time. Drama, literature, and poetry are examples. These imaginatively constructed worlds bring us delight, new experiences, and fresh ways of viewing the world. The world of games, sports, and athletics is one way we construct an imaginary world with goals, rules, and obstacles. Entering into this created world for a time can enrich our lives in various ways.

Sports and athletics flow from the kind of creatures God has created us to be.

According to Michael Novak, sport "feed[s] a deep human hunger" (cited in Hoffman, 1994, p. 139). However this is not because it is somehow religious as Novak suggests but because it corresponds to the way God made us.

Sports and athletics also grow out of the calling God gave humanity in the beginning, the so-called creation or cultural mandate (Gen 1:26–28; 2:15). Humanity was given the delightful task of exploring, discovering, and developing the potential God put in the creation in loving communion with himself. God's gift of sports was not given, of course, fully developed on a platter. The garden of Eden was not equipped with squash courts and baseball diamonds! Squash racquets and baseball bats did not grow on the trees. Rather God gave humanity formative power to explore, discover, and develop the potential of the creation in diverse ways. It is out of this foundational task that sports and athletics have arisen as one cultural product.

God's good gift of competition

I think many would be able to agree that sports and athletics are gifts from God. Perhaps fewer would agree further that competition is a good gift from God. In a recent trip to Australia I found that a number of Christian schools had a no competition policy for their playgrounds and athletic programs. Marvin Zuidema (1994) expresses the views of some in the Christian community about competition this way: "Competition is morally wrong because it pits one player or team against another in rivalry which often results in hate" (p. 185). Yet surely Zuidema is correct when he counters that competition is a "basic ingredient" (p. 184) of sports and athletics and that "no one can play responsibly to lose" (p. 185). Indeed the very nature of sports and athletics demands competition as an essential component. To eliminate competition is to destroy the very created nature of sport.

John Byl (1994) places the activity of "successfully overcoming unnecessary obstacles" at the heart of his definition of sports and athletics (p. 157). Various obstacles serve as necessary hindrances for one to enjoy the activity of sport and athletics. "Obstacles provide hindrances which prevent the player from using the most efficient way of accomplishing the goal. The joy in the game is in creating tactics to overcome the obstacles and accomplish the goal" (Frey et. al., 1986, p. 46). Competition is when a team or individuals agree to cooperatively oppose one another given the stated goals, rules, and obstacles of the game. In other words, rivalry is not at the heart of competition. Cooperation is cooperative agreement on the goals and rules of the game, and the cooperative desire to oppose one another (Frey et al.). Competition can enhance the joy and emotional intensity of whole athletic experience. Competition can sharpen one's skills and produce satisfying physical exertion. Competition can refine and improve the quality of the whole aesthetic or social experience. Thus an opponent is not first of all a rival but one who provides the opportunity for a more delightful experience of sport. Competition is an enriching part of God's gift. One loves one's neighbour in sport by providing stiff competition to enhance the athletic experience. I believe many athletes can resonate with Zuidema's (1994) statement that "competition can bring out cooperation, celebration, respect, and even love" (p. 185).

Yet it has to be recognised that competition, like sex, is a very powerful impulse that, because it has been twisted by sin, can easily turn ugly. It is necessary, therefore, to discern what is healthy and normative competition. Perhaps the most important thing that can be said here is that human obstacles are not simply hindrances like a barbell in weightlifting. They are not simply objects to be overcome. Human beings are created in God's image and therefore in the heat of competition must always be treated as such—with love, dignity, respect, and appreciation. Recently, I visited the site of the 2000 Sydney Olympics in Australia. In the observation tower that surveys the whole site they have pictures of athletes with quotes. The majority of quotes showed this violation of the creational intent of competition. "I don't care who I'm playing. I want to win more than they do," said one. "Intimidation is the key. You can have the other beaten before they hit the water" said another. The great football coach Vince Lombardi express this distortion and violation of competition in his well-known words: "Winning isn't everything; it is the only thing" and "To play this game you must have fire in you, and there is nothing that stokes fire like hate."

Sports, athletics and competition as one part of God's good creation

Sports, athletics and competition are good gifts given by God to his children. Yet these gifts must be received in certain ways if they are to remain good gifts. In other words, there are certain conditions of use if they are to be experienced as good. I mention two. The first is that sports and athletics must be seen as one part of the symphony of creation. An orchestra is made up of the differing sounds of many instruments all contributing to a single harmonious symphony. Human life in God's world was originally created that way.

This illustration implies, in the first place, that sports, athletics and competition have their own sound and part to play in the symphony of creation. Sport and competition is one valid (and good) God-given activity in life alongside of other valid (and good) God-given aspects of life (Spykman 1994, p. 53). Athletic activity is a unique part of the creation given by God and therefore has its rightful place in God's world. Unfortunately Christians have not always recognised this. There are attempts to justify sports and athletics because they serve some more noble utilitarian purpose. Hans Rookmaker (1978) used to say, "Art needs no justification." What he meant was that art is a good part of the creation given by God and can simply be enjoyed for its artistic beauty without any other utilitarian purpose. So it is with sports and athletics. It needs no justification. It is a good part of the creation and can bring delight as a gift of God. It does not need to be justified because it brings physical fitness, refreshment for work, psychological release, builds character and self-discipline, is a bridge for evangelism and so on. These all may or may not be valid. (In fact some of the ways sport is used for evangelism, even proselytism are, I believe, invalid. See Frey et al., 1986, p. 55, 56). In any case they are incidental and not needed to justify the existence of sports and athletics. Their existence is justified because God gave them as gifts to enjoy. As Shaughnessy (1977) puts it: "Essentially sport has no purpose at all: it is an end in itself . . . Its possible uses are incidental, like those of the fine arts, religion or friendship" (p. 180). If God gave it as a gift for human enjoyment it has its part to play in the diversity of human life.

> *Athletic activity is a unique part of the creation given by God and therefore has its rightful place in God's world.*

The illustration of symphony further implies that there is an organic connection between athletics and other aspects of God's creation. Creation is harmoniously interrelated. There are physical, emotional, economic, social and aesthetic components (among others) in all sport activity. On the one hand, this means that play suffers when other aspects of creation are weakened. John Byl (1994) says that play "is best realised when personal conflicts have been resolved" (p. 157). For Byl social and psychological harmony is an essential condition for sports. There are many other conditions as well. Can you imagine a competition where the athletes could not count, where they did not have the physical fitness to last longer than five minutes, or where they were incapable of any emotional expression? Could sport develop in a culture where economic conditions required people to spend all their waking hours making a living or where dishonesty was highly prized? On the other hand, other dimensions of our lives suffer when play is weakened. Recently, I spoke to a man with whom I used to play squash. I asked him if he still was playing squash. His response was that work made him too busy for any play. I suggested that the rest of his life would suffer if he didn't make time and his response was that he already recognised that.

The symphony metaphor also highlights a potential danger. When the sound of any one instrument is too strong or too weak the whole harmony suffers. It is possible for the sound of play and leisure to become too weak, where sports are depreciated. I think here, for example, of two dualisms that have degraded sports and athletics—the sacred/secular and body/soul dualisms. The sacred/secular splits God's interwoven and unified creation into two categories, the sacred and the secular. Sports are slotted into the inferior sphere of secular activities that are at best inferior and frivolous. The body/soul dichotomy sees sports and athletics as belonging to the body, the inferior part of man. Hoffman offers an example of this: " . . . games are things of the body, and thus of a lower order than things of the spirit" (cited in Wilson, 1987, p. 5). Both of these dualisms are rooted in pagan idolatry and ultimately corrupt an integral biblical understanding of creation, with sport as one valid God-given aspect of human life.

The other danger in any symphony is when any one instrument becomes too loud and destroys the harmony. When one part of creation is idolised and enlarged beyond its proper place, the harmony of creation is destroyed. This kind of idolatry is clearly seen in sports and athletics in the hedonism of our day. Charles Prebish (1984, p. 318) identifies sport as the fastest growing religion in America far outdistancing whatever is in second place. And when we absolutise sports we forfeit the delight it can bring. George Bernard Shaw is reputed to have said that an eternal life of leisure is like a perpetual holiday, which he wryly notes, is a good working definition of hell! *Our world belongs to God: A contemporary testimony* observes that "pursuing pleasure we lose the gift of joy." As Gordon Dahl (1971) puts it for millions of westerners, "leisure has come to mean little more than an ever more furious orgy of consumption. Whatever energies are left after working are spent in pursuing pleasure with the help of an endless array of goods and services. . . It offers men the choice of either working themselves to death or consuming themselves to death—or both" (p. 187). Pursuing athletics with an idolatrous abandon does not allow us the joy of receiving it as one of God's good gifts. In fact, idolatry brings death.

Conforming to God's created design

Sports, athletics and competition are good, then, when seen as one valid part of God's creational symphony. But secondly they are good when they conform to God's creational design. Sport is a unique creature. It is only when we understand and embody God's good creational design for sport and competition that we can see it is good. The Bible calls this wisdom. God's wisdom is seen in the order and design he established in creation. Human wisdom is when we conform ourselves to that order and design (Wolters, 1985, p. 25–28; Bergant, 1984, p. 3–6). This order is discovered as we experience that order in the fear of the Lord (Isa 28:23–29). In the same way that we seek to understand the creational structure and order of marriage or emotions so that we might increasingly become wise and conform ourselves to God's design for marriage and emotional response, so we need to struggle to understand the creational structure and order of sport and competition so that we might more and more conform to God's original design.

Theoretical reflection can make a contribution to this task: ". . . academic inquiry into what is going on in our play is both legitimate and important. It can be helpful in deepening, enriching and broadening our critical insight into recreational practices. It can help to account for leisure time habits. In so doing, it can also help in correcting and reforming this dimension of life" (Spykman, 1994, p. 54). That is why this kind of discussion is important. In the same way that sociologists might make a contribution to understanding the creational design of marriage or psychologists of emotions, so there is a need for scholars to study this important area of life to deepen the Christian community's understanding of God's original intent for sport.

Of course, a big part of understanding God's creational design for sport and competition will be to understand how sin has corrupted and polluted them. No athletic contest simply embodies the goodness of God's original design. Exploring God's creational design will mean becoming sensitive to those cultural spirits and idols that have perverted sport: a win at all costs mentality, sport driven by idolatrous economic forces, a hedonism that elevates athletics to the highest good, and so on (Frey et al., 1986, p. 51–56).

Delighting in God's good gift of competitive sports

In my own life competitive sports have played an important role. They have enriched my life immeasurably. I took the question I posed to the physical education teacher and asked myself, "What is it about sports, athletics and competition that delights you?" The following is a partial list. Probably the more devoted you have been to competitive sport, the more you will be able to resonate with the following.

There is an unmatched emotional intensity that accompanies competitive athletics. *Wide, Wide World of Sports* used to speak of "the thrill of victory and the agony of defeat." Any athlete or serious spectator understands that well. Zuidema (1994) notes this along with other things: "Athletes know the beauty of intensity of effort, the motivation of pursuit of goals, the feeling and being of fitness, the expressiveness of movement, the creativity of play, the excitement of total involvement, and the joy of sport" (p. 184). There is an emotional intensity way out of proportion with the importance of the event. As Huizinga (1950) puts it sport is "not serious" yet "at the same time absorb[s] the player intensely and utterly" (p. 13). The player is "absorbed in serious pursuit of a non-serious activity" (Frey et al., 1986, p. 43). The intensity of disappointment one feels in the loss of an important game or match is experienced acutely because one is so deeply absorbed, yet it is soon forgotten. So it is with the intensity of joy that comes with victory. And this joy and emotional vibrancy spills over into the rest of life. As Johnston has put it: "Play relativizes our 'over-seriousness' toward life, filling us with a spirit of joy and delight that carries over into all aspects of our existence" (Johnston, 1983, p. 48).

> *...a big part of understanding God's creational design for sport and competition will be to understand how sin has corrupted and polluted them.*

There is an immense physical satisfaction that comes from stretching oneself to the limit and finishing a match exhausted and physically spent. There is a certain joy and contentment that athletes know that comes with demanding physical exertion. I will often flop down after a hard match with the words, "That was good."

A social bonding takes place in competitive sport. I offer two examples. In my own university one person I have grown close to as a friend is John Byl, someone I play squash with more than any other. What is interesting is that there are few other social times where we get together outside the squash court. Yet a bonding has occurred that can be attributed almost exclusively to our games of squash. Another example comes from my recent trip to Australia. One of the teachers in my class was a physical education teacher named Neal Francis who was also a very good squash player, a good couple of notches above me. During that two-week period we played squash three or four times. Those times again brought about a bonding that exceeded any other relationship I had with others in the class. Others in the class were more verbal and intentional in engaging my attention during class. There were also other delightful social occasions with others, such as dinner. But that time of competitive struggle served to form a quick friendship.

Competitive sport brings about an aesthetic enjoyment. There is something that captures you in the creativity and unpredictability of each game. There is also something joyful about that perfect play. I often find myself rehearsing in my imagination that perfect squash shot right along the wall that dies in the corner or the take-down in wrestling perfectly executed and impossible to defend or that perfect throw to second base that catches a base stealer who got a great jump.

Competition sharpens skills in an iron-sharpening-iron effect. And there is an occasional glimpse of beauty experienced in a well-executed play that brings an aesthetic enjoyment that one wants to savour. Or one can dream!

There is finally a religious deepening that can take place as well. We are all created differently. Different parts of God's creation bring joy to different people. My wife, indeed my whole family, can take such delight in the beauty of music. I enjoy music but it does not touch my soul in the same way and bring me delight the way that competitive athletics can both as a participant and spectator. I'm sure my wife simply can't understand that. (When we play competitive board games like Scrabble, she wants to help everyone. She has little incentive to win herself.) Quite simply we are wired differently. I believe these different aspects that naturally bring delight (music for my wife, competition for me, and so on) can and should be opportunities for a religious deepening. What I mean is this: we are created to respond to God in joy, thanksgiving, love, and praise as we receive the whole of our lives as a gift from his hand. Those things that especially bring delight can be occasions that remind us of this fact, and opportunities to return to God the thanksgiving and praise that is due for every part of our lives.

Nothing matters but the kingdom but because of the kingdom everything matters

There is a well-known song that goes like this: "Turn your eyes upon Jesus. Look full in his wonderful face. And the things of earth grow strangely dim in the light of his glory and grace." That song used to characterise my life. If I turned my eyes upon Jesus, sports and athletics would grow strangely dim. They wouldn't matter much any more. I no longer believe that! I like that song and so I have changed the words and this is how my family now sings it: "Turn your eyes upon Jesus. Look full in his wonderful face. And the things of earth *take their rightful place* in the light of his glory and grace." That is because the Jesus we turn our eyes upon is Creator, Redeemer and Lord. With that vision, sports, athletics and competition take their rightful creational place.

Years ago, Gordon Spykman began a convocation address at Redeemer University College with these words: "Nothing matters but the kingdom", and he paused letting its truth sink in, and then continued, "but because of the kingdom everything matters." As a new Christian I had the first part down but I'm afraid I did not understand that the second must necessarily follow. Indeed, on that final day nothing will matter but the kingdom of God. "Only one life 't will soon be past; only what is done for Christ will last" is a little poem that ironically my grandmother wrote on the inside of an autograph book that she gave me to collect autographs of professional athletes. That poem sums it up. Nothing matters but the kingdom. However, since the kingdom narrated in the gospels is God's power in Jesus Christ by the Spirit to restore *all* of creation to again live under his liberating rule, it means that *everything* matters. Sports, athletics and competition matter because Christ created them and is restoring them to again conform to his rule. When we stand before the judgement seat of Christ only gold, silver and precious stones will last through the fire of God's judgement (I Cor. 3:12–15). I used to believe that included only evangelistic or ethical works and the like. Now I believe there will be athletic acts of gold and silver that will last. Spykman (1994), making reference to Revelation 21:24–26, rightly says: "The treasures of the nations will go into the new Jerusalem. Among those treasures, I believe, is good, sound, healthy leisure" (p. 58). I would add good, sound and healthy sports. May we receive the gift of sport with thanksgiving, praise God for his goodness, and conform all of our lives, including athletics, to God's design so that on that final day we hear "Well done good and faithful servant."

Questions for discussion

1. Goheen contends that both sport, and competition that accompanies it, are good gifts from God. How well does he sustain this position from a biblically informed perspective and if it is true, why does the same argument not apply to greed or individualism which are also integral components to much contemporary organised sport?

2. Identify several ways that a physical education teacher could foster in students "an attitude of delight and thanksgiving that joyfully acknowledges sports, athletics and competition as good gifts from God."

3. As Christian educators, discuss either of the following comments:

   i. "to eliminate competition is to destroy the very created nature of "sport".

   ii. "rivalry is not the heart of competition. Cooperation is cooperative agreement on the goals and rules of the game, and the cooperative desire to oppose one another."

4. What are the characteristics of effective Christian mentors for young people?

5. Goheen contends that God-honouring sport cannot exist without appropriately structured competition. Discuss this statement by replacing the word sport with schooling.

References

Bergant, D. (1984). *What are they saying about wisdom literature?* New York: Paulist Press.

Byl, J. (1994). Coming to terms with play, game, sport and athletics. In P. Heintzman, G. Van Andel, & T. Visker (Eds.), *Christianity and leisure: Issues in a pluralistic society* (pp. 155–163). Sioux Center, IA: Dordt College Press.

Christian Reformed Church, Board of Publication. (1987). *Our world belongs to God. A contemporary testimony.* Grand Rapids, MI: CRC Publications.

Dahl, G. (1971). Time and leisure today. *The Christian Century,* 10 February 1971, 187.

Frey, B., Ingram, W., McWhertor, T., & Romanowski. W. (1986). Sports and athletics: Playing to the glory of God. In *At work and play: Biblical insight to daily obedience* (pp. 36–59). Jordan Station, ON: Paideia Press.

Hoffman, S. (1994). Sport, play, and leisure in the Christian experience. In P. Heintzman, G. Van Andel, & T. Visker (Eds.), *Christianity and leisure: Issues in a pluralistic society* (pp. 139–154). Sioux Center, IA: Dordt College Press.

Huizinga, J. (1950). *Homo ludens: A study of the play element in culture.* Boston: Beacon Press.

Prebish, C. (1984). Heavenly Father, divine goalie: Sport and religion. *Antioch Review, 42*(3), 306–318.

Rookmaker, H. (1978.) *Art needs no justification.* Downers Grove, IL: Intervarsity Press.

Spykman, G. (1994). Toward a Christian perspective in the leisure sciences. In P. Heintzman, G. Van Andel, & T. Visker (Eds.), *Christianity and leisure: Issues in a pluralistic society* (pp. 53–60). Sioux Center, IA: Dordt College Press.

Wilson, J. (1987). Dilemmas of the Christian college athlete. *Imprimus, 16*(5), 1–6.

Wolters, A. M. (1985). *Creation regained: Biblical basics for a reformational worldview.* Grand Rapids, MI: Eerdmans.

Zuidema, M. (1994). Athletics from a Christian perspective. In P. Heintzman, G. Van Andel, & T. Visker (Eds.), *Christianity and leisure: Issues in a pluralistic society* (pp. 182–191). Sioux Center, IA: Dordt College Press.

Reflections on psychology

Tim Charles

Senior Management Team,
St Paul's Anglican Grammar School, Victoria

Tim has a Bachelor of Education from Deakin University and is currently studying for a Masters degree with the National Institute for Christian Education. He is an author of two psychology books and he has taught psychology for the International Baccalaureate at both the higher and subsidiary level, as well as Victoria Certificate of Education (VCE) psychology for many years. Tim is married to Jenny and they have three young children. He has taught in a number of grammar schools and is a former principal of a Christian Parent Controlled School. Tim was formerly an Australian Football League boundary umpire and umpires coach.

Abstract

This chapter highlights some of the ideas proposed by significant psychological theorists. It seeks to evaluate the schools of psychological thought and their particular worldview assumptions from a biblical perspective.

As Christian educators, all aspects of our teaching should enunciate a Christian worldview in which Scripture underpins our pedagogical approach. All knowledge is steeped in particular worldview assumptions. This is evident in psychology, particularly as it is a relatively new science with a controversial history. Psychology is growing in popularity and it has made immense contributions to our understanding of behaviour. We need to critique all of its assumptions and evaluate them in light of the truth in God's Word.

Introduction

As Christian educators, every aspect of our teaching should enunciate a worldview shaped by scripture. How often as teachers do we fall into the trap of doing the opposite of what Paul encourages us: "Do not conform ... to the pattern of this world" (Rom 12:2)? If we are serious about Christian education we should begin with the recognition that in Christ "are hidden all the treasures of wisdom and knowledge" (Col 2:3). If we get sidetracked, lazy or haphazard in our task as Christian educators we will begin to teach a curriculum steeped in secular worldview assumptions. In some ways we will do what Dewey proposed for the ideal school: "... the child becomes the sun about which the appliances of education revolve; he is the centre about which they are organised" (cited in Edlin, 1999, p. 45).

> *If we get sidetracked, lazy or haphazard in our task as Christian educators we will begin to teach a curriculum steeped in secular worldview assumptions.*

What then is a worldview and how does it impact on how we think and act? Wolters (1985) claims that a "worldview is the comprehensive framework of one's basic beliefs about things" (p. 2). He adds that we all have worldviews because they are simply part of being an adult human being. He argues that worldviews function as a guide to life and that they are human constructions, not divine revelation. A worldview is the lens, framework or grid through which we look at the world and every aspect of life. It is the foundation of our ideas and values, which in turn are the basis of our conduct. This raises some important questions about how well our children are being prepared to live out their faith in a post-Christian society. Most children growing up in church think they know all the answers, so long as the answer is God, the Bible, or Jesus. But when it comes to dealing with ideas and the world around them, many young people are unsure how to engage the culture, or how to respond with well-thought-out answers to life's pressing issues.

In his book *The scandal of the evangelical mind*, M Noll (1994) has put his finger on the problem. He writes that Christians have difficulty thinking "within a specifically Christian framework across the whole spectrum of modern living, including economics and political science, literary criticism and imaginative writing, historical inquiry and philosophical studies, linguistics and the history of science, social theory and the arts" (p. 7). What he means is that many Christians don't really understand how their faith intersects with most of life beyond their personal relationship with Christ. They know a little bit here and a little piece there, but what is missing is a comprehensive worldview, and the ability to see day-by-day issues from a biblical perspective.

Psychology has exploded across the academic and popular landscape in the last hundred years. Dozens of schools of thought have arisen and thousands of books have been written on the nature of our personalities, development, learning, relationships and inner well-being. The challenge for any Christian studying psychology is to test its assumptions against the full understanding of God's Word. This should be of interest to Christians because of the importance we place on a correct understanding of human nature. The key question to ask is what truths can be clarified from studying psychology?

Psychology often seems disconnected from, if not antithetical to, Christian perspectives on life. How do we relate our Christian beliefs about human beings to what psychology tells us? We are provided with glimpses of this battle when Elijah confronted Baal on Mount Carmel, when Jesus confronted Satan after his 40 days in the desert and when Paul took on the pagan philosophers at Mars Hill (Acts 17). Jesus quoted Scripture to Satan and this frame of reference deflated Satan's attack.

Similarly, Paul was prepared to critique the Athenians' worldview. He did not "become captive through hollow and deceptive philosophies, which depend on human tradition and the basic principles of this world rather than on Christ" (Col 2:8). Paul was faced with this reality when he was deeply troubled by the idols he saw in Athens. He addressed crowds at the Areopagus and confronted the stoics and epicurean philosophers whose own brand of truth stood in contrast to Christ's truth. Paul made a point of studying the stoic and epicurean philosophers. He used their ideas about "an unknown god" (Acts 18: 23) as a starting point in communicating with them. When told about Jesus and his resurrection, the stoics' response was: "He's a dreamer", or "He's pushing some foreign religion" (Acts 17:18). In this context there is a challenge for every Christian teacher to be equipped with the full armour of Christ's Word, as Paul was, to protect the integrity of God's message. To do this effectively Scripture needs to be the authoritative document that "demolishes all arguments and every pretension that sets itself up against the knowledge of God" (2 Cor 10:4–5). In our classrooms we will always face the challenge of uncovering God's truth in the midst of competing ideas in the education marketplace.

History of psychology

Significant debate surrounds the early history of psychology. There are scattered records which trace our earliest attempts to understand the complex ways in which humans think, feel and act. Early civilisations tried to explain human experiences in terms of the supernatural. The supernatural explained things that they couldn't otherwise account for, such as earthquakes, floods and drought. Many early civilisations put their trust in outside forces which they thought controlled their fates. They tried to foster good relations with these forces so that they could survive and prosper.

About five to six centuries before Christ the Greeks began to divorce themselves from superstitious thinking and to debate why humans behave the way they do.

About five to six centuries before Christ the Greeks began to divorce themselves from superstitious thinking and to debate why humans behave the way they do. The knowability of reality, the path to knowledge, and the idea that it was possible to investigate and shape the world were also introduced by the early Greeks. The earliest roots of psychology, however, can be traced to two different approaches to understanding human behaviour: philosophy, which is the study of human understanding of the fundamental truths of the universe, and physiology, which studies how living organisms function.

Ancient Greek philosophers and physiologists argued that one could come to an understanding of something without any supporting observations. Gradually as the two fields of physiology and philosophy diverged they had a significant influence on the way psychology evolved. Hippocrates, the ancient Greek physician and philosopher, left his mark on the overlapping fields of physiology and philosophy. He was particularly interested in uncovering the source of the mind, which he believed was a separate entity that controlled the body. Inherent in this belief was that the body and the mind (often referred to as spirit or soul) were qualitatively different. This concept is termed mind-body dualism. The body is made up of physical matter and the mind is not. Hippocrates proposed that the mind is located in the brain. For Hippocrates the agent of control lies within the body and not in external forces.

Two other philosophers, Plato and Aristotle, also laid out fundamental ideas about knowledge and methods for attaining it. Plato's contribution to science was the assumption that the universe was intelligible to human reason. He believed that there was a unity underlying perceived objects and that knowledge about the fundamental forms (similar to the modern laws of nature) could be attained through reason. Influenced by Heraclitus, Plato was concerned that true knowledge could not be attained through sense data and observation. Although the real world existed independently of the mind, the senses could only yield images or reflections of that real world. His pupil, Aristotle, debated this concept with him. Aristotle believed that the world could be known through objective observation. He himself used observation to learn about the world and for instance was the first to classify dolphins as mammals. He asserted that sense perception proper, free from any mixture of association and interpretation, is infallible. For perception does not arise by our own volition. It is stimulated by something which is independent of that which it stimulates. Using a combination of observation of natural phenomenon and deductive syllogisms, Aristotle believed that knowledge of the universe could be attained. The Western debate about whether the real world can be known through observation was formally initiated. Most of the Greek philosophers relied heavily on subjective thought and intellectual exercises at the expense of observation or experiment. They first developed ideas about how nature should work and then tried to fit nature to their ideas.

During medieval times philosophy was arguably a servant of theology. However, by the 17th century it established itself as an independent branch of study. It was Rene Descartes (1596–1650), arguably the founder of modern philosophy, who further delved into the relationship between mind and body. Like Hippocrates, Descartes embraced dualism. He also reasoned that the body is part of the physical world while the mind and its world of ideas is something different. Descartes was particularly influential in the development of psychology as a science. What he required, however, was a way of resolving these issues. Intuition and logic were seen to lack substance. During this period philosophers generally began from what they termed defensible assumptions and tried to reason their way to a conclusion.

The challenge with this methodology is that it could lead to incorrect conclusions. Descartes himself deduced that mind and body interacted at the pineal gland in the brain, while Aristotle claimed that thinking occurred in the heart.

The term psychology comes from two Greek words: psyche (meaning the soul or spirit) and logos (meaning the study of a subject). Thus, early use of the term often referred to the study of the spirit, soul or mind. It wasn't until the 18th century that the term acquired its literal meaning: "The study of behaviour". Today, psychology signifies the systematic and scientific study of human behaviour.

It was only approximately 130 years ago that psychology began to emerge as a scientific discipline. Compared to other sciences, the field of psychology is relatively new. By the early part of the 19th century physiologists were interested in how the mind receives and organises information from the senses.

Psychology is not a single homogenous discipline. The key schools of thought are behaviourism, psychoanalytic theory, humanism, and cognition, each of which has its respective foci, goals and beliefs. Since Christians need to understand the worldview assumptions and personal biases in each of the key theories to gain an accurate picture of behaviour, each of these will be discussed in more detail.

Behaviourism

The early directions of psychology were dramatically shaped by the behaviourists. The school of behaviourism was founded by American psychologist, John B. Watson. He argued that psychology should disassociate itself from philosophy and align itself with biology, focusing solely on behaviours that could be observed directly. Mental processes were not proper subjects to be studied scientifically because they were private events. He asserted that "if psychology was to be a science, it would have to give up studying consciousness as its subject matter and become instead the science of behaviour" (Weiten, 1995, p. 8).

According to Watson,

Psychology as the behaviourist views it is a purely objective natural science. Its theoretical goal is the prediction and control of behaviour. Introspection forms no essential part of its methods, nor is the scientific value of its data dependent upon the readiness with which they lend themselves to interpretation in terms of consciousness. The behaviourist ... recognizes no dividing line between man and brute (Gross 1996, p. 23).

Watson based his work on the experiments of Russian physiologist Ivan Pavlov, who had studied animals' responses to conditioning. In Pavlov's best known experiment, he rang a bell as he fed some dogs meat powder and every time the dogs heard the bell they knew they would be rewarded with a meal, which caused them to salivate. Pavlov then rang the bell without bringing food, but the dogs still salivated. They had been conditioned to salivate at the sound of a bell. Pavlov argued that the actions of animals can be accounted for in purely behaviourist terms and that humans react to stimuli in the same way. He declared that "the whole complicated behaviour of animals is based on nervous activity" (Noebel, 2000, p. 161). He also took the view that human beings could be controlled so that they only do good. Just prior to his death Pavlov told his associates that "now we can and must go forward … We may use all of the experimental material for the investigation of the human being, striving to perfect the human race of the future" (Noebel, 2000, p. 161). There is certainly no mention of God here in Pavlov's lexicon.

Behaviourism is mostly associated today with the name of B. F. Skinner. From his research Skinner developed the theory of operant conditioning. We behave the way we do because this kind of behaviour has had certain consequences in the past. For example, you are more likely to continue learning to water-ski if your initial experiences are positive rather than negative. Like Watson, however, Skinner denied that the mind or feelings play any part in determining behaviour. Instead, experience of reinforcement determines behaviour.

Although behaviourism originated in the field of psychology, it has had a much wider influence. Its concepts and methods are used extensively in education, and many education courses at universities are based on the same assumptions about humans and behaviourism. Behaviourism must be critiqued in the light of God's wisdom, and the following issues emerge for Christians to ponder.

1. Behaviourism has been termed naturalistic. This means that everything can be explained in terms of natural laws and that our material world is the ultimate reality. Behaviourists argue that human beings have no soul and no mind, only a brain that responds to external stimuli. There is an insidious view that behaviourism perceives humankind as simply a stimulus receptor, a creature capable of responding only in one predetermined way to any given set of circumstances in the environment. A Christian may ask what room behaviourism leaves for the sovereignty of God or free will.

2. Behaviourism teaches that human beings are biological machines and do not consciously act. Instead we are controlled by a learnt response to stimuli from our environment and can never make decisions in which we exercise free will. In fact, Skinner goes so far as to say that the mind and mental processes are metaphors and fictions. Behaviour is simply part of the biology of the organism and our brain is no more than a bundle of nerve fibres that synapse in particular ways in response to the environment. This is contrary to the biblical view that humankind is the very image of God, the image of a creative, planning, loving and thinking God.

3. Behaviourism teaches that we are not responsible for our actions. If we are mere machines, without minds or souls, reacting to stimuli and operating on our environment to attain certain ends, then anything we do is inevitable. This stands in contrast with a Christian worldview. Our past experiences and our environment do affect the way we act, but these factors cannot account for everything we do. The Bible teaches that we are basically covenantal creatures, not biological creatures. God himself is our nearest environment and we respond to him either in obedience to or rebellion against his Word.

4. Behaviourism is highly manipulative. Its key goal is to predict and control behaviour, rather than understand it. From his theories, Skinner developed the idea of shaping. By systematically controlling rewards and punishments, one can train another person to behave in a particular way. One of Skinner's goals is to shape his patients' behaviour so that they will react in more socially acceptable ways. Skinner is quite clear that his theories should be used to guide behaviour. His experimental analysis of behaviour has applications in education, psychotherapy, and the design of cultural practices in general. Of greatest concern, however, is that Skinner wants behaviourism to be the basis for manipulating patients, students, and whole societies. One needs to ask: Who will use the tools? Who will manipulate the technology? Arguably, Skinner would say that only someone trained in behavioural theory and practice would be well qualified to shape the behaviour of other persons. This stands in stark contrast to the biblical view, which commands us to love our neighbours, not to manipulate them. The ethical consequences of behaviourism are great. We end up with humans beings stripped of their responsibility, freedom, and dignity, reduced to purely biological beings, to be shaped by those who are able to use the tools of behaviourism effectively.

Psychoanalytic psychology

The psychoanalytic model of psychology is usually associated with a Viennese physician called Sigmund Freud. Sigmund Freud is known as the father of psychology and many view his developments of psychoanalysis, personality development and counselling as landmark events. He attracted a significant degree of notoriety and controversy with his theories of personality and behaviour. Occasionally Freudian terms are heard in general conversation, such as ego, unconscious, Oedipus complex, phallic symbol, repressed memory, displacement, projection, wish-fulfilment, neurosis, denial, and Freudian slip.

Freud focused his ideas on the belief that behaviour results from a person's inner forces and conflicts. Through studying fears, anxieties and obsessions of his patients and himself, Freud proposed that all people possess an unconscious part of their mind which contains the thoughts, memories and desires that are hidden well beneath the surface of conscious awareness but influence thinking, emotions and behaviour.

Freud believed people could be cured of their problems and mental conflicts by bringing to the surface their so-called repressed memories. Through studying people's dreams, their apparently innocent slips of the tongue, and their articulation of thoughts upon entering consciousness (known as free association), Freud believed it was possible to help individuals face their deep traumas and fears to find ways to help solve those problems. His theory of psychoanalysis attempted to explain personality, motivation and mental disorders by focusing on the unconscious aspects of our behaviour.

One of Freud's heroes was Charles Darwin; he is quoted as saying that before Darwin, man was set apart from the rest of the animal kingdom by virtue of having a soul. "The evolutionary doctrine made man a part of nature, an animal among animals" (Hall, 1954, p. 11). Freud was a materialist who believed that life and death were simply parts of the evolutionary process.

> *Freud believed people could be cured of their problems and mental conflicts by bringing to the surface their so-called repressed memories.*

Freud did not believe that God was the author of life, nor that all humankind is sinful. Rather he offered his own solutions to life and society in contrast to what he saw as superstition. Freud believed every human problem to be a result of repressed sexual desires. The cure for this would be to remove the repression.

Freud's philosophical interests were not those of the professional or academic philosopher. His philosophy was social and humanitarian. It took the form of building a philosophy of life. The Germans have a special word for it. They call it Weltanschauung, which means "world-view". Freud stood for a philosophy of life that is based on science rather than on metaphysics or religion. He felt that a philosophy of life worth having is one based upon a true knowledge of man's nature, knowledge that could only be gained by scientific study and research. Freud's own philosophy of life can be summed up in a phrase: "Knowledge through science" (Hall, 1954, p. 20).

Freudian concepts and terms have so permeated our society that they are generally treated as facts about human nature. For instance, people often refer to the id, ego, and superego as if these entities were self-evident. But these Freudian concepts are just that, concepts only, and are seen by many as a figment of Freud's own imagination. Historically, this is the way many psychological systems are formed. They are an attempt to define and explain the inner workings of all people, but the theorists end up defining and explaining themselves, according to their own subjective interpretation of their world. One needs to be increasingly vigilant to see that understanding humankind from this perspective is flawed. This is evidenced by the ever-increasing number of psychological theories that often contradict each other. Moreover, for the Christian, any such system should be seen as flawed because of the deceitfulness of the heart (Jer 19:9).

Numerous psychoanalytic myths devised by Freud are embedded in our culture, including:

1. Our conscious mind has less influence than the unconscious drives that determine our behaviour.

2. Our dreams and slips of the tongue are keys to understanding our unconscious motives.

3. Unresolved conflicts from childhood determine our current behaviour.

4. Many people are in denial because they have repressed unpleasant memories in their unconscious.

5. If children do not successfully pass through a series of psychosexual stages in their early years of life they will suffer from neurosis later in life.

Carl Jung

Another key figure in the psychoanalytic school of psychology was Carl Jung. From its inception psychotherapy undermined the doctrines of Christianity. While Freud called religion a universal obsessional neurosis, Jung viewed Christianity and all religions to be collective mythologies. He believed that they are not real in essence, but do have a real effect on personality. "Thus in Jung's view religions are indispensable spiritual supports, whereas in Freud's they are illusory crutches" (Szasz, 1978, p. 73).

Jung thought that religion was in fact a meaningful experience to many people and that religions could be useful as myths. His view of psychoanalysis was influenced by this choice to consider all religions as myths. According to Nelson (1957, p. 72), "Jung was the first to understand that psychoanalysis belonged in the sphere of religion". Jung's theories arguably constitute a religion because he viewed God as the collective unconscious, and thereby present in each person's unconscious. He believed that a person could become one with God by finding the god within. During his life he went through what he termed a deification process. He believed he became a god through an initiation in the "Land of the Dead". He delved deeply into the occult, and was involved in astrology, horoscopes, divination methods, necromancy and contact with disembodied spirits.

Jung is very popular among followers of New Age practices. He also had a desire to replace Christianity with his own version of psychoanalysis. This is documented in a letter he wrote to Freud:

> *He believed that a person could become one with God by finding the god within.*

I imagine a far finer and more comprehensive task for [psychoanalysis] than alliance with an ethical fraternity. I think we must give it time to infiltrate into people from many centers, to revivify among intellectuals a feeling for symbol and myth, ever so gently to transform Christ back into the soothsaying god of the vine, which he was, and in this way absorb those ecstatic instinctual forces of Christianity for the one purpose of making the cult and the sacred myth what they once were—a drunken feast of joy where man regained the ethos and holiness of an animal (R. Noll, 1994, p. 188).

Humanistic psychology

Humanism is said to have originated during the Renaissance when there was a revival of interest in the ancient writings of Greek and Roman philosophers. Since Constantine's conversion to Christianity the church had deliberately suppressed alternative views and this extended to the ancient classical writings. However, there were exceptions, with theologians such as St Augustine and Thomas Aquinas using ancient Greek philosophers such as Aristotle to support their Christian teachings and ideas. The attempt by the early humanists to return to a period prior to the triumph of Christianity in Europe may be regarded as the first tentative attempt to find an alternative to the teachings of Christianity. However, many of these early humanists did not abandon Christianity and were concerned with interpreting Christian teachings in what they considered to be a more humanistic light.

By the 19th century humanism had adopted a secular form, supported by the growth of science. Early scientists like Galileo were troubled by apparent conflict between the discoveries of science and Christian teaching. The church, unfortunately, was not sympathetic to this and regularly persecuted scientists such as Galileo. The advent of Darwinism was the catalyst for many humanists to separate theistic religion and science. Today, secular humanism is diametrically opposed to supernatural religion, which is based on the existence of God. Humanism's key objective is the advancement of humanity, and it does so using the methods of rational thinking and analysis to construct an ethical code that is conducive to human welfare.

Humanistic psychology is a value orientation that holds a positive, constructive view of human beings and of their capacity to be self-determining. It grew out of opposition to behaviourist theory and psychoanalytic theory, the two dominant schools of psychological thought during the first half of the 20th century. Neither psychoanalytical theory nor behaviourism fully acknowledged values, intentions and meaning as elements in conscious existence. It was felt that both of these schools of thought were too dehumanising. Psychoanalytic theory was rejected because of its belief that behaviour is dominated by primitive sexual urges. Behaviourism was roundly criticised because of its mechanistic outlook and overt alignment with biological reductionism.

During the latter stages of the 1950s a "third force" in psychology was beginning to form. Abraham Maslow and Clark Moustakas conducted a series of meetings for psychologists who were interested in founding a professional association dedicated to a more humanistic vision of life. The goal of this association was that themes such as self, self-actualisation, health, creativity, intrinsic nature, being, becoming, individuality, and meaning would become the future issues for psychology. In 1961, Brandeis University sponsored this new movement and the American Association for Humanistic Psychology was formally launched. A few years later the first invitational conference was held with a number of key psychologists significant to the new movement in attendance: Gordon Allport, J. F. T. Bugental, Charlotte Buhler, Abraham Maslow, Rollo May, Gardner Murphy, Henry Murray and Carl Rogers. The conferees considered why the two dominant versions of psychology (behaviourism and psychoanalytic theory) did not deal with human beings as uniquely human, or with many of the real problems people face in their lives.

Abraham Maslow, Carl Rogers and Rollo May remained the movement's most respected intellectual leaders for a significant period. Maslow developed his theory of human motivation which asserted that when certain basic needs are provided for, higher motives toward self-actualisation can emerge. Self-actualisation was embraced both as an empirical principle and an ethical idea. The vision and major theme of this new human potential movement believed that human nature was intrinsically good. Client-centred therapy was introduced by Carl Rogers. This type of therapy holds that a person's intrinsic tendencies toward self-actualisation can be expressed in a therapeutic relationship in which the therapist offers personal congruence, unconditional positive regard and accurate empathic understanding.

Throughout the 1970s and 80s humanistic psychology expanded its influence greatly. The three major areas of influence included the following:

1. It offered a new set of values for approaching an understanding of human nature and the human condition.

2. It offered an expanded horizon of methods of inquiry in the study of human behaviour.

3. It also offered a more diverse range of effective methods in the professional practice of psychotherapy.

The main assumptions underlying secular humanist psychology are that a relational, living and personal God does not exist and that humanity is a product of evolution. It emphasises the innate goodness of human beings in contrast to the scriptural view of humans as part of a fallen creation. Humanists are particularly uneasy with the idea of original sin. They have given their own interpretation of man's fall and believe that "the Christian interpretation of the story of man's act of disobedience as his 'fall' has obscured the clear meaning of the story. The Biblical text does not even mention the word 'sin'; man challenges the supreme power of God, and he is able to challenge it because he is potentially God" (Fromm, 1966, p. 7). This flies in the face of the first commandment that God gave Moses not to have other gods that replace our creator (Exod 20:3).

> *Humanists shift the blame for evil onto culture. It is not humankind who is evil. Rather it is societal influences.*

Watters (cited in Noebel, 2000, p. 154) states that "the Christian is brainwashed to believe that he or she is born wicked, should suffer as Christ suffered, and should aspire to a humanly impossible level of perfection nonetheless". He also makes the point that "the Christian must always be in a state of torment, since he or she can never really be certain that God has forgiven him or her". Watters believes that Christians are wound up in confusion and guilt which promotes mental illness. Kurtz (cited in Noebel, 2000, p. 152) adds that humankind is perfectible. Humanists shift the blame for evil onto culture. It is not humankind who is evil. Rather it is societal influences. Humanists argue that way despite the senseless destruction, war and cruelty evident in everyday life, for they cannot fathom that evil is an inherent part of our human nature. God opposes this view in Scripture by affirming that we are born into original sin and that we all "fall short of the glory of God" (Rom 3:23).

Humanism is a self-centred worldview. One of the foundational beliefs of humanism is that people in touch with their inner selves have better mental health: when humans rid themselves of the societal evils then they will progress towards fulfilling their unlimited potential. Marley (cited in Noebel, 2000, p. 154) emphasises this by stating that "to know humanism, first know the self in its relation to other selves. Trust thyself to stand alone; learn of others but lean not upon a single saviour".

Maslow (1968, p. 141) reinforces this:

Since this inner nature is good or neutral rather than bad, it is best to bring it out and encourage it rather than to suppress it. If it is permitted to guide our life, we grow healthy, fruitful, and happy.

This stands as a marked contrast to Jesus surrendering his life in complete obedience to God's will. Humanists argue that we have a basic need to continue to evolve as human beings as we strive to be fully self-actualised. This is only feasible when lower needs, such as physiological, social and safety, have been met. Maslow declared that only a few people in society are self-actualised and he refers to a number of significant leaders as being truly self-actualised (all Americans). The humanist assumes humankind's innate goodness is relative and that self-actualised people's "notions of right and wrong and of good and evil are often not the conventional ones" (Maslow, 1970, p. 140).

Humanists believe self-centredness is the philosophical direction of the future, building mental health and restructuring society. They also claim that we must focus on ourselves to determine what is right. We should not focus on helping others; rather we should simply concentrate on creating a good self. Hardeman (cited in Noebel, 2000, p. 155) affirms this by stating "it looks as if the best way to help other people grow toward self-actualisation is to become a good person yourself". In contrast, God encourages us to find our identity in Christ because we are his new creation (2 Cor 5:17). As Christians we need to embrace the challenge to "love the Lord our God with all our soul and strength" (Deut 6:4) and reject the centrality of self.

Humanism and education

From its inception secular humanist ideology has dominated Western public education, due largely to the influence of Horace Mann and John Dewey. While these men made some significant contributions to education they both deplored Christianity and their legacy has led state education down the road of opposing or excluding God and a Christian worldview. Dewey, one of the most significant educational theorists of the 20th century, embraced the atheistic secular humanistic worldview as part of his educational philosophy. When he was president of the American Humanist Association in 1933 he declared "that there was no God and no place for a belief in anything outside of ourselves in modern thinking" (cited in Edlin, 1999, p. 43). An example of the humanist dogma was promoted in the Humanist magazine in 1982 when it published an essay entitled "A religion for the new age". The article made the following comments:

I am convinced that the battle for humankind's future must be waged in the public school classroom by teachers who correctly perceive their role as the proselytisers of a new faith: a religion of humanity that recognizes and respects the spark of what theologians call divinity in every human being. These teachers must embody the same selfless dedication as the most rabid, fundamentalist preachers for they will be ministers of another sort utilizing a classroom instead of a pulpit, to convey humanist values in whatever subject they teach, regardless of the educational level: pre-school, day care, or large state universities. The classroom must, and will become, an arena of conflict between the old and the new, the rotting corpse of Christianity together with all its adjacent evils and misery and the new faith of humanism resplendent in its promise of a world in which the never realized Christian ideal of love thy neighbour will finally be achieved … It will undoubtedly be a long, arduous, painful struggle, replete with much sorrow and many tears, but humanism will emerge triumphant. It must if the family of humankind is to survive (cited in Edlin, 1999, p. 46).

Education has been strongly shaped by secular humanism, and Christians have remained largely silent. The challenge for Christians is to fight this human-centred, atheistic worldview with the full armour of God, so that our children's lives are modelled on those of mature Christian teachers and transformed by the wisdom of the Bible.

Cognitive perspective

In the 1870s during the emergence of psychology as a discipline, the cognitive perspective was recognised, with psychology seen as the study of consciousness. During the first half of the 20th century, the dominant theoretical approach in psychology was behaviourism which saw learning as a process of forming connections between stimuli and responses. This had limitations due to its sole focus on observable behaviour and not the underlying phenomena such as understanding, reasoning and thinking.

In the late 1950s the cognitive perspective reemerged into the mainstream of experimental psychology, largely because behaviourism is unable to adequately explain complex mental processes. More recently scientific research has made substantial progress in understanding the architecture and neural processes of the brain and mental life. Significant advances in technology and radiological imaging techniques have enabled cognitive scientists and psychologists to map the brain, understand thinking, problem solving, memory, attention, learning, language, different states of consciousness and a host of other information processing tasks. The more we understand about the nervous system and brain the more we need to marvel at God's incredible handiwork. Progress made on psychological, technological, biochemical, and philosophical fronts has also brought researchers closer to understanding the mind/brain/soul link than at any other time in human history.

> *Any attempt at understanding the deeper workings of our brain and mind must give due credit to God's creative majesty.*

Cognitive science has changed the way we conceptualise our mental life. Cognitive science helps us to gain a clearer vision of how God's creativity is displayed in some of his greatest gifts to us: our mental life and our ability to know him in a loving relationship. It would be improper for Christians to maintain a fragmented approach to studying these gifts. Consciousness is a topic that combines the simple essence of our own self-awareness with the complexity of the neural system that underlies it. As Christians, I believe that our task is to critique the recent discoveries made in cognitive science. However, we must be careful not to adopt definitions that might lead to a consciousness that ignores God. God created us in his own image (Gen 1:27) and we are the apex of his creation. Any attempt at understanding the deeper workings of our brain and mind must give due credit to God's creative majesty. Consciousness is not just about survival and reproduction, but is the vehicle through which we enter into relationships with our environment, each other, and, most importantly, our Creator.

Cognitive approach, constructivism and learning

The emergence of the cognitive revolution has had a significant and positive impact in education, particularly in its contribution to the learning process. Cognitive theories are concerned with the things that happen inside our brain as we learn. They take the view that we actively process information and learning takes place through our efforts as we organise, store and then find relationships between ideas, linking new to old knowledge. God has equipped us with our brain which facilitates these cognitive functions.

Watching my young children grow from infancy through their preschool years, I have often marvelled at the amount of learning they have acquired that has enabled them to understand the world. Those early years provided the basis for language, physical mobility, social understanding, and spiritual and emotional development. All of this knowledge is acquired before they have set foot in school. Through the help of my wife and me, our children have taught themselves by continually processing information and experiencing the world around them. This is an example of constructivism. Constructivism is a theory of how the learner constructs knowledge from experience. In many ways constructivism emphasises the importance of the knowledge, beliefs and skills we bring to learning. It recognises the construction of new understanding as a combination of prior learning, new information, and readiness to learn. All of our lives we all make choices about what new concepts or ideas to accept and how to fit them into our established understanding of the world.

In its radical form constructivism denies the existence of truth and thus is antithetical to Christianity. However, in its more restrained form called empirical constructivism, the theory offers us insights that align with biblical perspectives and are worthy of consideration.

Putting this into a school context enables us to understand that learning is not just about memorising facts but is an active process of integrating new experiences and information with existing concepts. Rather than simply absorbing ideas communicated to them by teachers, students take those ideas and assimilate them with their preexisting ideas and experience to modify their knowledge and understanding in a more complex, complete and refined way. Jesus' use of parables is a wonderful demonstration of this active approach to learning. Teaching, therefore, is a process which supports this construction and reconstruction of new knowledge rather than simply the communication of knowledge. Students are not sponges who absorb endless amounts of information but are active information processors. God designed our brain and mind to think about the construction and reconstruction of new knowledge.

The psychological theory of constructivism evolved out of the work of Lev Vygotsky and Jean Piaget. This theory has led to considerable debate between those who place greater emphasis on cognitive structuring processes as opposed to those who emphasise the social effects of learning.

Piaget suggests that humans cannot be given information which they will automatically understand and use. Rather, they must construct their own knowledge and they need to build their knowledge through experience. These experiences allow them to create mental images in their brain. The teacher should facilitate learning opportunities in the classroom which are full of interesting things to encourage students to construct their own knowledge through their own experiences and to have the ability to explore their world. There should be less emphasis on direct instruction and more emphasis on teaching specific skills and learning in a meaningful context.

Lev Vygotsky also made an immense contribution to social constructivism which is similar in many respects to Piaget's understanding of how children learn. In contrast, Vygotsky placed a greater emphasis on the social context of learning. Vygotsky felt that the students need to be guided by adults, but he also thought that it was very important for the students to be influenced by their peers as well as discover things on their own. Unlike cognitive constructivism, teachers in social constructivism do not just stand by and watch children explore and discover. The teacher may guide students as they approach problems, may encourage them to work in groups to think about issues and questions, and support them with encouragement.

The theories of Piaget and Vygotsky provide useful insight, but once again they must be critiqued against a biblically authentic worldview. While we can recognise the high value that they give to people, and the structure that they recognise in the maturational and learning processes, we should submit these processes to a Christian critique. This includes:

- recognition of the fallen nature of humankind

- the need for community that Piaget seems to deny

- the differentiation between truth discovery and truth creation

- a view of leadership from the Bible that is both much more structured and creative than modern cognitive theories allow

- the stewardly worship and service context of all learning as we indwell the great drama of God's creative and redemptive work in a world that he made and sustains moment by moment by his word of power.

Conclusion

This is only a brief overview of some of the "schools of thought" most dominant in psychology over its brief history and there is much here to ponder for Christians. It is important to continue to acknowledge that "Christ is Lord of all creation" and we need to discern and critique the secular worldview most dominant in academic literature today. As Christians we have a great story to tell; the challenge going forward is to construct this into a meaningful context that enables our children to approach Christ as a living reality who yearns to live inside our hearts and minds. In doing so we can draw out the positives and highlight the specific truths evident in the psychological worldview assumptions that I have alluded to. This aside, truth is ultimately found in the incarnate Christ.

Questions for discussion

1. How do you integrate a Christian worldview into your classroom teaching?

2. Are your students able to discern the difference between a Christian worldview and a secular worldview?

3. Why should teachers enunciate a Christian worldview in their teaching?

4. How do you teach your subject area in light of secular worldview assumptions?

5. What are the challenges for Christian teachers as they communicate God's truth in the classroom with so many other competing philosophies and ways of knowing?

6. Are there truths that might be derived from psychology? Discuss.

7. Reflect on the style of your teaching and discuss some examples where the constructivist approach to learning in your classroom is most evident.

References

Edlin, R. J. (1999) *The cause of Christian education* (3rd ed.). Sydney: National Institute for Christian Education.

Fromm, E. (1966). *You shall be as gods*. New York: Holt Rinehart & Winston.

Gross, R. (1996). *Psychology: The science of mind and behaviour* (3rd ed.). London: Hodder & Stoughton.

Hall, C. S. (1954). *A primer of Freudian psychology*. New York: The World Publishing.

Maslow, A. (1968). *Toward a psychology of being*. Van Nostrand Reinhold, New York.

Maslow, A. (1970). *Motivation and personality* (2nd ed.). New York: Harper & Row.

Nelson, B. (1957). *Freud and the Twentieth Century*. New York: Meridian (see p 7).

Noebel, D. A. (2000). *The battle for truth: Defending the Christian worldview in the marketplace of ideas*. City, OR: Harvest House.

Noll, M. A. (1994). *The scandal of the evangelical mind*. Grand Rapids, MI: Inter Varsity Press.

Noll, R. (1994). *The Jung cult*. State: Princeton University Press.

Szasz, T. (1978). *The myth of psychotherapy*. Garden City, State: Doubleday/Anchor Press.

Weiten, W. (1989). *Psychology: Themes and variations* (3rd ed.). City; State: Brooks/Cole Publishing.

Wolters, A. (1985). *Creation regained: Biblical basics for a reformational worldview*. Leicester, England: Inter-Varsity Press.

Chapter 13

The place of science in Christian Schools

Mitch O'Toole

School of Education, University of Newcastle

Dr John Mitchell O'Toole PhD Med(Hons) BSc(Ed) currently convenes the three secondary science education programs within the School of Education at the University of Newcastle, Australia and chairs the Academic Board of the Christian College of Higher Education. He coordinated science and personal development health and physical education (PDHPE) at the John Wycliffe Christian School between 1997 and 2000 and previously worked at a number of schools and universities. Mitch and his family spent a number of years teaching at Chinese universities in the 1980s. He is the author of a large number of books and articles for secondary school and university contexts. Mitch has an enduring interest in the history and nature of science, informed by his personal faith and sustained study of Scripture.

Abstract

Contemporary controversies can make science a problematic part of Christian schooling. This chapter explores the nature of science and the implications of that nature for Christian teachers. The discussion revolves around evolution/creation debates to make a more general case for a reformed critical realist approach to science teaching that helps pupils test the ideas they bring to class against syllabus, Scripture and alternative views.

Science is the study of the physical world, of the things that can be seen, touched, tasted, heard and smelt, and of the more subtle things of which they, in turn, are made. For those of us who share a common faith in the saving grace of God expressed through the sacrifice of Jesus, science is an attempt to understand the things he has made. Given that, the place of science in Christian schools seems fairly obvious. However, things are rarely as simple as they seem! Science is also a communal way of knowing and the community of science does not correspond to the community of faith, although there is more overlap than is often realised. The relationship between the two communities has been torrid, and members of each sometimes look on the other with considerable suspicion.

> *Science can be an uncomfortable topic in many Christian schools.*

The precise way in which mutual suspicion operates in education depends on the jurisdiction within which the interplay between home, school, church, university and legislature takes place. An entire number of The Christian Teachers Journal (Mitchell, 2005) was devoted to the way that the issue of science and Christian schooling works out in Australia. This chapter is an expanded version of one of the contributions to that illuminative special edition (O'Toole, 2005). Both the earlier paper and this chapter are firmly grounded in the situation prevailing in New South Wales (NSW) in 2005.

Taking sides

Science can be an uncomfortable topic in many Christian schools. The founding documents of some of the Australian schools established in the last third of the 20th century only mention science as part of a secular worldview that the school explicitly exists to challenge. This suspicion survives in the approach of some Christian academics (Goheen, 2004), in the attitudes of some parents who currently trust the schools with their children and among some members of school staff and executive. Suspicion is understandable in light of the use some people make of science in their attacks on faith. Some materialists undoubtedly use a simplistic account of "science" to argue that religious belief is irrational nonsense. Their view of religion is usually equally simplistic. Those of us for whom Christ's saving work is crucially important find such attacks irritating and distressing. Some of us consequently shift science into the enemy's camp and others subside into silence for fear of looking foolish. Neither response prepares the children in our schools to give a clear account of their faith in a world shaped by the technology that science has made possible.

Suspicion is heightened when developments in other jurisdictions raise the local temperature of historic points of tension between secular science and religious belief. The very existence of schools such as those to which we send our children, within which we work and which enjoy our support, is sometimes seen as detrimental to the common good. The suspicion with which secular science is treated within such schools is often seen as part of a constellation of commitments that are inimical to the maintenance of harmony in a culturally and religiously diverse society. For example, Paterson notes that US textbooks written specifically for Christian schools connect "Darwinism (and evolution generally), religious liberalism, communism and socialism, and political liberalism" (2003, p. 20). She sees Christian schooling as a reaction to perceptions of American public schools as promulgating godless evolution, denigrating religion, encouraging secular humanism and exposing children to occult content (p. 10) and suggests that they contribute to "a lack of civility and increased, ideologically driven stridency" (p. 1) in American public life. Similar concerns are sometimes expressed (though rarely so forcefully) in our own jurisdictions. Their impact on attitudes within our sector is understandable. Science is seen as part of a constellation of positions that are the focus of conflict and it can be hard to see clearly through the sweat in the heat of battle!

There is more disquiet within our schools about the life sciences than the physical sciences and most disquiet in the area of biological evolution. Viewed from within our jurisdiction, Paterson's concerns may seem exaggerated, if not offensive, but her assessment of the place of evolution at the heart of staff and parental concern seems accurate. It has become a *shibboleth*, a touchstone, a way of determining group membership and spiritual loyalty (Judg 12:5–6). The conflict between Gilead and Ephraim at the fords of the Jordan that day did not concern a nicety of pronunciation—"Sibboleth" or "Shibboleth". We are not reading about the first of the language wars. The issue was group membership. Evolution functions a bit like that today.

I have taught with people for whom acceptance of Darwinism was a mark of rationality: "It's not worth talking with someone who doesn't recognise the fact of evolution". I have taught with others for whom anything other than total repudiation of evolutionary biology and acceptance of the recent creation of the universe in six twenty-four-hour days was a mark of apostasy: "Anything other than what seems to me to be the plain meaning of what I read at the beginning of the Bible undermines the authority of everything that follows".

What matters?

The details of evolution may be as important (or unimportant) as the pronunciation of 'shibboleth': "Is evolution true? *It's hard to say and it doesn't really matter*" (Birkett, 2001, p. 128, her emphasis). She is probably accurate in noting (on p. 141) that what most people believe about the current state of most scientific theories has very little impact on their daily lives. However, as she acknowledges elsewhere in her helpful little book, this issue strikes a chord (or dischord!) because it touches our view of who we are and how we came to be.

Further, some of us are responsible for teaching these theories as part of state mandated science courses. For us, the details matter because we try to do the best we can for the children and families we serve in a situation more characterised by heat than by light. Those children will go on to encounter wide-ranging opinions on the origins and development of life. They need to be able to give an account of the hope that is within them (1 Pet 3:15) within the context of that wide range of views. Science teachers who share that apologetic imperative have the particular responsibility of helping their pupils to understand the strength and limitations of the mental models that have allowed science to shape the world within which we all live.

The arguments about evolution are simply the sharp end of a continuing debate between science and religion (Editor, 2000; Singham 2000a) but that very sharpness is what makes them important when Christians teach science. The debate matters to us because science is so often used as ammunition against faith and our students need to be able to sort the substance from the silliness. This paper will lay down the outlines of an approach based on a recognition of the strength and limitations of science and of the necessity for a considered position on the part of students coming out of Christian secondary schools. Any references provided need to be read critically. They appear to point to other sources, and the use of a reference should not be taken to imply endorsement of all it contains or all that its authors may have written in other contexts.

It's hot in the kitchen!

The interaction between science and religion (most sharply focused in discussions of evolution) continues to attract widespread interest. In 1996–97 there was a well-known controversy about Noah's ark, during which geologist Ian Plimer went so far as to mortgage his home to cover the legal costs of his unsuccessful Australian court challenge to the legality of fund raising to support expeditions to locate the ark (Plimer, 2000). Passions run deep in this area!

Controversies about evolution continue to flare in other jurisdictions. In 1999, the State Board of Education in Kansas (USA) adopted a science curriculum that made no reference to evolution (Boyce, 1999) and removed the topic from standardised tests taken by students in that state. The decision was reversed in 2001, following election of a new Board. Having a seat at the table (or preferably a majority of seats!) matters. In 2004, the Georgia Superintendent of Schools proposed a science curriculum where the word evolution was replaced by "changes over time". The proposal prompted widespread ridicule and was quickly dropped. Later in the same year, school officials from Cobb County, in the suburbs of Atlanta, placed stickers in the front of secondary science texts. The stickers described evolution as a theory that needed to be critically considered and were a response to complaints by more than 2,000 parents. Their use prompted a court challenge by another group of parents (Wyatt, 2004). A recent edition of a US professional journal for teachers has a caricature of "God as designer" on the cover and includes both a focused editorial (Smith, 2004) and a rather concerned lead article (Terry, 2004). Public meetings organised by Christians committed to a young earth are held in Australian church buildings and draw large and enthusiastic crowds.

Teaching material dealing with evolution often adopts a specifically anti-religious stance. For example, visual aids may begin with treatment of confrontational episodes such as the Scopes "Monkey Trial" (Hawkhill, 2002), textbooks may portray evolution as a settled question (Haire, Kennedy, Lofts & Evergreen, 2005) and student movement towards acceptance of evolution can be interpreted as reflective of successful science teaching (Scharmann, Smith, James & Jensen, 2005).

So, how does a Christian teach science?

Christian schools exist to provide a context within which our children might come to faith and move out in mission. This requires the commitment to submit everything to the lordship of Christ, and that "everything" includes curricular as well as organisational details.

In light of this, it seems obvious that Christians teaching science need to come to a clear understanding of what science is and of what Scripture teaches; and neither exercise is as simple as it sounds. It is important to recognise that while not everybody involved in this discussion is acting in good faith, neither are they all malicious deceivers, and to remember that you can't tell the difference by finding out whether they agree with you. Integrity, foolishness, wisdom and malice seem fairly well distributed across this field and some people just enjoy a good argument! Respect for the differing views that students bring with them to class is consequently essential, but we also need to help them to test their views against Scripture, science and other positions.

Scripture

As Birkett (2001, pp. 134–139) recognises, our Bible is made up of many different types of literature and reading one type as though it were another could lead to substantial misunderstandings, which she illustrates by reference to Psalm 19. Turn to that place and ask yourself whether the sky is a great tent, whether the sun has legs and whether your faith depends on the sun moving above a stationary earth. Then consider how similar figurative language might be recognised elsewhere in Scripture.

Questions like these point to a view of Scripture that elevates it to its full authority, rather than placing it under the epistemological and hermeneutic filter of contemporary controversy. What do the Scriptures say? How did the people who first heard or read them understand their message? What do they mean for us, today? These are not simple questions. Few of us are reading our Bibles in the languages in which they were written and even fewer are able to do so without the distortion of contemporary concerns. All of us need to take care as we make the inevitable move from comprehension to interpretation.

The first chapter of Genesis has long been seen as different from most of what follows. Long before any current controversies, Augustine (354–430 AD) suggested that the words in Genesis 1 cannot mean the same things that they mean elsewhere. He notes the obvious fact that the sun is created on "day" four (*City of God* Book 11, chapters 6 & 7). Throughout the bulk of Scripture (with the notable exceptions of John 5: 17, where Jesus implies that the "days" of Genesis 1 are not yet complete, and 2 Peter 3:8, which stresses the difference between God's perspective and our own) a day is the period from one sundown to the next. Three sundowns without a sun is a clearly inspired indication that God's central purpose is not to give us a lock-step recipe for creation events, any more than I am suggesting that the sun moves, rather than the earth, when I use the word sunset. He is telling us who he is (the creator), what that world is (his creation and not to be worshipped) and what we were (the part of that creation that reflected him most clearly).

The second (and succeeding) chapters tell us what happened after the world was created. The following chapters use the personal name of God, which the first chapter does not, and records a different order for the appearance of parts of his creation (plants appear before people in chapter 1 and between the creation of Adam and the formation of Eve in chapter 2). Again we have a clear and timeless indication that we are not looking at a recipe. We are reading how we left the place he made for us and how far he was eventually prepared to go to bring us back.

Science

The history and nature of science are the first two of the five Prescribed Focus Areas around which school science education in NSW is organised (Board of Studies [BofS], 2003a). Science teachers in this state deal with such issues on the basis of government mandate but the nature of science is also considered to be important in other jurisdictions (see, for example, Scharmann, Smith, James & Jensen, 2005).

Science is a spectacularly successful human activity that draws its power from a deliberate *limitation* of focus. Galileo's decision to limit his attention to the position of moving objects and their speed is as strong a candidate for the beginning of modern science as any other. Colour, taste, smell, beauty, composition, value and status all became irrelevant when he considered motion. They did not become unimportant, merely not relevant to the question at hand. Galileo, and those following him who later took the title scientist, built models of the world which excluded many things that were otherwise important. This reduction made their models manageable, but irrelevance to reductionist science does not imply triviality. The area of interest defined by science leaves untouched some things that are of very great importance.

> *Science is a spectacularly successful human activity that draws its power from a deliberate limitation of focus.*

There might have been no impact on the physics if Galileo had rolled highly polished balls manufactured from the skulls of murdered children down his runways. However, irrelevance to physics would not have made his choice of material unimportant. Consideration of the syphilis study that ran in Tuskegee, Alabama, from 1932 until 1972, or the wartime experiments in Germany and

Manchuria, indicate that the horrid possibility of research-motivated infanticide is more than a cheap shock. Notwithstanding the claims of some of the more enthusiastic apologists for science, irrelevance to experimentation does not equate to lack of importance or lack of reality. The limits of reductionism as a heuristic within science are also being publicly recognised (Marcum, 2005).

Using reductionist models in science

Scientists manipulate their models (either physically, electronically or mentally) and then watch what happens. Particular responses in the simplified model predict changes in the more complicated real world. When predicted changes happen, scientists become more confident about their models. When predicted changes do not happen, scientists may become uneasy but they will not abandon their model until a better alternative appears (Kuhn, 1970).

Models have a hard core and a protective belt. The core is usually taught to students and accepted as given by practising scientists. The belt provides the predictions and puzzles that define scientific work. The hard core of a model is rarely challenged as a model grows in power, while scientific reputations are built and destroyed by debates within the protective belt (Lakatos, 1978). Ptolemaic astronomy had a stationary earth and circular motion at its core and medieval astronomers occupied themselves with the problems of sphere, eclipse, conjunction and epicycle that made up the protective belt.

Models are always *less* than reality. That is not a shortcoming. It is what makes the models useful—reality is too complex to comprehend all at once or manipulate in intelligible ways. Powerful models make many predictions about the real world and those predictions lead to the development of many useful things. Less powerful models make fewer successful predictions. Less powerful models are replaced by more powerful models (when they emerge) and once replaced they disappear from scientists' view almost completely. Epicycles, N-rays, phlogiston, miogeosynclines, eugeosynclines, the ether and pangenes all formed part of scientific models which have collapsed to be replaced by more powerful ideas.

Blurring of the boundary between the core and belt is one of the signs of a lessening in the power of a model and it is usually signalled by debates about the model core. Copernicus thought that medieval astronomy had moved too far from circular motion (which he considered more central to the model core than a stationary earth), so he suggested that revolving the earth around a stationary sun would produce simpler calculations concerning a more circular universe; Tycho noticed a new star in the supposedly unchanging heavens; Kepler abandoned circularity of spheres for elliptical orbits and, eventually, Newton established a new model and left Ptolemy to the astrologers.

Science is that process of model proposal, elaboration, testing, collapse and replacement. This is the nature of science as understood by those who have looked most closely at it, and it sits at the core of contemporary state syllabi in NSW (BofS, 2003a, pp. 18–20, 58–59; 1999, p. 71). "If students are taught only current understanding, it is hard to avoid the consequence that they will learn that there is only one answer, now known and uncontentious" (BofS 2003a, p. 35).

The stickers calling for a critical view of evolutionary theory that were placed in Atlanta textbooks (Wyatt, 2004) are not necessary in NSW. Stronger statements are built into contemporary state curricula.

The discomforting impact of model transience

The transient nature of scientific models is an uncomfortable fact for students, who want a clear and simple answer that they can accept without too much effort. Some students respond to this transience by turning away from the study of the world around us and towards study of things that appear simpler and surer.

The transient nature of scientific models is uncomfortable for scientists, who deal with it on the small scale every day but find recognition of daily triviality on the large scale personally difficult. Some scientists respond to this transience by asserting the centrality of the work they do and repudiating the reduction at the core of science. They claim that only the things accessible to the tools of science exist, so moving from a legitimately reduced focus to a wilful denial of anything falling beyond that limited view.

The transient nature of scientific models is uncomfortable for parents who remember things from their own schooling that are no longer taught. Some parents respond to this transience by withdrawing from their children's lessons and other parents respond by withdrawing their children.

The transient nature of scientific models is uncomfortable for people drawing fun and profit from the science/religion controversy. Those attacking religion want to present science as truth and their opponents as fools, while those attacking science find it an elusive target, as scientists apparently keep shifting ground.

Much of the discomfort caused by the transient nature of scientific models stems from a lack of realisation that science also involves commitment that can be legitimately described as faith. Contemporary culture is much more comfortable with a dichotomy between true and false (with what "I" believe being true!) and the faith required to continue riding a model that will ultimately collapse sits uneasily with such a dichotomy.

However, science *does* change in predictable and cyclical ways (Singham, 2000b). The phenomenon of changing models is very clear in biological evolution. Lamarck (1744–1829) and Darwin (1809–1882) shared a model of inheritance as shaped by distributed, differentiated body memory (pangenes), although the Frenchman thought that individual use increased pangenes and consequently influenced subsequent generations while the Englishman thought that competition between individuals made certain pangenes become more common in the population as a whole. Mendel's experiments (published in 1866) suggested a new model of atomistic "factors" that were separated, combined and redistributed through sexual reproduction. The Austrian's paper was recognised in 1900 as others worked parallel to his earlier investigations. Morgan (1866–1945) showed that Mendel's "factors" were connected to bands on chromosomes and the genetic model of inheritance was up and running.

Mendel (or more accurately, Morgan) and Darwin were brought together by Dobzhansky, Simpson and Mayr to produce the neo-Darwinism that is still taught in most secondary school science classes today. Inheritance seemed to happen according to a basically Mendelian model with occasional mutations providing the raw material for that diversity whose response to environmental pressure produces change in species (few genes + mutation + natural selection = gradual species change: Haire, Kennedy, Lofts & Evergreen, 2005, pp. 208–229). The apparent simplicity of this explanation makes it a powerful tool in the hands of those wishing to make faith appear trivial. The mandatory junior science syllabus in NSW puts it like this:

5.8.3 the theory of evolution and natural selection

a. *discuss evidence that present day organisms have evolved from organisms in the distant past*

b. *relate natural selection to the theory of evolution* (BofS, 2003a, p. 35).

The optional senior Biology course includes a similar main idea:

1. *Evidence of evolution suggests that the mechanisms of inheritance, accompanied by selection, allow change over many generations* (BofS, 2003b, p. 43).

The current state of evolutionary thought

Neither of these quotes represents the current state of science in this area and the textbook shape of Darwin's impact has also been called into question (Depew, 2003; Maienschein, 2005). Inheritance has been found to be much more complex than Mendel proposed, Morgan elaborated or Mayr synthesised. Natural selection is proving to be inadequate as a motor for the diversity we see around us (Erwin, 2004). Many modern evolutionary biologists grant this inadequacy and acknowledge the existence of a range of other mechanisms, while blurring evolution into descent with modification from a parent population. Paradoxically, that does not seem all that far from the position taken by the Georgia Superintendent of Schools in early 2004.

In a further paradox, the sophisticated view of science in general embodied in the NSW curricula and the weakening explanatory power of neo-Darwinism allow us to use the contemporary situation in evolutionary biology as an example of the transience of scientific models. There are at least 10 versions of evolution in the science and school literature: classical Lamarckism, classical Darwinism, neo-Darwinism, mosaic evolution, polyphyletic descent, stasis, punctuated equilibria, saltationism, chromosomally directed evolution and the neo-animist Gaia hypothesis. The broad NSW emphasis on the role of models in the development of science helps us to see that the particular model specified by the syllabi is in trouble.

Practicing biologists recognise the inadequacy of natural selection as a motor for the changes they infer, so doubting a central part of the core of neo-Darwinism. Evolutionary biology is in that phase of scientific history that Thomas Kuhn described as crisis. This does not mean that the whole thing is about to fall down around scientists' ears, but it does mean that the simple story presented in most secondary science classes no longer guides research. The substance of the arguments (see, for example, Kerr, 2004 or Pust, 2004) is less important than the evidence their existence provides for weakening community confidence in the core of the neo-Darwinian synthesis. Birkett (2001, pp. 26–27) indicates that something similar happened to classical Darwinism at the beginning of the 20th century.

Evolutionary biology is in that phase of scientific history that Thomas Kuhn described as crisis.

It is not yet clear whether one of the existing models, or one not yet suggested, will provide the new orthodoxy. In the meantime, the heat of external arguments that continue to swirl around neo-Darwinism makes public expression of internal doubts risky for rising biologists (see, for example, Ayala's 2005 comments on the work of S. J. Gould). Something similar happened in early modern astronomy, when some priests continued to defend Ptolemy and attack Copernicus after their more technically minded brethren had quietly abandoned Ptolemy and ignored Copernicus in favour of Tycho or Kepler.

Such a sophisticated, model-based view of science explicitly recognises the role of external factors in the development of science. "Analyse information from secondary sources on the historical development of theories of evolution and use available evidence to assess social and political influences on these developments" (BofS, 2003b, p. 43).

This recognition has been translated into an examination question in at least one commercial trial Higher School Certificate examination in NSW. It will eventually appear in one of the high stakes external examinations that characterise this jurisdiction, with subsequent backwash into all biology classrooms.

Diversity

There is a range of responses to the somewhat complex situation described above. Some people argue that science defines rationality and that only measurable things, accessible to science, are real. This is the arrogant materialist position: we are nothing but wet bundles of electrochemical reactions produced by blind chance because that is all that their view of science allows them to see. Reaction against such views prompted the development of many of the founding documents of contemporary Christian schooling and collapse before it accounts for the public timidity of some of our brethren. Challenges to such worldviews remain crucially important (Birkett, 2001, pp. 113–123).

Some people attempt to make room for God in an essentially evolutionary context. This is the theistic evolution position, seen in its most developed form in the Roman Catholic idea that God gave a hominid a soul somewhere along the evolutionary line. Less developed forms are fairly common in many churches and the recent shift towards an intelligent design argument (Stroebel, 2004) may bring them closer to holders of the next position.

Some people lock their faith to an interpretation of Genesis that leads to a young earth and short human history. Conflict between such commitment and science will either result in collapse of the faith or repudiation of the science. The potential of intelligent design to combine this group (from which many supporters of Christian schooling come) and the larger former group probably accounts for the panic evident in some contemporary secular literature (see, for example, Terry, 2004).

Some people believe that the Scriptures have nothing to do with the physical world. This is the two realms view taken by many scientific organisations and individual scientists. It allows for polite, mutual coexistence without much interaction and relegates God and faith to what is considered to be the nonscientific personal faith aspects of life.

Evolution is simply the sharp point of wider interactions between science and religion and these views flow out into the rest of science. People who adopt a two-worlds view in response to the heat of the argument maintain the separation as Gould's non-overlapping magisteria. This can imply that science and religion do not often conflict but that science wins when they do. Those who adopt a young earth view take issue with much of modern earth science, physics and astronomy. People who put a theistic spin on evolution can take an uncritical approach to other models within contemporary science, and those who see only the material as real find evidence against faith wherever they look.

Respect, clarity and criticism

Examples of all of these positions, and variations on each, can be found in the science/religion literature and among the parent bodies of most of our schools. Clear examples appear in the afore-mentioned issue of *The Christian Teachers Journal* (Mitchell, 2005). There may even be parents holding the materialist position sending their children to Christian schools because of the perceived excellence of the education they offer. Consequently, there will be children in Christian school classes holding various versions of the materialist, theistic evolution, young earth and two-realms views. Fysh and Lucas (1998) describe an interesting study that exposed some combinations of these views in a Queensland Lutheran school.

These people need to be treated with respect in our classrooms and positions other than that we hold ourselves need room for expression. However, respect does not mean universal acceptance. As Paul notes in passing (1 Cor 11:19), differing opinions, even factional parties, are necessary if we are to distinguish between the flawed and the sound, the false and the genuine. Our pupils will rarely come to class with a coherent view of the position they think they support. Our science classes should allow room for them to develop the views they come with and see how those views interact with the history of science (which is directly in line with NSW syllabus imperatives), the witness of Scripture (which is directly in line with the Christian tradition from which most of our families come) and the other views that might be held.

Discussions of the interactions between science and religion might best be initially encouraged in less controversial areas of the science curriculum, so that pupils are able to become comfortable in such complex contexts before they move to the higher temperature area of origins. Cosmology is useful because it is an area that was once even more torrid than origins but has now cooled enough to provide a much more temperate context for discussion. Once pupils have some grasp of the nature of science and the use of Scripture, they will be more able to clarify and test their own positions.

This process may appear to emerge from a continuing and contemporary controversy in one area of science but its application across the broad sweep of science education prepares our children for the diversity of opinion they will find when they move beyond our schools. Their own views will be refined, they will recognise that other people hold different views and they will be better prepared to challenge arrogant materialism.

A personal postscript: What do I think about origins?

My own position in the creation/evolution fracas is visible around the edges of the argument made above. However, in a fraught context such as this, readers deserve an explicit statement!

I reject the views of both of the colleagues with whom I began this paper. On the one hand, evolution is not a fact—facts are facets of raw experience which models such as evolution attempt to explain. On the other hand, there are (and have long been) a variety of ways of understanding what Scripture says about creation. To claim that only one interpretation is biblical is as arrogant as to claim that only what can be measured exists.

> *It is my view that God made the universe but that he has not told us how.*

It is my view that God made the universe but that he has not told us how. We could not possibly understand him, if he had told us. He has told us who he is, who we are, how we got into the mess we see around us, and what he has done about it. We are saved because of the sacrifice of his Son and that is stumbling block enough. It is sad if my students, colleagues or friends turn away from the free gift of God, having heard it explained. It is literally a horrible thing if they turn away before that point because of the arrogant proclamation of one interpretation of Scripture.

I take a similarly reformed critical realist approach to both sides of this long argument. Science is neither as certain (or malevolent), nor religion as irrational (or simple) as those deriving fun and profit from origins disputes would have us believe. Scientific work is an act of faith that may be guided by a sterile materialism that takes methodological reductionism as ontologically sufficient, or it can be guided by a childlike joy in thinking God's thoughts after him. I suspect that the latter group of scientists are more capable of disinterested research, because they know that their worth rests in Jesus, not in the work that they do. It is probably worth noting that Christian academics are generally more common in university science and engineering faculties than they are in arts and humanities.

Science provides an inevitably limited, changing account of what his created universe is like. Arrogant attacks upon the faith by people who cannot see the limitations of science are best answered by pointing out those limitations, not to disprove any particular theory, which is transient anyway, but to help scientific materialists see the faith ideas and shifting sand upon which they stand. The stickers calling for a critical view of the theory of evolution that were put in the front of science books in Georgia in 2004 were quite accurate and, contrary to comments of one of the opposing attorneys, they apply just as strongly to theories of gravity.

In him [Jesus] everything in heaven and on earth was created, not only things visible but also the invisible orders of thrones, sovereignties authorities, and powers: the whole universe has been created through him and for him. He exists before all things, and all things are held together in him (Col 1:16–17).

Christians teaching science should be firm and sophisticated in their approach to the science they teach under the authority of Scripture. We cannot allow one interpretation of Scripture as it applies to one theory in science to become such a shibboleth that discussion ceases.

Questions for discussion

1. Comment on the role of jurisdiction in educational debates. Does where you are matter very much?

2. Is all materialism arrogant? How might we identify method sliding into dogma?

3. Draw upon your personal experience to explore a situation where the heat of a controversy made its resolution less likely. How can the truth be seen amid the turmoil?

4. Turn to the 'shibboleth' event in Judges 12. Read carefully around the events and consider the character and actions of Jephthah of Gilead. Comment on other such touchstones in our corporate life and consider how the life of Jephthah might influence our reactions to them.

5. What is your opinion of the relative merits of science and religion? Consider the sources and consequences of that opinion.

6. The US controversies form part of the background for this chapter. Go back over the chapter and produce a timeline for the wider controversies about evolution. Critically evaluate the position the chapter takes on the impact of differing educational jurisdictions.

7. Open your Bible and critically evaluate the section on 'Scripture'.

8. Do you agree that science is necessarily reductionist? Draw on your own experiences of school science to consider how widely the limitations of science are discussed.

9. Why do you think that changing models in science cause discomfort for so many people? Evaluate the impact of model change on our attitude to the current state of biological theory.

10. Evaluate the different views of the relationship between science and religion that are described towards the end of the chapter.

11. How do you think that issues of origins should be dealt with in Christian schools? The issue is far from settled!

References

Ayala, F. J. (2005). The structure of evolutionary theory: On Stephen Jay Gould's monumental master-piece. *Theology and Science, 3*(1), 97–117.

Birkett, K. (2001). *The essence of Darwinism*. Kingsford, NSW: Matthias Media.

Board of Studies. (1999). *Science Stages 4 and 5: Support document*. Sydney: Board of Studies New South Wales.

Board of Studies (2003a). *Stages 4 and 5 Science: Years 7–10 syllabus*. Sydney: Board of Studies New South Wales.

Board of Studies (2003b). *Biology Stage 6: Syllabus*. Sydney: Board of Studies New South Wales.

Boyce, N. (1999, August 21). Don't mention Darwin: Creationists have a new strategy in their assault on evolution. *New Scientist*, p. 4.

Depew, D. (2003). Protecting evolutionary theory from bad company. *The Review of Communication, 3*(4), 375–378.

Editor (2000, April 22). Beyond belief: Science isn't religion. You can't use one to justify the other. *New Scientist*, p. 3.

Erwin, D. H. (2004). One very long argument. *Biology and Philosophy, 19*, 17–28.

Fysh, R. & Lucas, K. (1998). Science and religion: Acknowledging student beliefs. *Australian Science Teachers Journal, 44*(2), 60–68.

Goheen, M. (2004). The gospel and the idolatrous power of secular science. In J. Ireland, R. Edlin, & K. Dickens (Eds.), *Pointing the way: Directions for Christian education in the new millennium* (pp. 33–54). Blacktown, NSW: National Institute for Christian Education.

Haire, M., Kennedy, E., Lofts, G. & Evergreen, M. J. (2005). *Core Science 4: Stage 5 essential content* (2nd ed.). Milton, Queensland: John Wiley & Sons.

Hawkhill Associates. (2002). *Evolution* [DVD]. Madison WI: Author.

Maienschein, J. (Ed.). (2005). The Darwinian Revolution [Special themed issue]. *Journal of the History of Biology, 38*(1), 1–152.

Kerr, B. (2004). The caucus-race of the dodo. *Biology and Philosophy, 19*, 781–799.

Kuhn, T. (1970). *The structure of scientific revolutions*. Chicago: University of Chicago Press.

Lakatos, I. (1978). *The methodology of scientific research programs*. New York: Cambridge University Press.

Marcum, J. A. (2005). Metaphysical presuppositions and scientific practices: Reductionism and organi-cism in cancer research. *International Studies in the Philosophy of Science, 19*(1), 31–45.

Mitchell, S. (2005). Science teaching: Is there one Christian approach? *The Christian Teachers Journal, 13*(2).

O'Toole, J. M. (2005). Weak in the head or soft on the scriptures: Science (in general), evolution (in particular) and Christian schools, *The Christian Teachers Journal, 13*(2), 20–24.

Paterson, F. R. A. (2003). *Democracy and intolerance: Christian school curricula, school choice and public policy.* Bloomington, IN: Phi Delta Kappa Educational Foundation.

Plimer, I. (2000, April 22). First person—Ian Plimer: I'd do it all again. *New Scientist,* p. 43.

Pust, J. (2004). Natural selection and the traits of individual organisms. *Biology and Philosophy, 19,* 765–779.

Scharmann, L. C., Smith, M. U., James, M. C. & Jensen, M. (2005). Explicit reflective nature of science instruction: Evolution, intelligent design and umbrellaology. *Journal of Science teacher Education, 16,* 27–41.

Singham, M. (2000a, February). The science and religion wars. *Phi Delta Kappan, 81*(6), 424–432

Singham, M, (2000b). *Quest for truth: Scientific progress and religious beliefs.* Bloomington, IN: Phi Delta Kappa Educational Foundation.

Smith, B. M. (2004, December). A perennial debate. *Phi Delta Kappan, 86*(4), 259.

Stroebel, L. (2004). *The case for a creator: A journalist investigates scientific evidence that points toward God.* Grand Rapids, MI: Zondervan.

Terry, M. (2004, December). One nation, under the designer. *Phi Delta Kappan, 86*(4), 265–270.

Wyatt, K. (2004, November 14). Atlanta schools' evolution dispute comes under fire [Electronic version]. *The Seattle Times.* Retrieved November 17, 2004, from http://seattletimes.nwsource. com/cgi-bi...68448411&slug=evolution14&date=20041114

Chapter 14

Preparing teachers to teach in a multicultural & multireligious context:
The approach of the National Institute for Christian Education

Charles Justins
Lecturer, NICE & Deputy Principal, Tyndale Christian School Sydney

Charlie has been a teacher for 29 years and, apart from one year at Marrara Christian School in Darwin and one at a NSW government school, these have been spent at Tyndale Christian School in Sydney. Many of those years have involved the teaching of mathematics, commerce and economics. He has been a deputy principal since 1991. In 2002, Charlie completed a doctorate in education on the topic *Christian Parent Controlled Schools in Australia: Foundational values and prevailing practice* and has taught part-time with the National Institute for Christian Education since 2001. Throughout his career, Charlie has been committed to the task of teaching from a distinctively Christian perspective and is keen to see that Christian schools are effective in their purpose of guiding and nurturing young people to be thoughtful and authentic followers of Jesus in every area of their lives.

The material in this chapter was originally prepared for a presentation at an IAPCHE (International Association for the Promotion of Christian Higher Education) conference in Chennai, India in January 2005.

Abstract

The preparation of Christian teachers to work in a multicultural and multireligious context requires preparation in biblical theology, worldview and embodied plausibility.

The chapter considers the multicultural context of Australia, Christian Parent Controlled Schools in Australia, the National Institute for Christian Education and the preparation of teachers for a multicultural and multireligious context.

The multicultural and multireligious context of Australia

Australia, with a population at the end of 2004 exceeding 20 million, is generally regarded as a multicultural nation. Kerkyasharian (1998) suggested that "multiculturalism is central to, and forms the basis of any discussion in Australia about our national identity and national future". Khalil (1999), similarly, argued that:

The preparation of Christian teachers to work in a multicultural and multireligious context requires preparation in biblical theology, worldview and embodied plausibility.

> *Australia has been and continues to be a multicultural society. The indigenous people have always been diverse culturally and linguistically. The first fleet that came to Australia in 1788 came from a number of ethnic backgrounds. Australia's diversity continues to grow with the flow of immigrants.*

Since 1945 about 6 million people have migrated to Australia. Over 25% of Australia's population was born overseas, including 7.5% from north-west Europe and 5.7% from Asia. Fifteen per cent speak a language other than English at home and 1% of the population cannot speak English at all. In 2001, it was estimated that the Indigenous population of Australia was 460 000 or 2.4% of the total population.

Since British settlement in 1788 and with the exception of its Indigenous population, Australia was for many years largely Anglo-Celtic, but this is no longer the case. In the mid-1990s, Tacey suggested that:

Australia has finally given up the myth that it is a homogeneous, unified Anglo-Saxon monoculture, a myth that was fiercely promoted during the major decades of Australian nationalism. Instead, a new myth has arisen which portrays Australia as a diverse, pluralistic, multicultural society, in which aboriginal people have a special place as the original inhabitants of this land ... In political and economic terms, Australia has given up the fantasy of itself as rugged, independent and materially self-sufficient ("riding on the sheep's back"). Politicians now tell us that Australia must participate more fully in the global and Asia–Pacific region, and that it must judge itself not by its own standards but by world economic indicators and by multinational standards (1995, p.117).

Not surprisingly, religious diversity in Australia is also increasing. In 1901 (the year that the various states of Australia decided by referendum to become one nation), 96% of a population of 3.7 million regarded themselves as Christians, but in the 2001 census this had dropped to 65%, with 25% regarding themselves as having no religion (or ignoring the question), and of the major non-Christian religions, 1.9% were Buddhists and 1.5% Moslems.

These statistics indicate that there is significant and increasing cultural and religious diversity in Australia and it is in this context that the issue of preparing teachers to teach in a multicultural and multireligious context will be addressed.

Christian schooling in Australia

Since European settlement, Christian schooling has been sponsored in Australia by a variety of churches. Initially, the official church of the colony, the Anglican Church, established schools. Hill (1997) has suggested "In the early settlement of Sydney, as the number of children on the loose in a mainly penal colony increased, Richard Johnson, the evangelical Anglican chaplain who accompanied the first fleet, initiated Christian schooling for them" (p. 280). In the intervening years, the Catholic Church has made the most significant contribution to Christian schooling and presently enrols over 20% of Australian students in its schools. Alongside a number of high-fee-paying elite church schools, a number of churches, notably the Lutherans and Adventists, have established schooling systems. More recently the newer Christian schools such as Christian Parent Controlled Schools, Christian Community Schools (now incorporated into Christian Schools Australia), schools under the auspices of Accelerated Christian Education and low-fee-paying Anglican schools have also commenced (Justins, 2002, pp. 12–28).

Christian Parent Controlled Schools

Christian Parent Controlled (CPC) schools began in Australia in the early 1960s as a result of the initiatives of Dutch immigrants of the Christian Reformed faith who gave a high priority to the provision of schooling for their children. The establishment of these schools coincided with a wider concern by many Christians that available Australian schools were not reflecting their beliefs and values. In particular, there were fears that the secularism and pluralism of state schools was undermining the Christian faith. Lambert (1997), suggested:

The reasons commonly given for the emergence of these relatively new alternative Christian schools centre on what their supporters perceive to be the failure of the multifaith approach in many state schools which they argue has led to chaos in the area of personal values and morality, and a devaluation and/or marginalisation of Christian perspectives in the curriculum in many state and traditional church schools (p. 275).

The reformed Dutch migrants who established CPC schools were part of the post-World War II influx of European settlers to Australia. Their distinctive educational philosophy was shaped by deeply held religious beliefs and convictions which compelled them to make Christian schooling a priority in spite of the difficult financial circumstances which afflicted most migrants of that time. These migrants, who also established the Reformed Churches of Australia (RCA), had left behind a schooling system in the Netherlands in which parents were able to choose from government, Catholic, or Protestant (Calvinist) schools and were thus able to take responsibility for the education of their children.

> *Developing a distinctively Christian approach in the construction of curricula is without doubt the most difficult task faced by parents and teachers in all Christian schools.*

The Christian reformed Dutch migrants were keenly aware of the schools they had left behind. Hoekzema (1990), one of the migrants himself and an early leader in this schooling movement, suggested:

Dutch migrants of Reformed persuasion arrived in this country in the early fifties and woke to the fact that something they had always taken for granted, a Christian school, was not available, non-existent. This was quite baffling for a supposedly Christian country and mind you, these migrants' grandparents had won the battle for equality of education only forty years before.

The first CPC school, Calvin Parent Controlled Christian School, the planning for which began in 1954, commenced in Hobart in 1962 with 77 students and three teachers. A national organisation which eventually became Christian Parent Controlled Schools (CPCS) Ltd was established in 1966, to support not only the three existing schools (two more commenced in 1966), but a number of other associations which were still in the planning stage. In 2004 CPCS Ltd had 58 member associations operating 85 schools with over 22 000 students.

Duyker (1987) argued that CPC schools had made a significant contribution to Australian society in their own right and that they had provided an important model for the emerging schools of other conservative Christian groups. Bouma (1997) in his discussion of religious groups in Australia also suggested that the emergence of this schooling movement was noteworthy:

The Reformed Churches of Australia [is] … a small denomination … it has had a significant impact on the religious scene in Australia. It has been active in promoting reformed theology beyond the borders of its own denomination. Its most notable contribution has been in the model of parent-controlled schools (p. 41).

Research involving analysis of early documents and interviews and surveys with CPC school pioneers and early school leaders identified four foundational values or fundamental principles of these schools:

1. Parents should control the education of their children;

2. The focus of the school should be on the needs of Christian families (including the importance of affordability and a protected environment);

3. The curriculum should be thoroughly Christian—guided by the Bible and with Christ at the centre of all school activities; and

4. All courses should be developed and taught by Christian teachers (Justins, 2002).

The National Institute for Christian Education (NICE)

The training of teachers has always been a significant priority for CPC schools. A national teacher education conference was held as early as 1973 and national conferences have generally been held every two years since. The reason that teacher training has had such a high priority is closely linked to the foundational purposes of these schools. If, as noted above, the movement desires teachers to construct and teach a curriculum which is thoroughly Christian—guided by the Bible and with Christ at the centre of all school activities—then these teachers need to be supported and trained for this task. The difficult nature of this task has never been underestimated by CPC educators. Mechielsen (1978), for example, argued:

Developing a distinctively Christian approach in the construction of curricula is without doubt the most difficult task faced by parents and teachers in all Christian schools. It is one thing to announce that such and such a Christian school has opened where the Lord is central and where all activities have the common goal of praising His great name, but quite another to put this into practice in the day-to-day operation of the school as an educational institution (p. 2).

Further evidence of this emphasis on the importance of teacher training was the decision by CPC schools not to join with other Christian schools in the establishment of a new umbrella organisation, CSA, in 2001. The Executive Director of CPCS at that time, John Metcalfe (personal communication, September 6, 2001), suggested that there were two main reasons for this. Firstly, it was believed that the new organisation would not have actively supported the concept of parent control, and secondly the new organisation would not have given sufficient support to Christian teacher education of the kind being provided by NICE.

In 1991, the Victorian (Australia) based Institute for Christian Education (ICE) formally came under the umbrella of the national Christian Parent Controlled Schools movement as NICE. ICE commenced in Victoria in 1979 with strong support from Victorian CPCS schools under the tutelage of Dr Stuart Fowler and Dr Doug Blomberg, offering postgraduate studies in education, essentially for teachers in CPC schools. The decision to extend these postgraduate studies to teachers in all CPC schools in Australia was a recognition that the preservation of a distinctively Christian approach to education required explicit and formalised training for teachers that reflected the reformational-philosophical stance of these schools.

In 1996, NICE collaborated with a similar organisation, the Institute for Christian Tertiary Education (ICTE, now trading as Southland College), which represented Christian Community Schools, to form the College of Christian Higher Education Inc. (CCHE) for the purposes of obtaining accreditation for their courses through the NSW Department of Education. CCHE uses the Oxbridge model where separate teaching institutes (NICE and Southland) come under one controlling body (CCHE) for academic affairs.

By 2004, NICE, through CCHE, had government accreditation for a number of courses:

- Bachelor of Education (Conversion)

- Graduate Diploma of Education

- Master of Education

- Master of Education (Professional Leadership and Training)

- Master of Education (Honours)

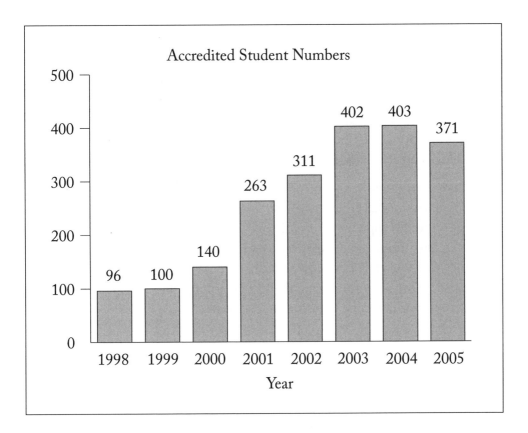

Accredited Student Numbers

The main teaching mode of NICE is distance education. Residential schools are also an important aspect of NICE's approach. The substantial interest in NICE courses is indicated in the above table. In 2004, NICE offered about 400 accredited student units and taught hundreds more students through non-accredited professional development days and also graduated its first South African cohort of 11 students. In a CPC school catchment with around 1200 teachers, to have 300 teachers or 25% of the total from that catchment (the other 100 come from non-CPC schools) studying with NICE is little short of remarkable.

In the context of its support for CPC schools, the explicit priorities of NICE are:

1. To provide Christian teacher education

2. To facilitate school and curriculum development

3. To articulate and nurture a biblical worldview

4. To promote international links and commitments to Christian education (National Institute for Christian Education [NICE], 2004).

The preparation of teachers

Preparing Christian teachers to teach in a multireligious and multicultural context requires preparation in three interrelated areas. Two of these areas are addressed by NICE through the two compulsory core units which focus on biblical theology and worldview issues. These units are intended to give teachers the necessary foundation upon which to teach from a Christian perspective. The third area provides an overarching approach that allows the first two areas to prosper.

It is important to note at the outset that every classroom is, to a greater or lesser extent, multicultural and multireligious. Even those classes in Christian schools with the outward appearance of cultural and religious homogeneity invariably contain children from families of diverse backgrounds. This issue is being addressed from the standpoint that Christian teachers need preparation in the three areas to be outlined below, notwithstanding the specific cultural and religious context they encounter in their particular schools and classrooms.

An emphasis on biblical theology

In the first compulsory unit, *Biblical Foundations of Christian Education*, it is suggested that teachers in Christian schools need to have a sound understanding of the Bible as a set of books with one divinely inspired overarching message: "In our understanding, it is the person and work of Jesus Christ that provides the central unity of Scripture. The gospel of Jesus, and its consequences—this is surely the centre of both the Old and New Testament Scriptures" (NICE, 2003, p. 8).

Thompson's (2004) doctoral research indicated that teachers in Christian schools in Australia possessed an understanding of the Bible shaped not by the whole canon of Scripture but largely by the early chapters of Genesis, by the New Testament accounts of Jesus and by a small selection of New Testament epistles. In particular, for these teachers, neither the Old Testament history of Israel nor the historic gospel events were decisive in shaping their worldviews. Through surveys and interviews teachers indicated that Jesus himself was influential, but it appeared to Thompson that the Jesus they spoke of was "sanitised, westernised and individualised" (2004, pp. 155–172).

In a survey of 295 teachers in CPC schools, while 94% agreed that "the Bible is essential for students to understand the world/human society", only 57% said "the Bible is often used in my class" (and this fell to 44% for secondary school teachers), and 38% felt that they had "not really been adequately prepared to teach from a completely biblical perspective" (Justins, 2002, p. 228).

As a corrective to these concerns, and to effectively and accurately understand and apply the Bible in the classroom, the Christian teacher needs an appropriate hermeneutical guide, a sound biblical theology. According to Goldsworthy:

Biblical theology examines the development of the biblical story from the Old Testament through to the New, and seeks to uncover the interrelationships between the two parts. Prophecy, law, narrative, wisdom saying, or apocalyptic vision are all related to *the coming of Jesus Christ* in some discernible way. Biblical theology is a methodical approach to showing these relationships so that the Old Testament can be understood as Christian Scripture (cited in NICE, 2003, p. 6).

While the specific cultural and religious context in which Christian teachers operate will impinge significantly on their manner and approach, it is crucial that they possess a sound understanding of biblical theology if they are to appropriately apply biblical principles in their classrooms. My own experience as a mathematics teacher in Christian schools testifies to this. A number of years ago, I received a copy of a maths text published by a Christian university which purported to be a Christian maths text for high school (secondary) students. A verse of Scripture was placed at the bottom of each page of maths theory and problems. Apart from this, the material was no different from that contained in any other secular mathematics text. There was no reflection on the nature or purpose of mathematics or any mention of the possibility that a Christian mathematician may have particular insights worthy of consideration.

> *Biblical theology examines the development of the biblical story from the Old Testament through to the New, and seeks to uncover the interrelationships between the two parts.*

I have also talked over the years with teachers who have suggested that a particularly biblical approach to mathematics is to organise activities where the content is taken from Scripture, for example a consideration of the dimensions of Noah's ark. A fully orbed biblical theology will reveal that such approaches are at best shallow and at worst detrimental to the gospel. A valuable discussion of mathematics and the Christian faith can be found in *Mathematics in a Postmodern Age* (Howell & Bradley, 2001).

An emphasis on worldview

The second compulsory NICE unit, *Worldviews in Education*, emphasises the importance of teachers having an awareness of their own worldview, of refining this worldview in the light of Scripture and of understanding the worldviews of others, particularly the dominant worldview assumptions of their own cultures and of their students.

A worldview could be considered as the perceptual framework through which we understand ourselves and the world around us, and therefore a Christian worldview is vital for a Christian view of education in general and for cultural sensitivity in particular. Walsh and Middleton (1984, p. 35) argue that a biblical worldview provides coherent, comprehensive and liveable answers to the fundamental issues of identity, location, evil and salvation (Who am I? Where am I? What is wrong? What is the remedy?). Sire (2004) suggests similarly that our worldview emerges in response to these questions:

What is prime reality—the really real?

What is the nature of external reality, that is, the world around us?

What is a human being?

What happens to persons at death?

Why is it possible to know anything at all?

How do we know what is right and wrong?

What is the meaning of history? (p. 20)

The NICE *Worldviews in Education* course outline suggests that:

It is recognised that it is not sufficient for Christian educators to proceed on the basis of an uncritical acceptance of a "Christian" worldview. The worldview that is embedded in our thinking and practice as Christians needs to be tested for its consistency with the Gospel just as rigorously as we test the worldview assumptions embedded in the practices of secular educators. We need to learn to "test everything" if, in our educational practice, we are "to hold fast to what is good" and avoid what is flawed—1 Thess 5:21 (NICE, 2005, p. 33).

An example of the way in which NICE students are prompted to engage in worldview analysis is the activity developed by Dr Richard Edlin, the current NICE principal, in which four scenarios based on actual events that have occurred in the context of Christian schools in Australia are examined and critiqued. In summary, the scenarios involve:

- A consideration of a share market competition that senior students in one school were involved in which the purpose was to "invest" a certain amount of money (simulated) in shares of their choice. The winning school was the one that received the greatest return on their "investment". While these students did not win the competition, they made a substantial profit and the principal of this school wrote glowingly of the students' performance in the school newsletter.

- A Remembrance Day ceremony in which those who have died in wars in which Australians were involved, particularly World Wars I and II, were remembered and honoured. The ceremony involved one minute silence as a mark of respect for those who had sacrificed their lives for their country.

- A gathering of Christian school principals in Canberra where a special dinner was held for the principals and specially invited members of parliament. A popular Australian (non-Christian) author was invited to speak and he addressed the audience on the power of individual aspirations and dreams and determination.

- A change in the way in which one school organised their annual class photos. They had traditionally gathered all the students in a class for a photo, but were now going to have a digital image of each student taken, from which a computer-generated collage would be constructed of the whole class.

Each of theses scenarios is examined by small groups of teachers, considering questions such as: How would contemporary society view this scenario? What worldview assumptions are illustrated by this scenario? Critique these assumptions. There is often considerable value for teachers in this type of activity, as many of their own hidden or unconsidered worldview assumptions are revealed.

These first two foundational perspectives are about teachers knowing—knowing how to appropriately read and apply the Bible and knowing how to appropriately read and understand themselves as cultural beings and the wider culture in which they live. Another way of putting this is that truth is important. Approaches that compromise biblical truth or desert the distinctive claims of Christianity such as the preeminence of Christ in the interest of peace or edifying inter-faith dialogues are, in the end, of no value.

NICE's fourth foundational pillar (see earlier, NICE, 2004) expresses the commitment of the organisation that helps fund it to another multicultural endeavour—the assistance of Christian communities involved in Christian teacher training in other parts of the world. Where possible, this is done on a cost-recovery basis. Where local resources are scarce, NICE funds its involvement from its own financial base.

In all these cases, however, NICE demonstrates its sensitivity to local contextual issues by linking with appropriate onsite indigenous partners.

As an alternative to efforts by other respected Christian tertiary educational institutions from North America which have come together to provide a multinational but Western-based educational qualification for Christian teachers, NICE's strategy has taken a different path. NICE seeks to oversee the local contextualisation and delivery under licence of its courses in overseas countries in a framework of reformed critical realism. After contextualisation, NICE courses usually are incorporated into qualifications of local partner institutes, delivered by suitably qualified and experienced Christian scholars with varying degrees of assistance and moderation from key NICE staff. Examples of these partnerships include the Heidelberg Institute in remote northern South Africa; Scott University in Kenya; Institute for Christian Studies in Canada; Emmanuel Schools Foundation in the United Kingdom; Masters Institute in New Zealand; and Kosin University in South Korea.

Embodied plausibility

Teaching in a multireligious context of any kind involves an interaction with people, and while a commitment to the promotion of truth is fundamental, teachers need to remember that their calling involves people. Teachers work with children or, for those involved in tertiary education, with adults. Truth is not disembodied—the gospel teaches that truth is embodied or incarnated in Christ and the New Testament in many places encourages us to follow the example of Christ and hold the primacy of truth together with the primacy of love.

The apostle Paul was undoubtedly one of the world's greatest promoters of truth. Think for example about his comments in Galatians 1:9 (ESV): "If anyone is preaching to you a gospel contrary to the one you received, let them be accursed". Nevertheless, he believed that people were important, that their backgrounds, contexts and identities were important. For their sake and for the sake of the gospel he was willing to change his own shape, to "become all things to all people" (1 Cor 9: 22 ESV). Clearly Paul was not suggesting that he was willing to become like others in idolatrous beliefs or inappropriate behaviour, but rather that he was willing to accommodate his own preferences and pleasures and eschew any privileges in order to draw close to people and form genuine relationships in order to win others to Christ.

For though I am free from all, I have made myself a servant to all, that I might win more of them. To the Jews I became as a Jew, in order to win Jews. To those under the law I became as one under the law (though not being myself under the law) that I might win those under the law. To those outside the law I became as one outside the law (not being outside the law of God but under the law of Christ) that I might win those outside the law. To the weak I became weak, that I might win the weak. I have become all things to all people, that by all means I might save some. I do it all for the sake of the gospel, that I may share with them in its blessings (1 Cor 9:19–23 ESV).

In Ephesians 4, Paul talks at length about the importance of truth. Without it, we are like children who are tossed to and fro by false doctrines and by deceitful and scheming teachers. Interestingly, he then marries truth and love. "Rather, speaking the truth in love, we are to grow up in every way into him who is the head, into Christ" (Eph 4:15 ESV). Even when beset by those promoting evil, our response (and this is extremely difficult under these circumstances) is to communicate the truth in love. There is no reason for Christian teachers to adopt a different paradigm from Paul. We ought to be all things to all students in order to communicate the truth lovingly and sensitively.

Pearcey (2004), toward the end of her book on Christianity and culture, suggests that "A verbal presentation of a Christian worldview message loses its power if it is not validated by the quality of our lives" (p. 355). She also suggests that people (and for our purposes we can read students from a variety of religious and cultural backgrounds) need to see new ideas lived out in practice before they can accept them. She calls this a plausibility structure. Christian teachers and Christian institutions need to construct plausibility structures in which others see the supernatural dimensions of love, power and goodness in the way that Christians live. We can dot every *i* and cross every *t*, in terms of our biblical theology and our worldview analysis, but without a genuine Christian lifestyle, an authentic following of Christ, which I would describe as an embodied plausibility, our biblical knowledge and deep understanding is of little value.

> *We ought to be all things to all students in order to communicate the truth lovingly and sensitively.*

The Japanese missionary and theologian Kosuke Koyama (1999) has also made a number of helpful observations in this regard. In his work in Thailand, he said that it took him some time to realise that the issue was his relationship with Buddhists, not with Buddhism.

It is the street-Buddhists who are the brothers and sisters whom I see, with whom I speak and with whom I live. To love them as they are *in all their complexity and not just to love anthropological, sociological, theological "formulations" of brothers and sisters is the command of God whom we have not seen (1 John 4:20) (p. 151).*

Koyama maintains that God's most profound communication to people was an incarnation of himself: "The ultimate and complete unity of the message (the Word) and person took place only in the person of Jesus Christ" (p. 155). This should also be true for Christians, i.e. that the message and the messenger must become one. While our teachers need knowledge and truth and a thorough understanding of the Bible and of the world in which they live, they need to embody their message, and approach their students with love and a desire to serve. Paul suggests that to Christians and non-Christians we ought to be the aroma or fragrance of Christ (2 Cor 2:15).

A short digression here. Embodying our message means that the classroom of a Christian teacher should be a safe environment for all students, regardless of their background. All students should be welcomed (and ideally feel welcome), with all opinions respected if conveyed respectfully and sarcasm and put-downs banished. The teacher's power should be exercised as servant-leadership. Van Dyk (1997) and Van Brummelen (1998) give wise and eloquent advice about the structure and environment of a Christian teachers' classroom.

> *All students should be welcomed (and ideally feel welcome), with all opinions respected if conveyed respectfully and sarcasm and put-downs banished.*

Finally, a few comments in regard to our institutions themselves. In preparing this chapter, I noted that a number of people were advocating the importance of a theology of the cross. Pearcey (2004), in the context of the proposition that Christians should embody their message, says:

As Martin Luther put it, Christians embrace a theology of the cross, not a theology of glory. The mystery of our salvation was effectuated by Jesus' descent to earth not as a conquering hero but as a suffering servant—mocked, beaten, hung on a cross. True knowledge of Christ comes only as we are willing to give up our dreams of glory, praying to be identified with Him on the cross (p. 358).

This perspective ought to impact not only individual Christians but also our institutions. Is the honour and glory of our school or educational institution important to us? If it is, are we in dangerous territory? How do we measure the success of our institutions? How do we promote or advertise our institutions? What impact would the failure of our institution have on us? What measures (or compromises) would we take in order to preserve our institution?

A theology of the cross, while holding steadfastly to the belief that truth is found definitively in Christ, is nevertheless modest, humble and respectful. A theology of the cross stands in stark contrast to a theology of glory, which Hall (2003) describes as triumphalism: "the tendency in all strongly held worldviews … to present themselves as full and complete accounts of reality, leaving little if any room for debate or difference of opinion and expecting of their adherents unflinching belief and loyalty" (2003, p. 17). Our institutions, and those of us in them, are limited, flawed and inadequate and ought to be seen as a means by which we promote the gospel rather than as divinely sanctioned, quasi-eternal ends in themselves.

In summary, while no teacher would ever be able to regard themselves as completely and unambiguously prepared, a (credibly) well-prepared Christian teacher would:

- have a familiarity with both the biblical narrative and the overarching gospel metanarrative

- possess a clear understanding of their own worldview and the worldview assumptions of their culture, particularly as those assumptions impact on the living and thinking of their students

- be committed to following Christ and embodying plausibly the Christian message, aware that they are flawed humans in need of the love and grace of God in Christ and willing to extend this love and grace in generous measure to their students.

Questions for discussion

1. Given the constraints of external exams and matriculation requirements, is it unrealistic to expect that teachers of senior (high school) students will use the Bible regularly in their classrooms?

2. Should teachers change their approach in response to a changing cultural and religious culture within their classes? If you think they should, give an illustration of what this might involve. What should a kindergarten teacher or a mathematics teacher do differently, for example?

3. Paul says, "I have become all things to all people" (1 Cor 9:22). What would it mean for a teacher to follow Paul's example in their schools and their classrooms? Provide examples of what this might look like.

4. Comment on Thompson's view that teachers in Christian schools in Australia possess an understanding of the Bible shaped not by the whole canon of Scripture but largely by the early chapters of Genesis, by the New Testament accounts of Jesus and by a small selection of New Testament epistles.

5. Christian schools are often large institutions with complex management structures, large numbers of students, teachers and parents and a multitude of rules, regulations, procedures, processes and systems. Is it inherently difficult for teachers in a school whose requirements have to be followed to plausibly embody the message of the gospel?

6. Can a theology of the cross epitomise the culture of a Christian school or is triumphalism an inevitable characteristic?

7. Assume that you are on the education committee of an embryonic Christian school. The school would like all teachers to be imbued with a sound biblical theology, equipped with a thorough understanding of worldview perspectives and wholehearted in their desire to plausibly embody the gospel. Suggest 7–10 strategies that the school could adopt which would assist teachers to develop in these areas.

References

Bouma, G. (Ed.). (1997). *Many religions, all Australians: Religious settlement, identity and cultural diversity*. Kew, Vic.: Christian Research Association.

Duyker, E. (1987). *The Dutch in Australia*. Melbourne: AE Press.

Goldsworthy, G. (1991). *According to plan*. Leicester, UK: Inter Varsity.

Hall, D. (2003). *The cross in our context: Jesus and the suffering world*. Minneapolis: Fortress Press.

Hill, B. (1997). Alternative Christian schooling: A search for meaning. In K. Watson, C. Modgil & S. Modgil (Eds.), *Educational dilemmas: Debate and diversity: Vol. 3. Power and responsibility in education* (pp. 280–287). London: Cassell.

Hoekzema, R. (1990, January). Unpublished paper presented to Tyndale Christian School staff.

Howell, R. and Bradley, W. (Eds.). (2001). *Mathematics in a postmodern age*. Grand Rapids, MI: Eerdmans.

Justins, C. (2002). *Christian Parent Controlled Schools in Australia: A study of the relationship between foundational values and prevailing practices*. Unpublished doctoral dissertation. Australian Catholic University.

Kerkyasharian, S. (1998, March 23). *Multiculturalism in Australia: today and tomorrow*. Address to the 1998 Annual Conference of the Federation of Ethnic Councils of Australia. Retrieved May 27, 2005 from www.crc.nsw.gov.au/publications/Multiculturalism_in_Australia.pdf

Khalil, M. (1999, 25 October). *Minimising the impacts and maximising the opportunities in a culturally diverse society*. Paper presented at the Living in the Olympic State II Conference. Retrieved May 27, 2005 from www.ncoss.org.au/bookshelf/conference/download/olympic2/khalil.rtf

Koyama, K. (1999). *Water buffalo theology* (25th Anniversary Edition). New York: Orbis.

Lambert, I. (1997). Alternative Christian schooling: The historical and contemporary context of the Australian experience. In K. Watson, C. Modgil and S. Modgil (Eds.), *Educational dilemmas: Debate and diversity: Vol. 3. Power and responsibility in education* (pp. 268–279). London: Cassell.

Mechielsen, J. (1978, October). *Mount Evelyn Christian School*. Unpublished paper.

National Institute for Christian Education. (2003). *Biblical Foundations of Christian Education* [Course notes]. Blacktown, NSW: Author.

National Institute for Christian Education. (2004). *Strategic pillars* [brochure]. Blacktown, NSW: Author.

National Institute for Christian Education. (2005). *NICE course handbook*. Blacktown, NSW: Author.

Pearcey, N. (2004). *Total truth: Liberating Christianity from its cultural captivity*. Wheaton IL: Crossway Books.

Sire, J. W. (2004). *Naming the elephant: Worldview as a concept*. Downers Grove, IL: Inter Varsity.

Tacey, D. (1995). *Edge of the sacred: Transformation in Australia.* North Blackburn, Vic., Australia: Harper Collins.

Thompson, R. (2004). Genesis and Jesus … and Christian worldview. In J. Ireland, R. Edlin and K. Dickens (Eds.), *Pointing the way: Directions for Christian education in a new millennium* (pp. 155–174). Blacktown, NSW: National Institute for Christian Education.

Van Brummelen, H. (1998). Walking with God in the classroom (2nd ed.). Seattle, WA: Alta Vista Press.

Van Dyk, J. (1997). *Letters to Lisa: Conversations with a Christian teacher.* Sioux Centre, IA: Dordt Press.

Walsh, B. and Middleton, J. (1984). *The transforming vision: Shaping a Christian worldview.* Downers Grove IL: Inter Varsity Press.

Glossary

antirealism—the belief that there is not an objective independent reality that can be known; similar to nonrealism; the antithesis of naïve realism.

astrology—quasi-religious system of prediction and explanation based on apparent positions of the stars and planets, as seen from the earth.

astronomy—study of the stars.

behaviourism—a school of psychology which says that psychology should only be concerned with the objective study of stimuli and responses, and should discard explanations of behaviour in terms of nonobservable events. All behaviour is the product of our conditioning, and mental processes such as thoughts, feelings, and intentions are superfluous to the purposes of psychological research.

chromosomally directed evolution—evolutionary change is "hard wired" into chromosomes through a system of more probable changes in nucleotide sequence leading to preferred mutations.

cognition—a school of psychology which includes all the mental processes concerned with the learning, manipulation and memorising of knowledge and ideas.

communicative language teaching—the most widespread current approach to language teaching, focusing on the use of language for communicative purposes rather than primarily language as grammatical structure.

conjunction—time at which two or more planets appear to come together in the night sky.

constructivism—a theory of how the learner constructs knowledge from experience.

constructivist approaches—approaches that regard knowledge as a human creation unrelated to any external reality.

contextualisation—an approach to theology that emphasises adapting the message to be relevant to the particular context of the receiver so that its equivalent meaning is transmitted.

Copernicus—late medieval astronomer (1473–1543) who worked out the mathematical implications of a moving earth.

cosmology—study of the structure of the universe.

creation mandate— the contention (or job description, as Nancy Pearcey puts it) that God has given human beings a special status of vice-regents or stewards over his creation with the authority and responsibility to give shape to the world in God-honouring ways. Thus all human activities like farming, fishing, building houses, making movies, designing computer programs, or forming governments are legitimate tasks that are performed either in obedience or disobedience to how God would have us care for his world and share in his redemptive purposes. Genesis 1:26–28 and Psalm 8 are seen as representative of the overall cultural mandate message of the Bible.

crisis—Kuhnian label for the time between loss of confidence in a model and the emergence of a superior alternative.

critical realism (see also secular critical realism)—a philosophical paradigm that acknowledges the existence of absolute truth but limits human understanding of that truth because of our cultural contextualisation; tends to prioritise science as the key to discovering that which can be known about truth; Roy Bhaskar is the recognised father of critical realism.

critical-historical approach (also called historical-critical approach)—an approach to biblical interpretation (hermeneutics) which starts with the presupposition that the Bible is a historical document which becomes God's Word as it is subjected to the processes of rational historical investigation, thus enabling one to discriminate between probable facts and the mythological products of the various writers' personal interpretive agendas and time-and-place cultural perspectives; it is compared to the thetical-critical advocacy of contemporary reformed hermeneutics which starts with the presupposition that the Bible is God's true Word and that it can only truly be understood when viewed as the divinely inspired, culture-embedded, unified drama of God's unfolding plan for the creation and redemption of the world through Jesus Christ. Other hermeneutical approaches include higher criticism (the erroneous assertion that the Bible can be interpreted free from belief structures and theology; liberationist perspective; reader-response analysis where multiple text interpretations are permitted when read in different socio-historical settings).

cultural mandate—see creation mandate.

Darwinism—a theory of biological evolution developed by Charles Darwin; species of organisms arising and developing through the natural selection of small, inherited variations that increase the individual's ability to compete, survive, and reproduce; competition between individuals caused some pangenes to become more common in a population.

data—factual information particularly when used as a basis for interpretation or analysis.

disequilibrium—the process of disrupting cognitive balance as a preliminary step to reforming thinking patterns so as to produce a reconfigured cognitive equilibrium.

dualism—the belief that existence is comprised of two parts: our secular or physical existence within the world around us which is essentially evil, and the sacred spiritual world of the soul which is made pure through the salvation of Jesus Christ. Dualism is often referred to (critically) as the nature/grace distinction.

ecological approaches—approaches to research in language education that understand the classroom as complex environment in which a very wide range of factors interact to produce particular effects, instead of trying to establish causal relationships between a particular action and a particular effect.

economic rationalism—the ideology that economic progress and development ultimately works for the good of all and societal progress, so that all other dimensions of a culture must be subservient to the goal of increasing economic performance; "If it's good for the economy, it's good for all"; concept developed by Michael Pusey in Australia.

educational constructivism—a child-centred approach to teaching and learning, where the learning moves from the known to the unknown, is child-initiated and child-directed, and where the teacher plays a supporting role in the learning.

elitism—the belief or attitude that people in a selected group are to be given an elevated status in society, often based on their socioeconomic accumulations or abstract academic qualifications and employment.

ellipse—oval shape.

empirical constructivism—a more relaxed form of constructivism than radical constructivism; in education, this is a child-centred approach that recognises the existence of reality but because of each person's contextualised point of view, claims that the search for a reality that we can live with is more important than the abstract reality itself.

epicurean philosophy—taught that our human mind was anxiety ridden and needed to lose its fear of deities (gods and goddesses). It believed that the gods existed, but they should not be feared because they did not dwell on earth. This philosophy also taught that the supreme good is happiness, but not mere momentary pleasure or temporary gratification.

epicycle—small sphere rotating on the edge of larger sphere: element of Ptolemaic and Copernican astronomy.

epistemology—the branch of philosophy that deals with the nature, origin and scope of knowledge; from the Greek words episteme (knowledge) and logos (word/speech).

ether—"subtle fluid" that was supposed to fill the universe.

eugeosynclines—classification of deep sedimentary deposits formed by vertical sags in an essentially static terrestrial crust, displaced after the acceptance of plate tectonics.

evaluation, formative—a technique for the ongoing assessment and evaluation of students and programs as a tool for program improvement; it examines the process rather then the outcome.

evaluation, summative—assessment that measures growth and understanding at the conclusion of an activity; it examines the outcome rather than the process.

experiential truth—that which one's experience indicates to be a close approximation to reality.

fact—data, commonly accepted observation.

Freud, S.—an Austrian neurologist and the founder of the psychoanalytic school of psychology, a movement that popularised the theory that unconscious motives control much behaviour.

Gaia—neo-animist belief that the earth is a living system involving interactions between lithosphere, hydrosphere, atmosphere and biosphere.

Galileo—early modern physicist (1564–1642) who established the basis for Newtonian dynamics and clashed with the Roman Catholic Church over his support for Copernicus.

general revelation—a response-requiring understanding of God that can be deduced from his creation. Often linked to the idea of common grace, which is the nonsaving but effective outpouring of God's grace and love to all people everywhere as evil is restrained and order maintained through God upholding his world moment by moment by his word of power (Heb 1).

Hebrew shema—see shema.

Hellenistic—of Greece; particularly referring to the period starting 323 BC (death of Alexander the Great) and extending to dates ranging from 144 BC to 300 AD.

hermeneutics—study of meaning.

heterogeneous—composed of a wide variety of parts.

holistic—taking a view of an issue that includes as many facets of the matter as possible, both quantifiable and nonquantifiable; often associated with a high respect for the person in any investigative activity, rather than just concentrating on one component of personhood.

hominid—fossil species resembling humans.

humanism—the "third force" in psychology which was founded as a reaction to the dominant schools of psychodynamics and behaviourism. Humanism views each person as a complete entity having values and goals which they seek to express and fulfil.

idealist/ism—philosophy, any view that stresses the central role of the ideal of the mind in understanding reality. Plato, Descartes, Hegel and Kant were idealists.

idolatry—worshipping a person, thing or idea in place of God. See Romans 1:25.

incarnation—God as Jesus Christ the second Person in the Trinity, becoming human and living on earth.

Jung, C.—a Swiss psychologist who parted with his teacher Sigmund Freud and developed his own theories. Jung disagreed with Freud that sexuality is the basic driving urge for human behaviour. He classified people as extroverts and introverts and argued that people share a collective unconscious, made up of symbols called archetypes.

Kepler—early modern astronomer (1571–1630) who abandoned the crystal spheres at the basis of Ptolemaic and Copernican explanations of the cosmos and replaced them with elliptical orbits.

Lamarckism—inheritance of acquired characteristics: blacksmiths had strong children because their work built up muscle pangenes that they passed down.

literal realism—(also called naïve realism) an approach that sees human knowledge as being a description of reality as it actually is.

literalism—understanding text in a non-figurative, literal manner.

metanarrative—an overarching, cohesive story that gives enduring meaning; as opposed to postmodernity which says there is no big story or metanarrative. Lyotard, Postman, Wright and Gohheen espouse a metanarrative perspective.

miogeosynclines—classification of deep sedimentary deposits formed by vertical sags in an essentially static terrestrial crust, displaced after the acceptance of plate tectonics.

model—mechanical, electronic or conceptual structured object that is used to link and explain data.

modernism—the mode of thinking, strong at least since the renaissance but having Aristotelian roots, that we can know things really, completely and definitively only through the rigorous application of rationality and the scientific method. Similar concepts are scientism, logical positivism.

modernity—the term used to describe a modern milieu.

mosaic evolution—organ systems change independent of changes in the entire organism: *Archaeopteryx* is a reptile with feathers.

naïve realism—see literal realism.

natural selection—survival of the fittest.

neo-Darwinism—few genes + mutation + natural selection = gradual species change.

neoplatonic—the revival and reinterpretation in the third century AD of Plato's (427 BC–347 BC) ideas.

nonrealism (see also antirealism)—the postmodern denial of any objective knowledge or reality.

N-rays—radioactive emissions that subsequently proved to be illusory.

ontology—study of the nature of being.

organic theologian—theologians who see their primary commitment as being to the Christian community and the calling of God rather than to the professional academic community.

oxbridge—where there are two separate teaching institutes (NICE and Southland College) coming under one controlling body for academic affairs (CCHE).

pangenes—"organic memory" distributed through the body; both Lamarck and Darwin used them to explain inheritance.

paradigm—a coherently developed and expressed approach, usually in the realm of thinking.

Pavlov, I.—a Russian physiologist who experimented with dogs and found that their reflexes could be conditioned by external stimuli. Specifically, after they were conditioned by the ringing of a bell at feeding time, they would reflexively salivate upon hearing the bell, whether or not food was present.

pedagogy—instruction of children; from the word Greek *paida* referring to children; sometimes used referring to education in general. However, its more limited use is preferred, with the word andragogy being used in reference to the education of adults.

philosopher-kings—the uppermost groupings in Plato's elitist nondemocratic hierarchy; they alone had the capacity to understand the ideal forms and they alone therefore were esteemed capable of accepting the burden to govern and rule.

phlogiston—supposed "element of fire" displaced after Lavoisier's work on nomenclature and reactions.

Piaget, J.—a Swiss zoologist who began studying psychology out of his interest in genetic epistemology, or the connection between biology and logic.

polyphyletic descent—existing organisms arose from many sources.

postmodern/ism—the late 20th and early 21st century response to modernity and scientism. The paradigm or worldview that believes there is no certainty and that truth is a human-bound, individualistic, nonbinding construction. By definition, it is difficult to say what postmodernism stands for because such an explanation would presuppose the very concept of metanarrative that postmodernism denies. Ideas associated with postmodernism are hermeneutic of suspicion, nonrealism and radical constructivism. Lyotard (1924–1998) and Baudrillard (1929–present) are postmodern philosophers; Stanley Grenz has been classed as a postmodern evangelical theologian.

postmodernity—the (prevailing contemporary) Western cultural milieu.

propositional truth—the declarations about the infinite, personal God and his world that are found in the infallible word of God (the Bible) and which transcend cultural limitations (Francis Schaeffer's "true truth") as opposed to the relativistic truth of postmodernity.

psychoanalysis—a method of treating mental disorders based on the teachings of Sigmund Freud.

psychoanalytic psychology—a school of psychology which focuses on the importance of the unconscious mind(with internal conflicts and instinctual energies) determining behaviour.

psychology—systematic and scientific study of behaviour.

Ptolemy—Hellenistic astronomer (2nd century AD), basis for medieval astronomy (and modern astrology).

punctuated equilibrium—species change is not gradual, species persist unchanged for long periods of time and then undergo rapid development.

qualitative methods—a research paradigm that focuses on the study of people rather than the gathering of quantifiable data for statistical analysis. Its ethnographic methods include focus groups, content analysis, participant observation and interviews, and participant observation which are then used to understand and explain social phenomena, activities and perspectives.

radical constructivism—the individualised construction of knowledge that denies the existence of any external truth or reference point beyond personal perception; propounded by Ernst von Glasersfeld (1917–present); the variant of postmodernism often taught in teacher education courses.

reductionism—the reduction of a complex reality to one of its component parts which often then becomes idolised as a replacement of the whole.

reformed critical realism—a philosophical and hermeneutical paradigm that declares the existence of absolute truth but limits human understanding of that truth because of our finite and fallen capacity to "see through a glass darkly"; it urges a proactive, humble engagement with the secular culture that starts from (1) a declared Christian presuppositional stance (thetical-critical method); (2) a high place of Scripture as the inspired, infallible unfolding drama of God's plan for the world; though reformed critical realism uses a similar descriptor to that of Bhaskar in order to indicate strategic parallels, reformed critical realism is a distinctive perspective that is reformed in a theological and foundational sense—it is not a mere synthetic reformulation of Bhaskar's critical realist theory.

resilience—the ability to function effectively in the face of stress and/or opposition.

saltationism—mutations occur in complex clumps to produce radically different organisms; the first bird hatched from a reptilian egg.

scientific method—the popularly held (but discredited) belief that through value-free, systematic observation and experimentation, one can refine a concept or idea to reach the truth of the matter, and this brings about an inevitable improvement in the lot of humankind; the assertion that any conclusions reached using paradigms other than the scientific method are mere beliefs or conjecture in comparison to scientific fact.

Scopes "Monkey Trial"—1925 court case, in Dayton, Tennessee, where J. T. Scopes was fined $100 for teaching evolution in defiance of state prohibition.

secular critical realism (see also critical realism)—a philosophical paradigm that acknowledges the existence of absolute truth but limits human understanding of that truth because of our cultural contextualisation; tends to prioritise science as the key to discovering that which can be known about truth; Roy Bhaskar is the recognised father of critical realism.

secular humanism—the idea that all explanations and reasons for being must ultimately find their cause and explanation in human beings, beyond whom there is no other; revealed knowledge is rejected in favour of a belief that the physical world is the totality of existence and must be the sole arbiter of morality and purpose; recognised as a nontheistic religion in the 1961 US Supreme Court case Torasco v. Watkins; it has been described by its adherents as a religion without revelation and as a new religion of humanity; naturalism is an associated term; John Dewey, Richard Dawkins are examples of secular humanists.

secular—a powerful faith commitment to the notion that God has no place in the explanation of the world, people or ideas.

shalom—the purpose, security and fulfilment that is the heritage of the Christian community as we move towards the restoration of all things and the coming of God's kingdom that has been and will be (the now and not yet) restored and fulfilled through the redemptive work of Christ, and of which Christians are the stewardly heralds in this present age.

shema—a Jewish liturgical prayer that declares the key tenets of the faith.

Skinner, B. F.—was a strong advocate of behaviourism, building on the conditioned response theories of Pavlov. He was the prominent figure of the school of psychology known as behaviourism which explains the behaviour of humans and other animals in terms of the physiological responses of the organism to external stimuli. Skinner maintained that learning occurred as a result of the organism responding to, or operating on, its environment, and coined the term *operant conditioning* to describe this phenomenon.

social reconstructionism—the conviction that education teaches beliefs and values and, as such, should overtly identify those values and beliefs that should be encouraged so that those values and beliefs can be incorporated into the curriculum and thus proactively shape society for the betterment of all. George Counts was a key social reconstructionist.

socratic method—a pedagogical problem-solving method using question and answer; the term comes from Socrates (470–399 BC) who used it as a teaching method which often exposed ignorance masquerading as wisdom.

special revelation—God's special and saving revelation of himself and his ways which is fulfilled completely in the living Word, Jesus Christ, and as unfolded for us in the drama of God's written Word, the Bible. Often linked to saving grace which is God moving to convict one of sin and draw one to himself through the working of his Holy Spirit on the basis of Jesus' substitutionary victory over sin and death at Calvary.

stasis—species persist until extinction.

stoic philosophy—taught that people should live in harmony with nature, recognise their own self-sufficiency and independence. The Stoic philosophers believed in being virtuous; they did not strongly differentiate God from nature and advocated that people should live in accord with nature.

streaming— the ethos and process of separating students and placing them into classes, groups or schools according to their academic ability; also called tracking.

subject cultures—the particular complexes of teaching practices, terminology, topics of discussion, taboo topics, etc. that grow up among teachers in particular curriculum areas.

teleology—the belief that there is a design or predictive purpose or final cause to existence, which in turn provides the meaning and purpose for life.

theism—belief in a personal god.

theory—well-supported proposed explanation.

thetical-critical method—philosophical paradigm suggested by the Dutch theologian Dirk Hendrik Theodoor Vollenhoven (1892–1978); asserted the *a priori* need of Christians to develop and articulate explicitly God-related presuppositions to their thinking as opposed to patterns that merely synthesise diverse strands of secular thought; it also involved the serious listening to and critiquing of other positions, always identifying first of all their religious presuppositions.

tracking—the ethos and process of separating students and placing them into classes, groups or schools according to their academic ability; also called streaming.

transience—change.

Tuskegee syphilis study—long-running US research project where Negro men suffering from a venereal disease were closely monitored but not treated long after an effective treatment existed.

Tycho—Tycho Brahe, early modern astronomer (1546–1601) last and greatest of the pre-telescope observers, suggested a compromise between Ptolemy and Copernicus: the rest of the planets revolved around the sun, which revolved around a stationary earth.

worldview—one's often unconscious, comprehensive framework for understanding of and living in the world; the lens that we use to give meaning to living.

Index